Africa's Golden Road

KWESI ARMAH

Africa's Golden Road

With a Foreword by
MZEE JOMO KENYATTA

HEINEMANN
LONDON

Published by
Heinemann Educational Books Ltd
48 Charles Street, London W.1
LONDON   MELBOURNE   TORONTO
AUCKLAND   HONG KONG
IBADAN   NAIROBI

© Kwesi Armah 1965
First published 1965

Printed in Great Britain by
Morrison & Gibb Ltd, London and Edinburgh

CONTENTS

I dedicate this book to my Comrades of the Committee of African Organizations; to the Pioneers of Pan-Africanism who imbued them and me with our abiding faith in Continental Union Government of Africa ; and to men and women everywhere whose devotion to Continental Union Government will certainly achieve this ideal and the happier life for Africans upon which, I believe sincerely, depends mankind's hope for a prosperous, peaceful future.

FOREWORD

by

HIS EXCELLENCY, MZEE JOMO KENYATTA

President of the Republic of Kenya

THIS is a sincere and thoughtful work. As a valuable exposition of African thinking, it reflects the expanding impact of the African personality in world affairs. Both statesmen and students of politics will find much to enlighten them in these pages. In the context of sheer humanity, Kwesi Armah has written a kind of *War and Peace* in miniature. His writing moves across a vast stage, on which he traces the emergence and the purpose of the African image and inspiration.

The author is one of the most promising of the younger African diplomats. As the High Commissioner of Ghana in London, he has presented African nationalism both as the flame and as the logic of an ideal. When attending constitutional conferences in London, prior to Kenya's independence, I met him several times. Always I found him interesting and helpful. His conscientious work for effective African Unity is itself renowned.

This book contains many accounts of historical and dramatic occasions in or relating to Africa. These are written with vigour, always with fairness, and often with such humour or penetrating comment as can help to make remoteness real. The whole work is one of perspective. It should do much to explain and interpret the approaches and attitudes of Africa, which to many outside observers still seem perplexing or strange.

The author describes the emergence of African democracy, and the pattern of collective decision, in an environment no longer containing distinction between the rulers and the ruled. He then gives an outline of Socialism, based on the idea of the extended family, in a society with social and moral values springing from the African tradition. These passages are well worthy of universal study.

vii

Kwesi Armah has constructed much of this book around the principle that the people of Africa would sooner starve in freedom than be the affluent pawns of ideological overlords, whether they call themselves Capitalists or Communists or anything else '. He explains the opposition in Africa to new forms of Colonialism, some rooted in economic evils, and some introducing class warfare as racialism in just another guise.

In all these sections, the author embarks on a critical and comprehensive study of non-alignment. He presents this as the positive and dynamic ideal which in fact it has become. And he does not lose sight of the influence of this philosophy in a world wherein reason and justice have been increasingly subjugated to the argument of military might. There is responsibility in Africa to uphold important principles, and counter the expediency and intrigues which have threatened to dominate mankind.

It is inappropriate to cover all the subject-matter here, but some items should be cited. On South Africa, the book poses the problem of how to translate what is morally accepted into action of some legal or political kind. The author calls for many reforms of the United Nations. The power of the veto – he says – must die ; China should be accepted into membership ; agreed ways must be found to manage any peace-keeping forces. He also proposes that the world body should establish an International Trade Organization, since history has shown how the road to prosperity and peace could be founded on trade.

Leading up to his conclusion, Kwesi Armah writes of the latent economic strength of Africa, and the dilemma of a continent with abundant natural resources, in which millions still go hungry in the midst of plenty. The solution he presents, which is shared by the statesmen and scholars and economists of all the African nations, is progressively to harness and exploit these riches through new forms of organization.

The author traces the growing African contribution to the counsels of the Commonwealth, and expresses the valid hope that the new Secretariat may give the Commonwealth an even fuller meaning. He tells the story of the old Committee of African Organizations, which served as a platform and a channel for political energies, prior to the Addis Ababa meeting at which 32 Heads of African States set up the Organization of African Unity.

The ultimate theme of this book is that, following the replacement of Colonialism by Nationalism in Africa, there should be a Union Government of Africa. In no other way can the author see the end-point of past political struggles, and the effectiveness of economic coordination.

Of course, this is not a new concept. It is the goal at which all of Africa might eventually come to aim. Readers will wish to judge for themselves the force and substance of the author's present reasoning. His purpose has clearly been to hold out inspiration for the future as appealing as that which strengthened Africa to break free from the bondage of the past.

I commend this book as a thoughtful and confidently written appraisal of the African scene.

INTRODUCTION

THIS book is a political testament, an expression of political faith.

I have lived through revolutionary events in my own country, Ghana, and in my own continent, Africa, and I have been privileged to observe at first hand the people of many other countries.

From these experiences, for which I shall be always grateful, many lessons can be learned, two of which have impelled me to write this book.

One is the continuing need to interpret Africa and Africans, their aspirations and inspirations, to other nations. The other is the need to stimulate the growing fellow-feeling between people everywhere which, alone, is our promise of peace and its assurance for ever.

The history of Africa was completely determined for the future when the first white men set foot in that continent. That history could have been a glorious one, a saga of collaboration between peoples who had different things to offer to the civilization of man. In fact, that history has been a most wretched one characterized for a long time by slavery and latterly by colonialism and Neo-colonialism. It is up to us Africans to salvage a continent from the ruins on our hands. We can obtain the best results in the shortest possible time if we attack our problems with one conscientiousness and as one man.

African Unity is our diamond of hope. Our problems are contemporary problems and are incapable of solution by an uncritical copying of the way of life of others, however successful this may be in its own setting.

Our concern is for our whole people and our democracy is the democracy of a mass society living like one organism with its own nodal control. This means One-Party Democracy with Democratic Centralism. This theory harmonizes our age-old African traditions with modern ideas of democratic participation in government. It is a process of political education and communication, and of popular action. It

xi

places power and the exercise of power in the hands of the people. Democratic Centralism has developed spontaneously in former French areas as well as in former British territories. It has given a new dimension to One-Party Democracy as now operating in many African states under many varied conditions. I am convinced that Democratic Centralism gives African democracy today a dynamic that will ensure the survival of democratic ideals for all time.

Africa, however, will not successfully solve its problems unless those who are more advanced avoid interference or any new attempt to subjugate the destiny of Africa to their own selfish ends. Africa must be insulated from the current ideological conflicts in which it can have no genuine part to play. A policy of non-alignment will ensure this insulation for Africa. Non-alignment is the basis of relations between African states, and between Africa and the world. This is neither mere neutralism, nor a withdrawal from the affairs of men with all their grave problems and grander hopes. It is positive neutralism with a positive programme designed, among other things, to make large areas of the world, including all Africa, nuclear-free zones. As African statesmen apply the principles of non-alignment more continuously, I believe the African continent will make an increasing and invaluable contribution to the abolition of war from this earth.

At all times, Africa must support the basic principles of the United Nations, which is the protector of the weak as well as of the strong. In this way, we can have the fullest confidence in all our tomorrows.

In the last chapter, I sum up my hopes for the future of Africa. These hopes essentially involve the idea of a Union · Government of Africa. Union Government was the dream of all the pioneers of Pan-Africanism. It is now the living inspiration of millions of young African men and women who have served its cause with zealous devotion, and often self-sacrifice. It is, I am convinced, the solid basis of the future prosperity and happiness of my beloved Mother Africa.

London
July 1965   KWESI ARMAH

CHAPTER ONE

CALL BACK YESTERDAY

YOUTH CHALLENGES OPPRESSION

POLITICAL awareness among the youth of Africa reached a dramatic climax in the year 1945. The din of Allied victory was about our ears. But so was the lamentation of anguish. Young Africans had battled bravely on many fronts, had suffered and died in the massive international effort to defeat racialism and Fascism. But the war was over now. Germany, Italy, and Japan, the aggressors, lay prostrate at the feet of the all-conquering Allies. Our surviving soldiers came back home. The combination of the elation of victory and a job well done, together with the melancholy of six years agonizingly spent, left in them a feeling of the necessity for a new deal.

There were also immediate problems. War, however necessary, is not an occupation ; and with its cessation must come the abandonment of a corrupting way of life. Returning soldiers needed a chance to earn a reasonable living, a chance to take part in the building of life, and so to cast aside the destructive skills of war. There were the disabled who were unfit for anything. The survivors of the war expected some arrangement whereby care could be provided for the disabled and the dependants of the dead, a little social security in what they were told was to be a world changed for the better. In the Gold Coast, our soldiers expected that the freedom which they had helped towards winning for other lands would be granted to their country too, the freedom which was promised by the Atlantic Charter to all nations of the earth.

They could not be certain, however, and this uncertainty for a while marred the joy of their homecoming. But then came the success of the Labour Party in the British General Election of 1945. This fired the imagination of my elders who communicated something of their excitement to my generation.

In Britain, ex-servicemen were returning to their homes with good gratuities and good hopes of self-respecting employment. The burdens of the aftermath of war were not falling on the poor alone, as they had done at the end of World War I; ' austerity ' was shared by the whole community. The Labour Government's brave decision to free India as the first step towards creating a new Commonwealth – surely a turning-point in world history of which British people will always be proud – encouraged and delighted those of us outside Britain. We too breathed the fresh promise of change.

Alas, the radicalism and social purposes of the Labour Government did not reach out to the Colonies of the old Empire ; these remained under the control of government-by-ordinance. Modest reforms in the Gold Coast legislature left the mass of the people there untouched. The hope that we would gain a little of the freedom for which our soldiers had fought and died was frustrated, as were the expectations of a real improvement in living standards.

Instead what some other areas of Africa did get was a flood of the new generation of White settlers, not as harbingers of the post-war ideals of the mother country but as self-styled ' refugees ' from democracy and social reform in England !

In 1947, the year of India's independence and also of the arrival of the new settlers in Kenya and Rhodesia, Kwame Nkrumah returned to the Gold Coast. He was more than a fresh and vivid voice of our discontent. He was the voice of positive action and a portent that the post-war map of Africa would be drawn neither by Empire-builders like Cecil Rhodes nor by alien politicians at a repetition of a colonial conference such as the Berlin Conference, where Africa had first been ' carved up ' by the European powers. Above all, Nkrumah caught the springtide of post-war youth in the Gold Coast. With growing maturity and the widening of political experience, which his dynamic leadership quickened, we became his admirers and adherents. A few years later I was proud to call him comrade-in-arms. Together with the beloved leader, my generation was to survive events that, sometimes, ' saddened our youth, yet made it great to live '.

Calling back yesterday, I think my final moment of dedica-tion to African Nationalism and the cause of African unity came in 1954. Then, Algeria defied the tyranny that had intensified since 1945 when Algerians, too, demanded a share of the freedom won in World War II, and launched their full-scale revolt against the might of France.

France had invaded Algeria in 1830, ostensibly in reprisal for an act of disrespect by the Turkish Dey of Algiers towards the French ambassador. In fact the primary motive was probably France's desire to reassert herself after her defeat and humiliation at the Congress of Vienna in 1815. She threw a huge military effort into the conquest of Algeria during the following decades, but – like Roman, Spanish, and Turkish invaders before her – she never managed to subjugate the fierce independent spirit of the tribes in the interior. In fact, the common enemy united these previously warring tribes in the desire to rid the country of alien invaders.

But before Algeria could unite to expel the colonialists, France did irreparable damage to the country. The tough, ruthless General Bugeaud was sent to take charge of the conquest in 1840. His policy was brutally simple : it was to subjugate Algerians by murder, pillage, and scorched-earth ruination of their land ; and then to re-populate the only reasonably fertile areas with European *colons*. Later, by mechanizing agriculture, France drove still more Algerians from even such poor land as they still cultivated, turning the country into a reservoir of cheap emigré labour to be exploited in France itself. As in the British colonial system, every effort was made to deny the people the truth of their own history and traditions in order to force upon them acceptance of a hopeless future.

All in vain. Algerians could not be assimilated. They rejected a French culture that had nothing but misery to offer them. They despised ' la Gloire '.

The modern struggle for Algerian independence, carried to final victory by the F.L.N. (Front de Libération Nationale), began as long ago as 1925. The movement then was called A.M.L. (Amis de Manifeste de la Liberté). Its leader, Ferhat Abbas, an enthusiast for the defeat of Fascism in World War II, emerged from hiding in Algiers to congratulate the French Governor-General on the Allied triumph. He was arrested.

In the demonstration of protest that followed, more than 4,500 friends of liberty were also arrested, 99 of them being sentenced to death and 64 to life imprisonment.

Meanwhile, some hundreds of miles eastwards, at Setief, near Constantine, even more terrifying and decisive events were in the making. There the defeat of Fascism was to be celebrated by a public parade on 8 May 1945. The Algerian population was to be permitted to gather at the Mosque, then lay a wreath on the town's war memorial. They were instructed not to carry banners and placards. Some, in festival mood, waved the Tricolor, the Union Jack, the Stars and Stripes, and the Hammer and Sickle. Others bore aloft placards with the words : 'Long live a Free Algeria' and 'Down with Colonialism'. In the Avenue Clemenceau a panic-stricken policeman fired a shot – a shot that was 'the shout before the avalanche'. Angry, despairing Algerians rioted. European casualties were 29 dead, 49 wounded. The Popular Front Government in Paris, the Vice-President of which was the leader of the French Communist Party, retaliated by air bombing, bombardment from the sea by warships, and the mass burning of villages. In a military action, which ranks high in the calendar of international crimes, there were officially 100 European and 1,002 Algerian casualties. Unofficial estimates, made by newspaper reporters, put the number of Algerian casualties at 18,000. So began nearly a decade of sporadic fighting while F.L.N. sought settlement by non-violent means – a decade of mounting terrorism until, on 1 November 1954, F.L.N. decided for freedom or death.

All Africa stood four-square behind F.L.N. during the savage seven years' war that followed. The courage of the Algerian population was sustained by the mighty popular effort to build their own administrative systems, schools and hospitals under enemy fire. Schoolteachers and doctors, north and south of the Sahara, gave up their holidays for voluntary service to the state emerging behind the flowing battle lines. Volunteers from all over the world, including France, flocked to work in the rescue-homes of Tunisia and Morocco where Algerian children were taken to escape the burning and bombing, and, especially, the brutalities of the French-controlled concentration camps. Fearless statesmen, like President Bourguiba of Tunisia and King Mohammed V of Morocco, offered all aid to Algeria while refusing to allow the Mahgreb to become a mere extension of the European battlefield and the Cold War raging there. Algeria's fight was our fight – against colonialist France and the *Organisation de l'Armée Secrète*, ugly instrument of the alien settlers. Like all young Africans, I felt I was in it and of it until Algeria was free. The struggle epitomized Africa's will for freedom, its capacity to endure through long, long years of military and legislative aggression and – this was Africa's undying glory – its determination to sustain and maintain its own culture against all the hazards of time and colonial spite.

*   *   *   *

I came to London in 1957, the year after the Convention People's Party achieved its third and decisive General Election victory in the Gold Coast. I found my fellow students, as I had expected, animated by the vision and inspiration of the new state of Ghana. I was very proud of Ghana's leadership and was devoted to its development. I recalled ' Aggrey of Africa ' – James Emman Kwegyir Aggrey – the founder, in association with Sir Gordon Guggisberg, at that time Governor of the Gold Coast, the Rev. A. G. Fraser, from Scotland, and Nana Sir Ofori Atta, of the Prince of Wales College at Achimota, near Accra, built to celebrate the visit of Edward, Prince of Wales, now the Duke of Windsor.

Aggrey – the name in Akan means ' valiant ' – was born in Anomabu in 1876 and died in 1927 in New York where, at Columbia University, he was compiling his thesis for a Doctorate in Philosophy. He revolted, like all men of gentle spirit, against an orchestra of life to which hungry bellies contributed their groans and overfull bellies their hiccoughs. He preached the theme of the oneness of the human race ; as on the piano keyboard, he often said, true harmony is attained only by the combination of the black and white keys. Central to this theme was his constant plea that to educate the women was to educate the nation. For him Achimota – a co-educational centre ranging from kindergarten to university with a highly qualified staff drawn from the four quarters of the earth – was a dream come true. His image of the black and white keys of the harmonium, symbolizing his faith in humanity rid of racialism, humanity seeking fulfilment in unity was visually represented by the college crest of Achimota. Aggrey witnessed the end of slavery and the beginning of education in Ghana. He nourished yet another dream and, in the nineteen-twenties, expressed it in a prophecy which we students believed it was our privilege and duty to realize. ' There is a Youth Movement coming in Africa that some day may startle the world,' he wrote. ' This restlessness all over Africa stands for self-discovery, self-realization. It tells of power just breaking through.'

The ' power just breaking through ' was finding expression in the organizations of African students in London and all over the world.

The Committee of African Organizations

African students abroad, whether in England, America, or France, had always tended to gravitate into groups for friendship and mutual aid. Their first impressions were usually of shock and disappointment. Never well off financially, their lot was cast among the slums of great industrial cities, slums which they didn't expect to find at all in the wealthy nations of the West. People who allowed themselves to get to know Africans quickly entered into easy relationships with them ; with their African qualities of gaiety and loyalty, serious pursuit of study and willingness to work they won goodwill and affection. Slums, however, are the breeding ground of the *lumpenproletariat* whose own terrifying sense of insecurity makes it treat every strange face as the face of a foe. White snobbery expressed itself – and, alas, still does – in discrimination against black students, discrimination made harsher by the fact that the student, as a rule, was better educated and spoke better English than his tormentors, as well as possessing attributes of personality which capitalist society had denied them. Racial discrimination is unknown to childhood. It is an adult disease, a reflection of the adult's lack of confidence in his own community.

These associations of African students gradually assumed an organizational form. As long ago as 1925, responding to Aggrey's inspiration, a Nigerian student in London, Ladipo Solanke, combined four small groups into the West African Students' Union. They established W.A.S.U. branches in Africa to keep in touch with each other in later life. As membership grew, W.A.S.U. also grew in political conscious-ness and activity. Its horizon extended to all African affairs. It carried into every movement for colonial freedom a new and militant radicalism which rejected the ideologies of the West as a solvent for African problems. W.A.S.U. members were worthy inheritors of the Pan-African ideals formulated by our magnificent ' Old Guard ' – among them Kenyatta, Azikiwe, Nkrumah, Awolowo, and Johnson – and strong links of unity began to be formed between the youth of many African countries.

I found that the exciting march of events in Africa was stirring my fellow-students to a new fervour for freedom. We created, in March 1958, a Committee of African Organizations as a new, effective pivot for all student bodies. By November 1958 we had established our headquarters at 200 Gower Street in London. We responded readily to the eager demand from all members that we should widen our membership to include Europe and develop an all-embracing political platform.

Soon, colonialism provided the catalyst. Southern Rhodesia, in preparation for the move towards independence of the ill-fated Central African Federation, established in 1951, pro-jected a federal franchise offering the vast African majority 15 out of 65 seats in the Legislative Assembly. The strong probability that the British Government would accept this unjust proposal sent a wave of indignation across Africa and stirred in all African students the fear that progress towards independence would be slowed down in every African state.

These fears were, as it turned out, not to materialize. For one thing, African political parties were already springing up which were destined to pursue national independence with an uncompromising single-mindedness. Our people knew that the colonial administration would not rule indefinitely against the will of the people. Independence was therefore assured as long as the will to independence could be sustained.

The youth were not left out of all this. It was Edmund Burke who said : ' Tell me what are the prevailing sentiments that occupy the minds of your young men, and I will tell you what is to be the character of the next generation '. Independence was to be won not just for now, but for all time. It was, therefore, important that the minds and souls of the youth should be fired with the same passion for freedom which had driven their elders.

The policy of C.A.O. was simple. It was unity for Africa and freedom for all African countries. Our officers and Committee members are today to be found in distinguished offices in the service of our continent. These names include those of Abu Mayanja, who became Minister of Education in the Kabaka's Government of Buganda (a federal component of Uganda) ; Maiza Chona, now Zambia Minister of Home Affairs ; Oscar Kambona, well-known External Affairs and Defence Minister of Tanzania ; M. Sipalo, who became Minister of Health in Zambia ; Oliver Tambo, now Vice-President of the African National Congress of South Africa ; Peter Kionange, now Minister of Education in Kenya ; Burudi Nabwere, now Kenya's Permanent Representative at the United Nations ; S. M. Kapwepwe, now Minister of Foreign Affairs in Zambia ; Moses Obiekwe, prominent member of the Nigeria N.C.N.C. ; Salim Rashid, Junior Minister of Finance in Tanzania ; L. Lubowa, now Minister of Commerce and Industry in Uganda; Isaac Chinebuah, Headmaster of Achimota School in Ghana and now a Minister of the Government in Ghana ; W. E. C. Daniels, Director of Legal Studies in Ghana and now a Cabinet Minister ; Willie Abraham, M.P., well known as Professor of Philosophy in the University of Ghana. John Pire, Oscar Kambona, and I were made responsible for the task of devising an up-to-date constitution for the joint organization.

The resolution to extend our interests to Europe led to the Committee's being responsible for a number of Youth Conferences in Moscow, London, Paris, Belgrade, and other places. It is a realization of our African youth that the age in which we live demands pluck. We are at the barrier of a new frontier at which the spirit of Africa must realistically and truthfully plan the new thinking in Africa and develop the united continent we dream about.

C.A.O. as a Common Platform

In Africa itself at this time alliances between the newly independent countries were being established. The two planks of C.A.O. policy were, as I have said before, unity for Africa and freedom for all African countries. Freedom for individual countries was being achieved. The danger to the future of our campaign for true African unity was that the newly forming political groups might become power blocs, on the pattern of European power-politics, which would hinder unity of purpose for the whole continent.

In London C.A.O. had an invaluable task to perform as a bridge between these groups. The Committe was unceasing in its efforts to bring leaders of the new countries together, to meet each other and to meet the people of each other's country. C.A.O. provided a sanctum and a forum where our leaders could think aloud about the aims and purposes of African unity and could converse privately with their young followers about the tremendous problems arising in our homelands. Public statements of the highest authority were delivered, under the Committee's auspices, by Kwame Nkrumah, Nnamdi Azikiwe, Jomo Kenyatta, Julius Nyerere, Joshua Nkomo, Ben Barka, Oginga Odinga, Kenneth Kaunda, Milton Obote, Hastings Banda, Chief Albert Lutuli, and my good friend Dr David Pitt. At private sessions our members were enabled to exchange views with Houphouet-Boigny, Modibo Keita, Sekou Touré, and William Tubman.

Almost all the African political leaders gravitated, one after the other, to London and London, through the activities of C.A.O., became the centre for a great deal of Pan-African activity. Each of these leaders made important statements on the common platform thus provided by C.A.O.

Jomo Kenyatta had served seven long years of imprisonment for allegedly organizing terrorism in Kenya. Neither the charge nor the trial that followed gave any convincing proof

of the much-acclaimed British justice. All Kenya and all
Freedom Fighters in Africa awaited his release. The Colonial
Office, afraid of the increased prominence which the long
imprisonment had given Jomo, fought shy. He was first taken
out of prison but confined to a house built for him in a small
village. Three months later he was released. Kenya was
jubilant and soon he was at the head of the Kenya African
National Union and leading its delegation to constitutional
talks in London.

In London he addressed a meeting organized by C.A.O. at
the African Unity House – his subject ' African Freedom and
Unity '. He paid tribute to Kwame Nkrumah and said that
the independence of Ghana marked the end of the white man's
rule in Africa. The independence of the other states might be
delayed a little but was unpreventable. The white settler must
descend from his pedestal of arrogance and cease to pretend
that he was in Africa as a lord. He thanked the Executive of
C.A.O. for continuing the Pan-African movement among the
students and wished them success. Needless to say, the
presence of Jomo Kenyatta in our midst was a great inspiration.
He embodied the hard fight that was the African's lot and the
victory that was surely to crown the African's struggle for
freedom under God's sun and in his homeland.

Another veteran Pan-Africanist to speak on the C.A.O.
platform was H.E. Dr Nnamdi Azikiwe, Governor-General
(as he then was) of the Federation of Nigeria. His subject was
' The Future of Pan-Africanism '. C.A.O. was fortunate
indeed to hear this talk. The Patron felt that the opportunity
afforded by Zik's presence in London should not be lost in
view of the emphasis which the British press was placing on
what it regarded as a sure division of the Pan-African camp.
The British press never took kindly to the idea of all the states
of Africa coming together and pulling together politically,
economically, militarily, and culturally. Some papers con-
ceded that the idea was a fine one but added that it could at
best only remain a dream. The fact that a ' Monrovia Group '
appeared to be meeting independently of another group called
by them the ' Casablanca Group ' lent colour to their doubts.
As Nigeria was in the Monrovia Group and was particularly

acclaimed by the British press as providing a new, better, and moderate leadership in Africa, it was important that the view of the greatest of Nigerian politicians should be known to C.A.O. and the African population in Britain and Europe. For the more serious among us were worried by this rift in the Pan-African movement at home ; Zik's talk was encouraging and brilliant. It was heard by a large audience at Friends House on 12 August 1961, and covered the whole ground and assured us that, in spite of the temporary rift, African States would surely come together. Summing up he said :

The Accra Conference of African States demonstrated that African States are amenable to reasoned appeals for Unity. The All-African Conference showed that African politicians can sink their individual differences. The Sanniquelli Conference vindicated African statesmanship. The Conferences of the Brazzaville States – Members of the French Community – are examples of realism in tackling the problems of African Unity. The Casablanca Conference shamed those who thought that African Leaders were mainly moderates and tongue-tied marionettes. The Monrovia Conference presaged the emergence of reasonable and statesmanlike leadership on a wider scale in Africa. The Tananarive and Coquilhatville Conferences depict the African as a compère of his European and American comrades when it comes to hard bargaining and power politics.[1] The All-African Trades Union Conference advertised to the world the role which African labour plays in the solution of African problems.

If this evidence of a sincere attempt to resolve the problems created by the interplay of social forces can be a guide, then it is patent that no matter what may be the difficulties in the way, African Unity is possible in the foreseeable future. Deep-seated fears exist, it is true, but they are being gradually replaced by mutual confidence. Granted that complex problems rear their heads and often confuse the honest efforts of those who believe in African Unity, nevertheless solutions have been suggested and analyses are being conducted to discover the best methods of resolving these human problems.

In conclusion, it is my firm belief that an African leviathan must emerge ultimately ; it may be in the form of an association of African States or in the form of a concert of African States ;

[1] For detailed descriptions of these conferences and groupings see p. 16 *et seq.*

but my main point is that so long as the form of government is clearly understood and an efficient machinery for organization and administration is devised, backed by multilateral conventions which would enhance the standard of living of Africans, safeguard their existence by collective security, and guarantee to them freedom under the law in addition to the fundamental human rights, the dream of Pan-Africanism is destined to come true.

Finally, one of the leading Africanists of all times, Edward Wilmot Blyden, said : ' It is really high time that a unity of spirit should pervade the people of the world for the regeneration of a Continent so long despoiled by the unity or consent of these same people. Thinking Negroes should ask themselves what part they will take in this magnificent work of reclaiming a continent – their own continent. In what way will they illustrate their participation in the unity of spirit which pervades the people of their fatherland ? ' That was Dr Blyden preaching Pan-Africanism in the nineteenth century. On our part, what shall we do ? History will chronicle the choice made by us in the twentieth century.

Zik's talk had the desired effect. From then on those among the Nigerians who hitherto had only paid lip service to C.A.O. began to participate earnestly in it. They had been told that there were no permanent rifts in the Pan-African camp in Africa, as the British and American press would have had the world believe. There were only various routes towards the one and only goal – the African leviathan. The learned Zik was emphatic about this. ' As I see it,' he said, ' there is bound to arise an African leviathan in the form of a political organization or association or union or concert of States.'

Even though some press reporters were present when Zik spoke no report of the speech appeared in any of the Anglo-Saxon newspapers. For these papers refrained, as usual, from publishing anything that agreed with the vision that encouraged Pan-Africanism, especially anything that agreed with the concept of it in terms of political union. And it is this view of it that Dr Azikiwe's speech endorsed. C.A.O., by getting Zik to speak, bridged the gap which threatened to divide the Pan-African movement on the continent itself.

Dr Kenneth Kaunda visited London before Zambia became independent and said at a C.A.O. meeting that students had a special responsibility in bringing about African unity. He said that no African or friend of Africa could be in doubt as to the correctness of African unity. But unity was not possible without brotherhood, and students in the Committee of African Organizations had the unique opportunity of making that brotherhood real.

At another meeting President Julius Nyerere of Tanzania dwelt on the fact that African Unity could be attained only if we were prepared to overcome the difficulties involved. It would be foolish to suppose that there were no difficulties. He called upon all African youth to lead exemplary lives and develop in themselves that strength of character in whose absence great nations cannot be built.

The Prime Minister of Uganda, Dr Milton Obote, said African unity was inevitable but that youth did not need a Union Government in order to achieve unity. He pointed out that we must set a forceful example of unity by closing our ranks in service to one another, and as a means of achieving African unity more quickly.

A more sombre note was struck in a speech given by Dr Hastings Banda of Malawi, who warned that some of us might have to die for Africa. He told us that unity could only come at a price and that we must always be prepared to pay that price.

The Committee of African Organizations was also active in supporting the campaigns that arose in London to boycott South African goods and destroy the devilries of apartheid and racial discrimination. We played our part in the 1961 Trafalgar Square protest against the British Government's Congo policy ; we demanded that Patrice Lumumba be released from imprisonment by United Nations forces before hired mercenaries were permitted to murder him. A couple of weeks later we joined the London demonstrations against Dr Verwoerd, then attending the Commonwealth talks which resulted in South Africa's expulsion from the Commonwealth. The intensification of our activities provoked retaliation. Some racialist hoodlums set fire to our office and destroyed many of our records. Dr Nkrumah at once answered a plea to which he had listened sympathetically on a previous visit to

England.   He provided funds to enable us to buy and re-construct as the permanent headquarters of the Committee premises now called Africa Unity House at Collingham Gardens, London S.W.5.   Africa Unity House is a beautifully decorated and gracious club with a full-time Warden and ample office accommodation.   There are rooms allocated to West Africans, East Africans, North Africans, and Southern Africans for their specialized interests, and an office for C.A.O.   The House combines every amenity of a social centre and political power house with the atmosphere of a home from home.

Meantime, in October 1960, the Committee of African Organizations had convened in London the most impressive Conference of young Africans yet held anywhere in the world. Messages of goodwill and support came from all over Africa, from Eire, Czechoslovakia, the United Arab Republic, China, and Korea, and from political parties and societies in every part of the globe.   Naturally, the Congo tragedy occupied all our thoughts, and I recall the deep emotion evoked by the speech of Mr Dionje Arsene, President of the Congo Youth Union.   'Every time that an honest African Government wishes to work in the interest of the people,' he said, ' this Government is labelled " Communist " by the Western bloc ... Everything depends upon us alone . . . to lead Africa towards a better destiny.   There are no boundaries separating Africans.   One sees Ghanaians in Leopoldville, Congolese in Morocco, Moroccans in Guinea.'

Mr G. M. J. Cabral, of the Revolutionary Front of National Independence for Portuguese Colonies, explained the meaning of Fascism in everyday life. ' How difficult it is to organize a movement, how difficult for two people to meet, to send a letter abroad, to come out from our countries . . . the devilish brutality of the régime . . . the silent massacres that go on.'

Young Mohammed Messaud Kellon brought a report from the Algerian battle-front.   In a solemn, uplifting occasion representatives of missions of young Africans pledged themselves anew to the modern programme of Pan-Africa.

We pledged ourselves to support the single-minded purpose of all our leaders to secure independence for the Congo and majority rule and the defeat of apartheid throughout Africa.

They had won our full confidence in their determination to solve the problems of the balkanization of the Continent bequeathed by colonial rule, and to create the conditions for all-African co-operation. Yet we were concerned also about differences of opinion on the strategy of progress, and of differences of opinion on political action that was taking place during this time in the continent of Africa itself.

Several factors aggravated these differences, and were seized upon avidly by Africa's enemies abroad and exploited in the hope of provoking dissension – still a simple operation in a land mass of over eleven million square miles containing 250 million people speaking twelve different languages with more than 800 dialects, and poor communications. Most important among these factors was the diversity of constitutions which emerged from the agreements with the former colonial powers about independence ; some of them served to perpetuate the divisions of tribalism. There was also the natural desire of African states within the British Commonwealth of Nations to cherish that association while other states were equally eager to retain their links with the French Community. With the quickening approach of independence, all Africa was involved in the debate, as significant for the future of the world as for the future of Africa, about ways and means to African unity. The debate, inevitably, highlighted the questions that divided us, that being the primary purpose of debate ; it obscured for too many of us the more vital aims that united us.

At the same time, all leaders and governments were involved in the giant task of building up their countries and economics, from, often, meagre beginnings, and of securing the peace and integrity of their own states. The most urgent duty of all leaders was to ease the grinding poverty of the masses of ordinary folk who expected, quite properly, that the revolution sweeping Africa would bring some speedy relief from their long social misery. In this tense atmosphere, the differences that arose were almost bound to be exaggerated. They were finding expression in various groupings, each desirable in itself since each represented a long step forward to inter-state cooperation, yet all tending to encourage cross-currents that could impede progress towards the final Pan-African objective.

Let me digress now, to describe briefly the origin of these groupings.

THE AFRICAN GROUPINGS – PRECURSOR OF THE O.A.U.

In the end, it can be argued, these early alliances contributed powerfully to modern Pan-Africanism by posing, at a developing stage, many of the basic questions to which African unity alone can provide the answers. They were part of the democratic process of debate and discussion. They have an important place in the story of the African revolution.

The first Conference of Independent African States, held in Accra, in April 1958, soon after Ghana won freedom, was attended by Ghana, Liberia, Egypt, Tunisia, Libya, Sudan, Morocco, and Ethiopia, which began a faithful and fruitful relationship with her African neighbours. This epoch-making conference came to clear decisions on broad policy. All its members committed themselves to positive action for African freedom. They undertook to give direct support from within Africa to the F.L.N. in Algeria and to the opponents of apartheid in South Africa. They accepted the inspiration of the African Personality – postulating the re-birth of African culture and an understanding of Africa's distinctive contribution to the history of civilization – as the source of their own unity and their determination to secure, at once, a common African policy on international affairs. They agreed that the practice of this policy must imply support for the Charter of the United Nations, full acceptance of United Nations decisions, and loyalty to the Afro-Asian Bandung Declaration of 1955 which formulated the principle of Non-Alignment in these words : ' Abstention from the use of arrangements of collective defence to serve the particular interests of any of the Big Powers ; abstention by any country from exerting pressure on other countries '. Accordingly, they affirmed their respect for each other's political and territorial integrity and their willingness to seek conciliation on any disputes that might arise between them. They did more than condemn racialism in other countries. They determined ' to eradicate where they arise, vestiges of racial discrimination in their respective countries '.

In December 1958 there met, also in Accra, a Conference of the All-African Peoples' Organization. This, as a non-official assembly, exercised the privilege of all such assemblies to dot the ' i's ' and cross the ' t's ' of the great conference of the previous April. Referring to the slogan ' Africa for the Africans ', Chairman Tom Mboya declared : ' Once the principle of " one man one vote " is established, we will not practise racism in reverse '. Dr Nkrumah supported this view with an equally emphatic statement. ' when I speak of " Africa for the Africans ",' he said, ' this should be interpreted in the light of my emphatic declaration that I do not believe in racialism and colonialism. The concept – " Africa for the Africans " – does not mean that other races are excluded from it. No. It only means that Africans, who naturally are in the majority in Africa, shall and must govern themselves in their own countries.' Both speakers were voicing the views of all responsible African leaders. Our brothers of the F.L.N. raised the question of the use of force in the struggle for freedom, a question upon which they commanded the sympathy of the conference. The delegates pledged ' full support . . . to all those who are compelled to retaliate against violence to attain national independence and freedom for the people ', but wisely decided that national independence could be gained peacefully ' in territories where democratic means are available '. A third important principle of political action was enunciated by Dr Nkrumah. ' The independence of Ghana will be meaningless unless it is linked up with the total liberation of Africa.' It is a principle to which faithful adherence down the years has attracted the support of all independent African states. This conference was the authentic voice of the African masses. It was followed by an upsurge of the liberation movement in the Congo and in Southern Rhodesia, and by action in Malawi which carried nationalism to victory there.

In Chapter Four I shall explain the circumstances in which Ghana aided Guinea in her defiance of General de Gaulle, from which there developed the Ghana-Guinea Union in November 1958. That Union, the first ever entered into by Africans and between Africans, symbolized the expulsion of European and alien power from Africa. It was an historic

occasion.   On 2 May 1959, Guinea and Ghana 'solemnly
agreed to seal the Ghana-Guinea Union in practice' and, in
the Conakry Declaration of 24 December 1960, described the
basic principles of the Union of Independent African States.
African Unity, at last, had found its feet – they were on the
path to progress.

On 19 July 1959, President Tubman of Liberia met President
Sekou Touré and President Nkrumah at the village of Sanni-
quellie and issued a new Declaration calling for the creation
of the Community of Independent African States and describing the operations and objectives of such a Community.

My story switches now to the French-African Community
established by General de Gaulle under the constitution of the
Fifth Republic.   There, symptoms of the speed of change in
modern Africa were appearing.   Eleven countries had opted
for membership within the Community, but President Sekou
Touré's courageous rejection of de Gaulle and Guinea's
decision for independence had precipitated a precedent that
set public opinion alight throughout the Community.   In
April 1959, Senegal and the French Sudan formed the Mali
Federation, despite the neo-colonial intrigues of France.
Ivory Coast at once entered into economic arrangements with
Upper Volta, Niger and Dahomey – forming the *Conseil
de l'Entente*.   Political divergencies had brought the Mali
Federation close to collapse when, suddenly, de Gaulle granted
it independence within the Community, whereupon President
Houphouet-Boigny demanded independence for the *Entente*
outside the Community.   The result was that all the remaining
French territories south of the Sahara, except French Somaliland gained their independence by the autumn of 1960 ; a
result that indicated to intelligent observers that de Gaulle was
about to attempt a solution in Algeria.   Ex-French Sudan
retained the name Mali and on 24 December 1960, joined
Ghana and Guinea in a Union of African States.   On 1 July
1961, the three Presidents issued a detailed constitution containing an invitation to every state or federation of African
states accepting its aims and objects to join it.

Beyond all doubt, the political differences that led to the
formation of separate groupings were, basically, about the

tactics of attaining the Pan-African ideal to which all were committed. Should it be approached by way of federation and by what kind of federation, or by immediate positive action to build a Union Government of Africa ?

Those who were in favour of a federation were evolutionists who sincerely believed that federation must be evolved from a practical experience of working together in chosen fields like communications and regional economic collaboration. There were on the other side the instant men, who believed with equal sincerity that given the same agreed end of a Union of Africa there must, right at the outset, be a political agency whose task it would be to plan and relate the specific fields of collaboration in order that they should singly and together point at the same end.

The Union of African States and Madagascar – the Brazzaville Group – grew out of a conference called by the Ivory Coast in October 1960 to consider mediation between France and Algeria. By January 1961, the group – comprising Congo (Brazzaville), Ivory Coast, Senegal, Mauritania, Upper Volta, Niger, Dahomey, Chad, Gabon, the Central African Republic, Cameroun, and Madagascar – was able to publicize its Declaration. This asked France ' to conclude the war in Algeria in 1961, and after frank negotiations to apply honestly the principle of self-determination '. It supported United Nations action in the Congo, stating that what, above all, ' is required in the Congo (Leopoldville) is that no other State intervenes in her domestic affairs through the intermediary of soldiers or diplomats '. It created a Commission to study and propose ' a plan of African and Madagascan economic co-operation '.

The Casablanca Group – comprising Morocco, Guinea, Ghana, Mali, the United Arab Republic, Libya, and the Algerian Provisional Government – met early in January 1961, Ceylon also being represented. It issued an African Charter proposing the creation of ' an African Consultative Assembly, as soon as conditions permit, composed of the representatives of every African State, having a permanent seat and holding periodical sessions '. It established an African Political Committee, an African Economic Committee, an African Cultural

Committee and a Joint African High Command. It affirmed unshakeable adherence to the United Nations Charter and to the Declaration of the Afro-Asian Conference of Bandung, with the aim of promoting co-operation among all the peoples of the world and of consolidating international peace. A resolution on Algeria invited all countries ' to take steps forthwith to prevent their territories from being used directly or indirectly against the Algerian people ' ; called for the immediate withdrawal of all African troops serving under French command in Algeria ; and approved the enlistment of African and other volunteers in the Army of National Liberation.

As regards the Congo situation, the Group decided to withdraw troops placed under the United Nations Operational Command there. It demanded that the Command take immediate action to disarm and disband lawless rebels ; release from prison and detention all members of the Parliament and Government of the Republic ; re-convene the Parliament of the Republic ; eliminate all Belgian and other military and para-military personnel not belonging to the United Nations Operational Command whether operating as such or in disguise ; release to the legitimate Government all civil and military airports, radio stations and other establishments now unlawfully withheld from that Government ; and prevent the Belgians from using the United Nations Trust Territory of Ruanda-Urundi as a base to commit aggression – direct or indirect – and to launch armed attacks against the Congolese Republic.

The third significant group – Monrovia – was brought to birth in the Liberian capital on 8 May 1961. It comprised the twelve members of the Brazzaville group who were joined by Liberia, Nigeria, Somalia, Sierra Leone, Togo, Ethiopia, and Libya. Tunisia was present as an observer. Its major resolution was ' on the means of Promoting better understanding and Cooperation Towards achieving Unity in Africa and Malagasy '. This resolution declared that ' the Unity that is aimed to be achieved at the moment is not the political integration of sovereign African States, but unity of aspiration and of action considered from the point of view of African social solidarity and political identity '. Concrete measures proposed were the creation of an inter-African and Malagasy Advisory Organization and the setting up of a technical commission to work out ' detailed plans for economic, educational, cultural, scientific, and technical cooperation, as well as for communications and transportation among African and Malagasy States '.

On the grave, immediate questions facing Africa and the world, the conference made these decisions :

'. . . to give material and moral assistance to all dependent territories of colonial Powers with a view to accelerating their accession to independence '.

It welcomed the proposed opening of negotiations, on 20 May 1961, between France and Algeria, and appealed to the French Government and the Provisional Government of the Algerian Republic to ' conclude an agreement putting an end to the war and accord to Algeria its independence and territorial integrity '.

It re-affirmed its faith in the United Nations ' as the only Organization which, in spite of past weaknesses and mistakes in its work, is best adapted to achieve a real solution of the Congo problem '.

It condemned unreservedly ' the theory and practice of apartheid by the Government of the Union of South Africa ' and urged all African states and Malagasy ' to apply immediately political and economic sanctions, collectively and individually, against the Government of the Union of South Africa '.

The Monrovia Powers met again in Lagos in January 1962, when two important statements emerged. Emperor Haile Selassie declared that ' no fundamental irreparable rift ' existed in Africa ; President Azikiwe announced that those Powers absent from Lagos would be ' welcomed with open arms '.

The great debate within and between African countries was conducted with fierce and fervent vigour, often in strong words uttered bluntly by strong men – the future of the ideals all had pursued with passionate zeal and the fate of millions who loved them and were loved by them were at stake. It was conducted, too, at every level of African society, social, political, and trade union. And the urgent question could be put in these terms : Could the Pan-African movement build a real framework of Unity ? Summing up an exhaustive review of Pan-Africanism in 1962 in all its many manifestations, Mr Colin Legum wrote :

> If we look at Pan-Africanism today, just four years after its transplantation to Africa's soil, we see unmistakable signs of severe strains developing between its component parts. But we see something else as well. Despite all the setbacks, quarrels, and divisions the desire for unity has grown stronger, not weaker, in these last four years. More, not fewer, leaders, movements, and governments have embraced the cause of unity. Their argument is not over the need of Unity, but about the best way of achieving it. Admittedly, such arguments often produce a divisive rather than a unifying result, because in the end the argument becomes more important than the objective. But this has not yet happened in Africa.[1]

C.A.O.'s INITIATIVE

This, briefly, is the background of events in Africa itself which led the Committee of African Organizations, the youth of the Continent, to resolve to direct all their efforts towards helping to produce a unifying result.

Our Easter, 1962, Conference in London had many successes to record. Nyasaland had added her name to the African Freedom Roll. The F.L.N. had triumphed in Algeria. World moral opinion had learned the truth about the black hell we call South Africa as we grieved over the massacre of seventy-one Africans at Sharpeville. Chief Albert Luthuli had been awarded the 1961 Nobel Peace Prize and had delivered an oration of noble worth and humanity. Portugal had not dared to allow a seven-man Commission from the United Nations to inquire into conditions in her African colonies. Dr Nkrumah had declared his belief that African Unity was no longer a dream since both the Monrovia and the Casablanca Powers were agreed upon its desirability, indeed, its necessity. Dr Azikiwe, receiving Ghana's High Commissioner

[1] *Pan-Africanism : a Short Political Guide*, Pall Mall Press, 1962, p. 130.

to Nigeria, announced that he felt a moral obligation to help to strengthen Ghana-Nigerian ties because it was in the Gold Coast that ' I had a foretaste of the imperialism which nationalists of Ghana and Nigeria ultimately succeeded in dislodging ' ; and the then Governor-General added : ' The links between Ghana and Nigeria transcend the vagaries of politics and have stood the test of time '.

All the efforts of the West, and of the newspapers of the West, to divide Nigeria and Ghana and cast doubt on the future of Pan-Africanism had been confounded.

The Congo, unhappily, remained an ever-darkening tragedy. Mr Dag Hammerskjøld, Secretary-General of the United Nations, was *en route* to Katanga to implement the Security Council's resolution to expel the mercenaries when he was invited to meet a British Secretary of State with Mr Tshombe and Sir Roy Welensky at a village in Northern Rhodesia. The plane crashed on landing, and a staunch friend of international peace was killed.

Disturbing, too, was the possibility that the third conference of Independent African States, due to be held in Tunis, was unlikely to be convened. The second conference – following the inspiring assembly at Accra in 1958 – had been held in Addis Ababa in June 1960 and had done a fine job of consolidation, especially in relation to co-ordination of the African delegations to the United Nations. The suggestion of delay in organizing the third conference induced the Easter, 1962, meeting of the Committee of African Organizations to instruct their executive to act, and with speed. Already the Committee had incorporated thirty-nine African organizations. It had secured the affiliation of youth and student bodies in France, West Germany, East Germany, and Czechoslovakia. It was producing, under the brilliant editorship of Mr Antwi Akuako, who laboured without financial reward, its own official organ, *United Africa*, which was winning a growing audience and expanding influence among Africans at all levels from leadership to rank-and-file. A dedicated Secretary, Mr Dennis Phombeah, of Tanganyika, supported enthusiastically by his Chairman, Mr B. Chango Machyo, of Uganda, had gathered around him a devoted and efficient staff. The executive decided to interpret its mandate for action by convening a Conference which, in the cause of African Unity, would bring together representatives of students and young people from all over the world, and to convene this conference within the next months.

The Committee chose Belgrade as the city sited most conveniently to receive students from East and West. Yugoslavia is among the non-aligned powers of Europe, and Marshall Tito assured the Committee a generous, warm welcome. The date was fixed for 29 August ; delegates were to be presented with the Constitution of the All-African Students' Union in Europe and were to be invited to define afresh, as young people saw them, the immediate aims of Pan-Africanism. The current issue of *United Africa*, flown to Belgrade, carried on its front cover ' the flag of the Continental Union ' drawn by the editor on the design described in the Conakry Declaration of 1959. The map of Africa, in gold and mounted on a green background, showed thirty-nine black stars representing the African states, all of them linked by red lines signifying the bonds of blood and brotherhood. Located north-eastwards, the red rays from a yellow sun shone on the Continent. Delegates received the flag of the Continental Union with acclamation.

The draft Constitution is among the important historical documents of Pan-Africanism – precise, scholarly and, in some respects, a model for the constitution of the Union Government of young Africa's ambition. The preamble to the Constitution read :

We, the youth of Africa, possessing a glorious tradition and history from time immemorial, following the great spirit of independence as manifested in the achievement of freedom in a large number of African States and now being engaged in demonstrating to various African States that the emergence of a United States of Africa is essential for the salvation of that great Continent are determined :

(*a*) to promote understanding and unity amongst the youth of Africa and to develop a feeling of one community ;

(*b*) to accelerate the total liberation of Africa from imperialism, colonialism and neo-colonialism by working towards :

(1) the breaking up of all unholy alliances or associations with imperialist powers ;

(2) the removal of all foreign military bases from the national soil and evacuation of foreign troops therefrom ;

(3) the liquidation of monopolists and creation of national economy ;

(4) the establishment of democratic institutions eliminating evil social customs of all kinds ;

(c) to work hand-in-hand with all forces which are resolutely anti-imperialist and anti-colonialist, with a view to the realization of African Unity ;

(d) to work towards the achievement of a common policy, common foreign policy, and a common defence programme in Africa ;

(e) to work for the social and cultural development of Africa ;

(f) to work towards the eradication of ignorance, illiteracy, poverty, and the improvement of medical facilities in Africa ;

(g) to co-ordinate the activities of the youth organizations of Africa ;

(h) to mobilize world opinion in support of African liberation ;

(i) to ensure that this Union is truly independent ;

(j) to formulate concrete measures for the achievement of these objectives.[1]

Having approved the Constitution, which ensured a continuing life for the Committee of African Organizations, the delegates went into separate commissions to debate the problems of African unity in detail. The conference then met in plenary sessions to finalize a policy statement which harmonized all the issues our governments and leaders had been discussing during four tremendous years. This Communiqué[2] made the theme of African unity transcendent among Africans in Africa and young Africans all over the world.

The next step for the Committee of African Organizations was clear. Men and movements were crossing, gladly, the bridges of friendship and unity they had built. The all-embracing programme and the common platform it had

---

[1] The Constitution's seven Articles are printed in Appendix I, p. 275.

[2] Appendix II, p. 277.

laboured, with so many noble pioneers – past and present – to create, had won acceptance. The Committee decided to convert its Easter 1963 Conference into a second meeting of the Parliament of the All-African Students' Union, and summon representatives from all over the world to its sessions.

Parliament met in Friends House, London, on 17–19 April 1963. Young people rallied from thirteen European countries, from North, Central and South America, and from Canada. Their countries of origin were Algeria, Angola, Bechuanaland, Basutoland, Cameroon, Congo (Leopoldville), Gambia, Ghana, Kenya, Liberia, Morocco, Nigeria, Northern Rhodesia (Zambia), Nyasaland (Malawi), Mali, Portugal, Guinea, Senegal, Sierra Leone, Somalia, South Africa, Southern Rhodesia (Zimbabwe), Sudan, Tunisia, United Arab Republic, Uganda, and Zanzibar. They passed unanimously, for transmission to all Heads of African States and Governments, a simple, four-point manifesto :[1]

1. The Youth of Africa expect the leaders of Africa meeting at Addis Ababa to perform one clear and honest duty – the duty to unite all the States of Africa.
2. To this end, they should as individuals sink all their personal differences and as groups should disband the Casablanca, the Monrovia, and the Brazzaville Groups, so-called.
3. They should draw up a Charter of African Unity to which all the States should subscribe.
4. The Addis Ababa Conference should give a name to the Union and appoint a Secretariat as well as the seat of its operation.

These four major policy decisions, together with the full Manifesto, were unanimously approved for transmission to all African States and Governments. It had already been announced, in March 1963, that the third Conference of Independent African States would be held in Addis Ababa in May 1963. We in C.A.O. could have no doubt that the Belgrade Conference and its final communiqué, addressed to

[1] The full Manifesto of the Conference is printed as Appendix III, p. 283.

all Heads of States and Governments, had played no little part in bringing this about.

At Addis Ababa I was proud and happy to join the Ghana delegation where all the 32 Heads of States and Governments drew up and subscribed to the Charter of the Organization of African Unity. That was an occasion that will live in song and story. Yet, calling back yesterday, I shall remember and glory always in the courage, patriotism, self-sacrifice, and affectionate brotherhood of these young men and women of the Committee of African Organizations.

Our young people faced a challenge never before met by the youth of any continent. They revealed all the moral and mental qualities that will make our homeland great again. They bore aloft, with all the fearless generosity of the young in heart, the torch of unity which our leaders had lit, and they raised it proudly in days of darkness and doubt. Union Government, a dream of yesterday, is the assured reality of tomorrow. Young Africans helped to make it so. In their hands the future of united Africa will be secure and mighty and benign – for them and their children, and for the future of all mankind.

CHAPTER TWO

CONTINENTAL UNION GOVERNMENT FOR AFRICA : OUR DIAMOND OF HOPE

TRAGIC ANTECEDENTS

The first shipments of natural gas have recently been delivered by Algeria to Great Britain and Europe, and the Sahara oil strike is opening up another important supply of chemical products for the world. These physical facts establish in the Maghreb the most vital element of national development and independence – an internal source of physical power. Yet they leave the potential wealth of the Sahara virtually un-tapped ! And they are only part of the background to the question : how rich is Africa ?

The waters and rivers of Tanzania and Ethiopia are still unharnessed, and the vast hydro-electric possibilities of the African continent, estimated to represent more than 40 per cent of the potential still available to the world, are un-developed. Many other estimates suggest exciting possibilities : that the Congo basin, for example, could produce enough food crops to feed half the world – this in under-nourished Africa !

These facts are beyond dispute : Africa supplies more than 60 per cent of the world's gold ; most of its diamonds ; some of its copper, rubber, platinum, and iron ores ; much of its cocoa and a substantial part of its coffee, to say nothing of raw cotton, sisal, groundnuts, palm oil, citrus and hard woods.

Indeed, we are rich ; potentially, I believe, the richest un-developed land mass under the sun. Nevertheless, we are hungry in the midst of our plenty. And the reason is not far to seek. It can be found in the hundreds of surveys pigeon-holed in the governmental offices of all the former colonial powers. These surveys crumble into the dust of decay because, down the years, colonial investment has been concentrated on the get-rich-quick policy of extracting the resources of Africa – gold and diamonds especially – to the exclusion of colonial enterprise which might have ensured balanced industrial growth and social progress for the citizens of Africa.

Let me cite an example from Bechuanaland, whose lack of progress has always been attributed, and attributed wrongly, to the backwardness of the Africans.

In the early 1930's, radicals in Great Britain, the protecting power, were expressing alarm at Imperial neglect of the three Protectorates – Bechuanaland, Basutoland, and Swaziland – in the light of South Africa's threat to annex them and the growing fear that apartheid was turning the Union of South Africa into a swamp of indecency. The Protectorates had been reduced to mere labour reserves from which poorly-paid labour could be recruited for the Rand gold mines. Meantime, the lands were being scourged by wind and sun and flood.

The British Government sent Sir Alan Pim, K.C.I.E., a former Indian Civil Servant, on a tour of the Protectorates, Kenya and Northern Rhodesia. His report on Bechuanaland was published in 1933.[1] It revealed shocking poverty, malnutrition, disease, and a neglect of social services. The contribution from general revenue for educating 8,000 African children attending school was £100 per annum and for 180 European children £1,000. There was one hospital bed for every 2,800 Africans. Sir Alan stressed the urgent need for additional water supplies, better breeding of cattle and technical instruction in preparing skins and hides. He denounced South Africa's effective application of economic sanctions against the Territory and its dynamic young leader, Tshekedi Khama, Chief of the Bamangwato, in the form of a cattle embargo. This embargo had operated against cattle below a certain weight since 1925. It was poverty's whip lashing young labour into Johannesburg's jungle. The British Government ignored its responsibility to examine and aid water development and the cattle industry. It did nothing to crack down on South African sanctions. It allocated a grant-in-aid of £177,000 to the Protectorate and, no doubt, expected God's blessing on its Imperial generosity !

Just over ten years later, the Agricultural Adviser to the British Administration proposed that the Mbabe Depression,

[1] Cmd. 4368.

containing soil 'of high quality' and capable of withstanding
'heavy grazing', should be irrigated. Meantime, Tshekedi,
an enthusiastic rancher, had improved the quality of his cattle
and was exporting increasing quantities to the Belgian Congo
and surrounding countries. He had created a growing dairy
milk industry. He was pressing for technical and financial
help to establish canning facilities. He was pleading for the
construction of a port in the natural harbour at Walvis Bay,
in South-West Africa, for two important reasons. Such a port
would increase and cheapen access between Great Britain,
the Protectorates, and the Rhodesias, stimulating trade
between them and the outside world. It would also defeat
South Africa's policy of charging higher freight rates on food
and grain sent to Palapye than on the same freight carried 800
miles farther, on the same trains, to Salisbury.

Nothing was done. The British failed to protect their
Protectorate. South Africa retained all her inhuman rights
to impose cattle and grain sanctions on Bechuanaland.

Another aspect of Tshekedi Khama's long and tragic struggle
to communicate his African initiative and imagination to his
white bosses was his refusal, despite British Government pressure, to endorse a concession, granted in 1893 and later
withdrawn, to the British South Africa Company to mine
coal and other minerals in his territory. Presented with a
virtual *fait accompli* in 1929, Tshekedi resisted on the advice of
his tribe in Kgotla. Had he been willing to concede his
tribe's ownership of mineral rights under the Protectorate
agreement, and betrayed his people's need and desire for
social progress, investment money would have poured into
Bechuanaland in the twinkling of an eye.

Perhaps I am unkind to the British. Maybe the real truth
is that too many of them in high office know too little about
Africa. In her interesting story of Tshekedi's life,[1] Mary
Benson tells a charming and illuminating tale told by the late
Douglas Buchanan, K.C., a hero among Africans in the Cape
and one of their vigorous representatives in the South African
Parliament before representation of the Coloureds by white
M.P.'s was withdrawn by the Verwoerd régime. Buchanan

[1] *Tshekedi Khama*, Faber and Faber, 1960, p. 114.

accompanied Tshekedi to London as his legal adviser to meet Mr Malcolm MacDonald, then Under-Secretary of State for the Dominions, and now a considerable authority on, and a good friend of, Africa. Miss Benson then relates Buchanan's own account of his lunch with Mr MacDonald.

> We arrived on time to find MacDonald and two other gentlemen awaiting us, the permanent head of the department and his deputy. When we were seated Mr MacDonald said : ' I have always been kept so busy with major dominion affairs that I had never even heard of the Bechuanaland Protectorate, much less the Bamangwato, so I am going to ask you, Mr Buchanan, to start from the beginning and tell me how Bechuanaland became a Protectorate and bring us right up to date.' He then turned to the permanent head and said : ' You must just be patient as you know all that Mr Buchanan will have to say.' To that the permanent head replied : ' I am in exactly the same position as yourself, sir, and that is why I have brought my next in rank.' To which that person added : ' Well, sir, I am in the same position, as my time has been so fully taken up with Ireland.'

And Douglas Buchanan's tail-piece ?
' Well ! Our lunch party continued till about four o'clock. I did not get much lunch as I was kept talking all the time.'

Debate about whether, without the advent of Colonialism, Africa would have emerged, in her own way, as a great modern industrial complex, is speculation made futile by time and fate. Certainly, the harnessing of animals from elephants to camels to the colourful caravans of trade, was an African equivalent of the West's horse-and-buggy. In devising tools to satisfy his immediate needs, the African has always been as ingenious as any other man. He has revealed aptitude and courage and endurance in modern war. His innate capacity for hard work and enterprise is admitted and demonstrable – in the dramatic, indigenous development of cocoa in the Gold Coast (Ghana), and in the fact that, even today, no man works harder for less reward than the Egyptian fellah. The stimulant of economic enterprise and machine production is trade, and no visitor to the bazaars of Cairo or the street markets of West Africa would deny that, to Africans, trade is an exciting, skilful adventure.

' In West Africa,' writes Mr Ken Post,[1] ' there was a tradition of trade with the European extending back to the fifteenth-century contacts with the Portuguese. Places like Gorée, Cape Coast, and Calabar had been centres of trade in commodities such as slaves, ivory, and gold-dust for centuries. Whole kingdoms, Dahomey and Benin the most famous, had flourished upon trade with foreign merchants, and the coastal areas with their hinterland, the whole of the " forest belt " in fact, were no strangers to Europeans and European merchandise.' Similar patterns of trade have been traced north, south, and east in Africa. While Africans controlled the political areas of trade, the possibility of creating stable, economically progressive societies was always present. So, too, was the possibility of individual and collective accumulation of capital, essential for the introduction of machine production. Colonialism, and its conquest of the political areas of trade, denied these possibilities to Africans. The Africans' reaction to Europeans hell-bent on making change but with little or no understanding of what they were determined to change, is reflected in the explorer Mungo Park's *Travels in the Interior Districts of Africa* : '. . . even the poor Africans whom we affect to consider as barbarians, look upon us, I fear, as little better than a race of formidable but ignorant heathens.'

Slave-trading, as Dr Eric Williams, Prime Minister of Trinidad and Tobago, points out in his classic study of the subject,[2] was economic, not racial, in its origin. It was an extension of the system of transporting convict labour as indentured servants from England to the West Indies to open up the sugar plantations. ' The need of the plantations outstripped the English convictions.' It was found, also, that ' the money which procured a white man's services for ten years could buy a Negro for life . . . Kidnapping in Africa encountered no such difficulties as were encountered in England. Captains and ships had the experience of the one

[1] *The New States of West Africa*, Penguin, 1964, p. 43.
[2] *Capitalism and Slavery*, Andre Deutsch, 1964 ed., p. 19.

trade to guide them in the other. Bristol, the centre of the servant trade, became one of the centres of the slave trade. Capital accumulated from the one financed the other. White servitude was the historic base upon which Negro slavery was constructed. The felon-drivers in the plantations became without effort slave-drivers. " In significant numbers . . . the Africans were latecomers fitted into a system already developed ! " '[1]

The ambition of every slave-trader, British, Dutch, Portuguese or whatever, was monopoly ownership of the human being and free trade in selling him, body and soul, in the market-places of the world. Industrialism – largely the accident of geography in the distribution of the world's resources of coal and iron, steam and power – was fashioning a fresh manifestation of the Imperial idea. This was to exploit African slaves in their own homeland. Colonists, backed by Governments, grabbed Africa's mineral wealth, applying their growing industrial techniques to its extraction. They dominated the areas of trade politically with the support of Imperial arms. They acquired authority over the entire economy. For Africans, there remained only the development of cash and subsistence crops.

SERFS TO ALIEN MASTERS

The new pattern of trade made Africans not partners in their national heritage but serfs to the alien masters of a changing economy. In addition to existing tribal boundaries, many new frontiers imposed by alien dictatorship divided them. True, slavery gradually ceased to be politically condoned ; even the Churches of the West felt compelled to condemn it. Economic domination, however, was justified on both religious and political grounds, at home and abroad. It was the apotheosis of the profit motive. Colonialism pursued it with a passionate joy in its dividend-making results.

Yet Colonialism, in the Marxist phrase, contained within itself the seeds of its own destruction. Although it intensified

---

[1] Professor V. B. Phillipps : *Life and Labours in the Old South*, p. 25, (Boston, 1924), as quoted by Dr Eric Williams, *op. cit.*

the backwardness of Africa's backward areas, it promoted new interests in the areas producing cash crops and developed a taste for consumer goods. Many of its civil administrators, shocked by the brutality of the system, pursued the ideals of trusteeship with a single-mindedness for which Africans will always honour them. Colonial economic interests effected a mixing of the African populations through travel. This, and the minimal education provided to serve colonial needs, created an awareness in the African political leaders of the importance of social services and a social infrastructure. Colonialism's failure to do a reasonable social job stimulated social discontent.

Colonialism required, and gave many Africans, a *lingua franca*. Social discontent, divine discontent, forced the rise of the mighty nationalist movements which united us. The *lingua franca* – French or English – enabled our leaders to communicate the unifying power of nationalism and the moral purposes which set our continent ablaze. Today, African unity is still a rainbow shining ' on storm-driven skies and the dark tribulations of men '. Tomorrow, African unity will bring peace and freedom into African affairs and, I believe in my heart, into the affairs of all mankind.

These general reflections on the reaction and interaction of slavery and colonialism on the economy and social life of Africa lead me, naturally, to a rather more detailed, comparative study of our pre-independence development ; development about which even some of the chiefs were ignorant until they discovered that alien politicians had robbed them of their country and their native wealth.

Europe had her first predominantly economic contacts with Africa at the start of the slave trade. These contacts began south of the Sahara and they were tied up with the trade to the East Indies. Commerce in African slaves originated in Imperial Rome and, say some of the historians, continued under the Muslim domination of North Africa.

African slaves were common in ancient Arabia, Turkey, Persia, and India. Europe's thrust into the Americas demanded able-bodied people to boost the new economy. From the early years of the sixteenth century this demand was supplied by the sons and daughters of Africa. Spanish, Flemish, and Genoese merchants were all involved in the slave trade. After 1560 the English began to take part. The earliest victims came mostly from the rivers between Cape Verde and the Niger. Territories as far south as Angola were bereft of men and became blighted. The Portuguese had established a series of stations from Cape Verde to the Congo. Then began the search for gold, giving an added stimulus to the greed of the early European explorers. As soon as the trade route to India became known, the east coast of Africa was colonized. Thus both the west and east coasts, as well as the area we now know as the Cape, were opened up for exploration. The explorers, however, kept their colonies close to the coast and built forts to protect themselves from attack by those Africans who were keen enough to sense the future. And so for nearly five hundred years the slave trade flourished. The trade was discriminating. The Portuguese-created forts gradually became, not places of defence, as many historians would have us believe, but auction marts for human beings. Not all the unhappy people who were press-ganged were accepted for the American plantations. The auctions were held mainly to weed out the men of normal physical fitness and to market those who were stronger than average.

Africa south of the Sahara was drained of its strongest and most virile citizens for well-nigh five centuries. An interesting sidelight on this iniquity can be seen at the present stage of world history. I refer to the distinctions which Africans in the United States have won for that country in the areas of world sport. They have distinguished themselves too in music, in the arts, and in medicine. These successes in no way compensate for the evil visited upon their ancestors, who, after all, did more to build up the wealth of Europe and the New World, by the sweat of their brow, than any other race in the world.

Another shameful part of colonial history concerns the merchant adventurers and their visits to the west coast of Africa. The English among them received a charter from Elizabeth I which was continued under Charles II when these pirates were given the title of the Royal Africa Company. The main purpose of this Company was to capture some of the lucrative slave-trade, previously monopolized by the Dutch, between West Africa and British settlements in North America and the West Indies. It was a case of the European powers quarrelling over the spoils of conquest. But powerful associations of merchants often given some sort of quasi-official charter by their European country of origin continued to administer the forts and trading stations of the west coast of Africa.

Then, further south, diamonds were discovered in 1866 and gold began to be mined in the Transvaal, on the Rand, in 1886. Diamond diggings helped to demonstrate the field in which African labour could collaborate most profitably with European overseers. In mining, the close supervision of the more routine tasks increased the relative efficiency of Native labour, and the burden of transport costs was reduced considerably.

Development through the agency of companies grew considerably during the years preceding and following the Berlin Conference, a gathering of European powers summoned to slice up Africa into economic units which were then parcelled out among the participating powers as ' spheres of influence '. Having denuded West Africa of her manhood, the merchants now decided to exploit the rest of the continent and continue the process of enslavement although, by this time, slavery as such had been officially abolished by the British Government.

In British territories the Royal Niger Company, the Imperial East Africa Company, and the British South Africa Chartered Company all served to expand British trade and influence. In the Belgian territories the Congo Company for Industry and Commerce, founded in 1886, established a series of subsidiary companies for the development of particular areas or activities. In French Equatorial Africa an epoch of Concessions to the Companies opened in 1899. In the Portuguese possessions the Mozambique Company and the Company of Mossamedes, among others, exercised almost unlimited power over a wide terrain. In the German territories the Deutsche Ostafrikanische Gesellschaft and the privileged companies in South-West Africa and in the North and South Cameroons operated on similar lines.

The companies varied greatly in size and in the methods they employed. Some accepted more responsibility towards Africans than others ; even where responsibilities were normally assumed some took them more seriously than others. In territories unsuited to European settlement, early attempts to develop trade involved much wastage of the resources of the colony. Rubber and forest timber were exhausted without proper replacement ; trees were ' mined ' instead of being cropped. Accumulations of ivory were for a period obtained by exchange of cheap imports.

The first decade of the twentieth century saw the revocation of the earlier grants of concessions and the separation of the functions of trading from those of government. French and Belgian policy moved early in this direction. In the British territories, administration was transferred from the chartered companies to the Crown by more gradual stages.

Quite early in the lives of the chartered companies it was realized that the larger combines could afford organization to control the conditions and welfare of the native employees. This was one cause of the apartheid policy of South Africa and the Rhodesias and to a less marked extent, that of Kenya. To increase further the stability of the European populations, the plantation system was devised in the development of the agricultural resources of the country. The White Highlands of Kenya, for example, were set aside for settlers. Apartheid, already a harsh economic fact, now became a social disease. This was the evil against which the Kikuyu people, deprived of their rightful lands, naturally rebelled.

The Economic Tragedy of Africa

At the turn of the century, Africa was producing a large proportion of the world's exports of palm and palm-kernel, oil, wool, and cocoa, and was making a substantial contribution to the export of groundnuts. It was, however, its mineral wealth which offered the strongest attraction to European capitalists. To win the fullest benefit from Africa's immense mineral resources, railways, ports, and towns were built. Where minerals were found in areas climatically attractive to

Europeans, as in South Africa and the Rhodesias, colonies of white settlers and planters were established. Where conditions were favourable for farming after the European pattern, more plantations were established. Hence, flue-cured tobacco and tea were grown in Central Africa and sisal in East Africa.

Africa, inevitably, was caught up in the Great Slump of the late twenties and the early thirties : inevitably, because all the dependent territories were tethered to the banks and stock exchanges of the outside world. During these years Sierra Leone and Nigeria suffered falls of 53 per cent in their revenues. Kenya and Uganda suffered a decline of 39 per cent ; Tanganyika and the Gold Coast, declines of 56 per cent and 39 per cent respectively. And this in spite of an increase in the value of gold production. Taken as a whole, Africa's revenues fell by 48 per cent. Remember that the African peoples were geared to the economies of Europe and were living as European finance determined they should live – that is, in miserable poverty. Yet the depression was less damaging to the African economies than to other more developed areas. The total recorded value of world exports declined by 66 per cent in the period 1929–34, compared with a decline of 73 per cent in North America and only 48 per cent in Africa. European farmers in Africa were financially embarrassed and were often driven to seek government assistance. The drift of European agricultural labourers to the towns of the Union of South Africa produced a serious ' white ' unemployment problem. Wage-earning Africans, wisely, had never abandoned the cultivation of subsistence crops and were able to return to full-time subsistence production when displaced from other employment.

Another important aspect of the labour situation must be noted here. Employment in the mines of the Belgian Congo, the Rhodesias, and South Africa had become the source of cash income for the populations of adjacent countries. This labour was acquired and organized in the most arbitrary way. In Angola and the territories of equatorial Africa poverty and hunger were imposed deliberately on the native population to ensure that they would seek work beyond the borders of their home countries. The system of forced labour, full details of which have only recently come to light, was an accepted method of enabling great corporations to continue exploiting Africa and the Africans. Fifty-seven per cent of Africans employed in South Africa's gold mines in 1947 came from outside the Union's borders. In West Africa the coastal towns which had grown in response to the regular export of cash crops, were becoming increasingly dependent on outside sources for their livelihood ; in Nigeria and the Gold Coast there was more specialization on particular crops and expanding external trade between one area and another. While African rural communities remained relatively unaffected by the economic crises in Europe and the Americas, those Africans who were driven out of the European-designated reserves to become urbanized in the shanty towns south of the Sahara did not fare well. The death roll from hunger probably rose to tens of thousands. The facts were hushed up at the time.

Then came World War II. Miraculously and, as it were, overnight, the picture changed. Once again there was great demand for foodstuffs and raw materials. Yet the lot of the African people remained as miserable as ever. Those who were making huge profits out of their labour and out of the raw material from their soil gave no thought to what is known as common justice. The shanty towns are still there as witness to their absolute greed.

Although tropical Africa accounts for only a comparatively small percentage of total world trade, in a number of important commodities it is the largest single exporter. The following table is reproduced from the Food and Agricultural Organization Africa Survey, published by the United Nations :

Share of World Trade of Principal African Commodities, 1959

Commodity	Share of World Exports %
Palm kernels .	93·4
Groundnuts .	83·8
Diamonds	80·0
Sesame seeds .	72·4

Commodotity	*Share of World Exports* %
Cocoa	70·5
Groundnut oil	69·5
Palm oil	65·3
Sisal	61·2
Cotton seed	60·2
Palm kernel oil	55·1
Copper – by quantity, not value . .	26·6
Coffee	19·6
Cotton lint	17·5
Tobacco	11·2
Lumber – by quantity, not value . .	7·2
Natural rubber	5·2

Gambia today derives the main part of its export revenues from groundnuts, Uganda from cotton, Zanzibar from cloves, the Union of South Africa from gold and diamonds, Rhodesia from tobacco and minerals, Zambia from copper, Ghana from cocoa, Sierra Leone from diamonds, iron ore, and palm kernels, and Nigeria from cocoa, groundnuts, and palm kernels.[1] Malawi is still largely agricultural, yet it obtains 9 per cent of its revenue from the labour of its migrants working in the mines and factories of adjacent territories. Similarly for Mozambique. In 1952 it was estimated that more than 260,000 Africans were away from home at work in South Africa or Southern Rhodesia. An even greater dependence on migrant labour holds in the High Commission territories of Bechuanaland, Swaziland, and Basutoland. By June 1953, there were some three-quarters of a million non-indigenous Africans from these territories living in the Union of South Africa.

Outside the areas of European settlement, the greatest advances in industrialization have been made in what was called formerly the Belgian Congo. There, the index of manufacturing production, including electricity supply,

[1] Since the oil strike in Eastern Nigeria, oil has displaced cocoa as Nigeria's main foreign exchange earner.

increased in value by three-quarters and in volume by 90 per cent in the period 1950–53. The most important enterprises have been electricity and metal, which depend entirely upon the mining industry, and textiles, beer, tobacco, and food for local consumption. The main market for consumer goods is an African urban population of just over two million people living outside their customary environment and, consequently, outside the basic subsistence economy.

In other parts of Africa not blessed with the mining industry or a European community, the scale of industrialization and specialization following the growth of markets has been much smaller. These considerations should not incline us to overlook the human and other factors inherent in the economic conditions. The African is essentially agricultural in his outlook. Europeans have always been industrially minded, especially where there was cheap African labour available for factories and mines. Within the restricted range of industrial production open to tropical African countries there is a variety of possibilities for small-scale local initiative. Cotton-ginning is well established in the cotton producing areas of Uganda, the Congo, and Malawi. In what was formerly French West Africa, groundnut oil is produced and refined together with its by-products, oil cake, soap, and glycerine. In Angola the most important secondary industry produces dried fish, fish cake, and fish oil. Textile, cigarettes and soap factories are to be found in the least industrialized areas. Cement factories have been erected in ex-French West Africa, ex-French Equatorial Africa, Mozambique, and Uganda, as well as in the Congo, Kenya, Nigeria, Zambia, and Rhodesia ; and there are oil refineries in Ghana and Nigeria.

In general, however, there must be markets for even the smallest factory industry. Without the market, the industry is not viable. Outlay is wasted. Thus it follows that in some territories the existence of a well-developed cottage industry may offer better opportunities for steady economic advance than large-scale undertakings. In Nigeria, for example, only a decade ago, production by factory methods as distinct from

native crafts was estimated to contribute less than £1 million
to the gross domestic product of £596·7 million, whereas rural
industries like spinning and weaving, tailoring, leather work,
illicit gin-distilling, wood carving, and other native crafts were
estimated to contribute as much as £8·5 million. Even where
the village industry is limited to subsistence or semi-subsistence
output, the volume of the output may constitute an appreciable
part of the gross domestic product.

International comparisons of *per capita* national income can
never be more than a very rough guide to the relative real
income per head. Even where statistical methods are similar,
price variations and other factors affect the precision of the
comparisons. Overall averages are highest where the mineral
industry is well-developed and where the European population
is large enough for the characteristically high European
averages to have a significant effect on the national average.
Actually these statistics, however well founded, must be suspect.
Africans in all territories controlled by European colonialists
are paid such minute salaries and wages that they would
probably be better off in their own cottage industries. The
average European wage is so far above any that the African
is permitted to earn that there is no real comparison at
all.

Dr A. J. Hanna has written of Southern Rhodesia :[1]

> The white trade unionists have taken their stand on the
> principle of 'equal pay for equal work', by which they mean
> equal pay for holding the same category of job, regardless of
> competence to do it. Provided that employers will pay Africans
> the full, artificially high European wage rate, they will not object
> – because they well know that employers will not pay it . . .
>
> The statistics published by the Federal Government show that
> in 1958 African wages and salaries averaged £80, while non-
> African (almost wholly European, but including Indian and
> 'coloured') averaged £995. Whatever allowance may have to
> be made for the relative inefficiency of African labour, the gap
> which separates these figures is striking when compared with
> the 'differentials' in Britain, or any socially homogeneous
> country, between the wages of skilled and unskilled workers.

[1] *The Story of the Rhodesias and Nyasaland*, Faber, 1960, pp. 191–2.

The truth is that *per capita* income figures can always be weighted towards whatever argument the author is trying to prove. On the back cover of *Africa Report* for August 1963 – the journal is published by the African-American Institute in Washington – there is a comparative table of *per capita income* in Africa in 1961 printed without any explanatory material. This table puts Gabon's average at $200. The figure is suspect ; it purports to make the per capita income of Gabon higher than Ghana, which it puts at $199. A sounder source, the F.A.O. African Survey, relating to the year 1959, spurns definite figures which, it says, cannot be accurately calculated and instead groups countries into income ranges. Ghana, Senegal, Rhodesia, and Nyasaland fall into the top group of $151–200, Gabon falls into the second group, in company with Liberia, Ivory Coast, and Congo (Brazzaville), $101–50.

In Liberia [says *African Survey*] 44 per cent of the income accrues to foreign firms. The Federation of Rhodesia and Nyasaland is in the highest income group, mainly because of the high level of income of foreign individuals and companies. Relative high average incomes in Gabon and Congo (Brazzaville) give little impression of the extreme poverty which prevails in these countries. In Gabon, where about one-third of the income accrues to the European population, which accounts for a bare one per cent of the total, it is estimated that the average African family earns Fr.CFA 50,000 (203 dollars) in contrast to the average foreign family, which earns Fr.CFA 1,500,000 (6,076 dollars).

Clearly, the share of the indigenous African in his country's wealth is miserly, especially where the African himself is not fully in control of his country's economy but depends upon colonial masters or foreign investment. The following conclusions are significant for the African.

First, political control of its own trade area is vital to every independent African state if African standards of living are to reflect faithfully the tremendous effort now being made by all states to escape from the morass of poverty in a potentially rich continent.

Second, only overall political direction of economic development by a Union Government can achieve these aims : a reasonable price level for primary products in the commodity markets of the world together with marketing arrangements to even out booms and slumps ; and the retention, in Africa and for Africans, of enough of the profit of its export trade as will enable capital accumulation and capital growth to finance expanding industries.

Third, the assurance, which only a Union Government whose authority extends throughout the continent can guarantee, that foreign investment and enterprise will be rewarded fairly, even generously, without the threat arising of neo-colonialism and a return to the conditions which, for centuries, have made Africans aliens in their own homeland.

Positive Steps

Obviously, the grand design for all-African unity had to begin as a political idea. ' Seek ye first the political kingdom ' was the theme preached, year in and year out, by the Leader of the Convention People's Party in Ghana. As it inspired the hearts and informed the minds of his fellow-countrymen, Kwame Nkrumah expanded the theme, always basic to Pan-African propaganda, that only freedom for all Africa could ensure freedom for all the individual sister states of Africa. So the idea of continental unity was woven into the very fabric of the nationalism which swept the new leaders to victory and their countries to independence. Ghana, followed in quick time by other progressive independent states, provided for the supra-sovereignty of Union Government in her constitution.

Sovereignty and security are synonymous. That is why modern states fear, and act on the fear, that any sacrifice of any part of one must involve loss of the other. African nationalists soon came to grips with the sophisticated idea, not yet appreciated in the West, that if no part of sovereignty and security can be sacrificed in order to avoid threat to other countries, both principles endanger national integrity and international cooperation for peace. This same idea was stirring among Asian nations. It attracted Ethiopian representatives and Ghanaian observers to the Bandung (Indonesia)

Conference of April 1955 ; a conference made notable by two facts. 'At last the non-white peoples seemed to be coming together' and 'the news spread widely of a common bond between peoples who had suffered, and people who still suffered, from the evils of colonial rule ';[1] and here it was that the new President of Egypt, Colonel Nasser, gave full and powerful support to the policy of a dynamic neutralism endorsed by all free countries with no interest in oppressing or exploiting other nations.

I quote Mr Ken Post again, and at some length. His summing up fills in the background to the mighty efforts that blazed the golden trail to Addis Ababa in May 1963, when the Organization of African Unity finally converted the propaganda for unity into an organized, purposeful force for positive action. It also enables the reader to dismiss from his mind the doubts and sneers and misrepresentations with which too many Western commentators treated one of the most important meetings in world history.

The themes of the Bandung Conference, writes Mr Post,[2]

were again explored at the Afro-Asian People's Solidarity Conference held in Cairo in January 1958, but at the same time certain new important features emerged. First of all, the ' Cold War ' became more obtrusive ; both the People's Republic of China and the U.S.S.R. were invited to attend, and, although the neutrality of the Afro-Asian countries was emphasized, the leader of the Soviet delegation seized the opportunity to offer aid for development for newly-independent states. Secondly, it became apparent that the Africans did not necessarily consider their ties with the Arab or Asian countries to be particularly close. In March 1957, at the time of Ghana's independence, Kwame Nkrumah had already announced that he would call a Pan-African Nationalist Conference at Accra in the near future. After April 1958, when the first conference of Independent African States was held at Accra, it was Ghana which more often than not set the pace. The will of Kwame Nkrumah towards Pan-African unity and the opportunity given him by the comparatively early independence of Ghana ensured this central role,

[1] Ken Post : *The New States of West Africa*, Penguin, 1964, p. 154.
[2] Post, *op. cit.*, pp. 154–5.

which was reinforced by the holding of another meeting, the All-African People's Conference, at Accra in December 1958.

Bandung, Cairo, and the second Accra meeting of 1958 thus introduced a theme which has dominated the foreign relations of the African states, and introduced it even before most of them became independent. This theme was the solidarity of all peoples who had been subjected to colonial rule, and the need to free those who remained subjects of the ' imperialists ', or, as in South Africa, of a dominant white minority. Afro-Asian solidarity Conferences have continued to be held, at Conakry in April 1960 and Moshi (in Tanganyika) in February 1963. The first All-African People's Conference set up a permanent secretariat, the All-African People's Organization, and further Conferences have been held, at Tunis in January and Cairo in March 1961.

This first All-African People's Conference also introduced a second theme, which has dominated relations between the African states themselves. One of the resolutions stated that the ' ultimate objective of African nations is a Commonwealth of Free African States ', and Pan-African Unity, the dream of Nkrumah and other nationalist leaders, found itself proclaimed as a goal while only a small part of the continent was free. Debate on the right way to achieve what most African leaders accepted without question as a desirable objective was to occupy much attention during the next five years.

The debate was fast, free, furious, and – yes, almost always – fraternal !

The idealists among us soon learned that it is not the number of countries struggling towards freedom that counts when, as the English say, ' the chips are down ', but the spirit of the people in those countries. Often enough the spirit of the people is reflected in the varying temperaments, ambitions, even suspicions of their leaders and of the leaders of the separate political parties within the country. Did not the late Lord Beaverbrook make the propaganda-machines he called his newspapers the most widely read and the most fiercely hated in Great Britain by ' personalizing ' political issues ? The conflicts of personalities within parties frequently exceeds in sheer venom the clash on principles between parties. Moreover, the colonial powers still possessed an ace of trumps which has taken many tricks since it was first played by the

Roman Imperial machine. To African, Asians, and Europeans subjected to their ruthless conquest, the Romans offered hope of *order*. Life having been disordered by invasion and plunder, *order* was the main benefit to be earned by submission to invasion and plunder ! The modern equivalent of the Pax Romanus through all debate about African Unity lies in the promise of economic advancement for all the peoples, as peoples and as citizens of a continent. Could African leaders, with their meagre resources (and with enormous demands for reform becoming increasingly urgent) insist that aid from outside should be treated, not in relation to the requirements of the donors, but in relation to the long-term needs of all African states ? Aid – aid with strings – was colonialism's ace of trumps. It has been at the root of most of the differences over the principles upon which unity should be based and for many states it poisoned and undermined their power of choice. It explains why, throughout this book, I have stressed the importance of all aid being funnelled through and administered by the United Nations.

The vigour of debate in Africa on the methods of achieving unity developed support for two ideas which have always been implicit in the Convention People's Party's case for African Unity. One was that an African Common Market offered immediately realizable hopes of raising the level of Africa's economic activity and that the project could be stimulated by the creation of a common African currency. The other idea was that all African states, whatever their form of government, could escape dependence on foreign aid only if they exercised effective control over the produce of their extractive industries. These industries offer a major source, in some states the only source, for capitalizing our natural assets and accumulating development finance. They are also a major objective for colonial penetration and re-entry into the African economy – for neo-colonialism and all the dangers it represents to our societies.

The first of the two Conferences held in Accra in 1959 hammered out these three principles of action :

1. Cooperation on foreign policy and concerted effort in diplomacy.

2. Unified economic planning to cover all Africa.
3. Common defence planning leading to the creation of an African Military High Command.

The conception of the African Personality, now accepted as a philosophical symbol of the release of African personality and a guide to thought on unity, was discussed at a high intellectual level; it gave birth to the proposition that an African literature should be encouraged – one that was free from misrepresentations of the history and culture of the African people. Following the Conference, President Nkrumah led a goodwill mission from Ghana to all countries taking part – Ethiopia, Libya, Tunisia, Morocco, Egypt, Liberia, and the Sudan – thus giving clear physical expression to the fact he had thundered home when opening the first session: ' Today we are one. If in the past the Sahara divided us, now it unites us. And an injury to one of us is an injury to all of us. From this Conference must go out a new message: ' Hands off Africa! Africa must be free.'

In the fierce ferment of new ideas, and in face of the growing demands of the African masses for federation, differences and difficulties – some of them serious – arose. These were our growing pains: severe enough, yet less permanent than the growing pains of federation in Europe and America, where our critics often forget that self-interest, so dominant in the history of their own continents, has been a factor shaping events in Africa too. Important above all deviations and desertions and disappointments is that the great cause lived on, African leaders learned well the lessons of history in the making, history of their making. The Organization of African Unity is the most dynamic force in Africa today, and a power of growing dimensions in the world of today and tomorrow.

TRIALS OF THE TIMES

The student of African politics might find useful some first-hand observations on the Accra Conference and on the various congresses and meetings that preceded the great Assembly of Heads of States at Addis Ababa in 1963. First, however, I must note the groupings inspired by the intensity of an African situation in which colonialism was collapsing and the popular clamour for independence was growing. I disapproved of the policy of most of these groups; each of them disapproved of almost all the others! Nevertheless, they were an important reflection of the turmoil of the times and a living proof of the political awakening of Africa, and the realization that the artificial divisions left over from colonial times were entirely unsatisfactory. All Africa realized that a regrouping was necessary. But few African countries were in a position fully to appreciate the radical nature of the regrouping which was called for. The regrouping which actually took place and resulted in the formation of the Casablanca Group, the Brazzaville Group, and the Monrovia Group represented a historic and inevitable stage in the African revolution, but it contained in itself the seeds of its own destruction, for it was inadequate and did not offer a thorough solution to the socio-economic problems of Africa.

The members of the Casablanca group, which had cultural and military committee meetings twice a year, were Egypt, Morocco, Ghana, Guinea, Mali, and Algeria, with representatives from Libya in attendance. The political committee of the Casablanca group sometimes met at Heads of State level.

The Monrovia group sought to produce a draft constitution for an Organization of African States. The Conference (May 1961) which bears its name was attended by representatives from Cameroun, the Central African Republic, Chad, Congo (Brazzaville), Dahomey, Ethiopia, Ivory Coast, Liberia, Malagasy, Mauritania, Niger, Nigeria, Senegal, Sierra Leone, Somalia, Togo, Upper Volta, Libya, and Tunisia. At its Lagos Conference (August 1961) all the above states participated except for Libya and Tunisia but with the addition of Tanganyika and Congo (Leopoldville).

In addition there were the Brazzaville Group and the Afro-Malagasy Union which met at six-monthly intervals at Heads of State level. Both had defence, economic development, and other specialized agencies which met regularly. The Brazzaville Group included Cameroun, the Central African Republic, Chad, and, of course, Congo (Brazzaville). Members of the Malagasy Union are Dahomey, Gabon, Ivory Coast, Malagasy, Mauritania, Niger, Senegal, and Upper Volta.

Other important organizations were the West African Customs Union – Ivory Coast, Dahomey, Upper Volta, Mali, Senegal, Mauritania, Niger, and Togo – and the Equatorial Heads of States Conference in which Chad, Gabon, Congo (Brazzaville), and the Central African Republic all took part.

In the eighteen months following the first and founding conference of Independent African States in Accra, there arose the Ghana-Guinea association, the first Union of African States in which Ghana and Guinea were joined by Mali, the Prime Ministers' Conference of Equatorial States, and the West African Customs Union. During that same time there was promoted the Guinea Declaration of a Union of African States, the Ghana-Guinea-Liberia proposal for an integrated community of Independent States and, finally, at Monrovia, a conference of Independent States to help our brothers in the Algerian war.

Who, in face of these facts, will deny that the democratic process of discussion – and disagreement! – contributed mightily to the speed and quality of our unity?

Now, back to the Accra Conference. There, three vital contributions from ' the floor of the house '. After Prince Sahle Selassie, leader of the Ethiopian delegation and representative of Emperor Haile Selassie, had emphasized the importance of bringing the latest scientific and technological know-how to Africa, a co-delegate from his country pointed to the immense natural wealth of the continent, considered as a whole, and discussed the issue of its effective exploitation and control. So was mooted, for the first time, the idea of unified economic planning as an essential condition and vital result of African unity. Powerful and penetrating were the remarks of President Tubman of Liberia. Long before the Congo was precipitated into the centre of world conflict by the misuse of the veto by the Big Powers at the United Nations, he demanded the abrogation of the veto in all United Nations affairs. His proposal at Accra, that a majority vote ought to be worth more than a minority veto, offered an example of shrewd foresight; today, it is the supreme condition for the survival of the United Nations. Dr Eilbury, of Libya, pleaded for religious tolerance north and south of the Sahara and aroused the conference to lively awareness of the malicious propaganda disseminated by racial fanatics.

Casablanca was the beautiful home of our second conference – a graceful tribute to the late King Mohammed V, who courted death rather than abdicate at the behest of French imperialism, and to the tough, hard-working Moroccan people who have always served well the cause of African freedom. His Excellency Ahmed Balifry, Minister of Foreign Affairs, gave the conference the thought that became its keynote: ' Love between people is a *sine qua non* of successful cooperation between them '. His country, he said, had decided to remain outside the spheres of influence of all the big blocs because its geographical position exposed it to imperialist greed. A great and good man from the Sudan, Sayed Mohammed Ahmed Mahgoub, reported on the support his people had given to freedom fighters in the Cameroons and Cyprus, and expressed our confidence in the victory of Algeria, still fighting France and her *colons*. Dr Mohammed Fawzy affirmed Egypt's solidarity with Africans and Algerians, and with other Arabs in protesting against the alienation of their lands in Palestine.

Inspiring in rhetoric, the Casablanca Conference was also instructive in its realism. It deplored the division of the world into power blocs. It expressed unswerving support for the Charter of the United Nations and respect for the decisions of the Organization. It upheld the principle of abstention from interference in the internal affairs of other countries, and from involvement in the collective defence arrangements of the Big Powers. It condemned racialism. It carried a step further the exchange of scientific information especially in relation to industrial planning and agricultural development, by setting up a Joint Economic Research Commission. It inaugurated a study of African raw materials and minerals and the possibilities of interchange within Africa of these vital assets. To expand education for Africans and about Africa, it proposed the establishment of publishing houses.

In May 1961, representatives of twenty African and Malagasy states began a ' break-away ' five-day summit meeting in Monrovia. Ostensibly, the purpose of this meeting was to make a fresh appraisal of the problems of inter-African cooperation and to build a bridge between the Brazzaville powers and the Casablanca powers; and to this end the conference was sponsored by six states representing all the conflicting political groups in Africa – two Brazzaville powers (Ivory Coast and Cameroun); two Casablanca powers (Guinea and Mali); and two uncommitted powers (Liberia and Nigeria). A few days before the conference opened, the Foreign Ministers of the Casablanca group met in Ghana and, as a result, Guinea and Mali withdrew their sponsorship. The subject of dispute was the plain fact, which the conference was to find quite unescapable, that Africa needed unity and that African people everywhere were insisting upon leadership pointing the way to unity. Ten months later, at the Lagos meeting of the Monrovia group, Azikiwe himself delivered the opening address. This meeting endorsed in all essentials the policies of the Casablanca powers – and Nigeria and Ghana, the two most thrusting states south of the Sahara, began to walk the same path to progress.

Still another landmark conference was held in Casablanca in January 1961. Its subject was the Congo. Morocco, Egypt, Ghana, Guinea, and Mali were represented by their Heads of State. The Provisional Government of the Algerian Republic spoke through its Prime Minister, Mr Ferhat Abbas. Libya's Minister of Foreign Affairs, Mr Abdelkader el Allam, was present; so, also, was Mr Alwin B. Perera, Ambassador Extraordinary of Ceylon. King Mohammed V's moving speech contained this key passage:

> When we received the appeal from the Prime Minister of the Congo, Mr Lumumba, followed by the request from the United Nations General Secretary to participate in the implementation of the Security Council's decisions concerning the Congo, we who are here today did not hesitate in our response. In doing so we acted in accordance with our obligations to the United Nations, loyal to the pledge of African solidarity and with the aim of stifling neo-colonialism in its infancy before it could infect the body politic of our liberated nations. We took this action in order that our continent should not become an area for bargaining, a field over which raged conflicts and bitter antagonism.

Remember, these are the words of a leader whose integrity, and the integrity of whose soldiers, had been tested over many years of colonial pressure. Now recall how these skilled, experienced troops, and the troops of other nations faithful to the United Nations, were pilloried in the Congo. All the propaganda machinery of imperialism throughout the world was intent on proving that the only good troops in the Congo were the money-crazed criminals rushed in there to defy the authority of the United Nations. And the purpose? To divert public attention from the fact that, by use of the veto to obstruct majority decisions at the United Nations, soldiers were deflected from their real task; instead of defending the popular and legitimate government of the Congo, they took its Prime Minister, Patrice Lumumba, into custody, treated him like a felon and stood by while he was done to death. There was some sparkling oratory from President Nasser, President Nkrumah, and President Modibo Keita of Mali; and a moving affirmation of Asian solidarity with Africa by Ceylon.

The second conference of the Monrovia group at Lagos, as I have suggested above, revealed how African leadership was maturing. It got down to discussion of a great variety of problems from currency to pest control. References to other African groups were free from acerbity. There was a growing consciousness of the inward meaning of the words of our Ghanaian scholar, Dr Aggrey:

' The hour strikes for Africa's quickened forward march:
With closed ranks, eyes on the highest goal;
Success is certain under devoted leadership '.

There was never any lack of devoted leadership in any of our groups, whether radical or moderate. Our lack, present in some measure in every group, was of experience of walking the tightrope of politics under new conditions in a revolutionary area in our revolutionary continent. All of us were learning the importance of internal security to the stability of our states. We were being taught that, in practical politics, priorities, which Aneurin Bevan once described as ' the language of Socialism ', are in truth the language of simple survival in all political systems based, like ours, on mass democratic support. All African leaders had to face courageously the problem of inspiring poor people, deprived of many of the amenities of the good life, to sacrifice today in order to expand the education and training and capital investment that, alone, could ensure a happier tomorrow. We were groping, above all, towards an understanding of the importance of defining and applying a political ideology of positive action to provide an adequate flow of leaders and administrators for the years ahead, supported by a disciplined, because intelligent and well-informed, electorate.

We soon saw that in the multifarious groupings of Africa we were missing many opportunities of doing the best for ourselves even though the vituperation and acerbity which characterized early relations between the various groupings were dying out. The conviction was growing and spreading that it was in a unitary framework that our common hopes stood the best chance of fulfilment. The initiative to create such a framework began to gather force.

In May 1962, Presidents Senghor and Sekou Touré agreed in a communiqué which was issued after their meeting at Labé in Guinea to increase their joint effort for African Unity. A coming together of the Casablanca Group and the Monrovia Group was regarded by them as constituting the all-important step towards African Unity. President Houphouet-Boigny of Ivory Coast also visited Conakry in August of 1962 and announced that he acknowledged the necessity of bringing the Casablanca and the Monrovia Groups together, and agreed that an opportunity should be sought to begin discussions for unity between the two groups. In the same month, the King of Morocco repeated an earlier appeal for states to seek unity on the basis of the African (Casablanca) Charter. At the same time, the Secretary-General of the Casablanca Group said that as Algerian independence had been achieved he saw no reason why there should not be a rapprochement between Casablanca and Monrovia.

Also in August of the same year, President Modibo Keita said during a visit to the Ivory Coast that in future there would be nothing fundamental to separate the two groups. In September, President Sekou Touré sent an emissary to the Union of African and Malagasy States Conference at Libreville and the Casablanca Group Secretary-General, Mr M. Ouazzini, was able to welcome the statements on African Unity which were made at Libreville.

Following this conference, the Mauritanian permanent representative at the United Nations stated that it had been decided at Libreville to withdraw Mauritania's candidacy for one of the non-permanent seats on the United Nations Security Council, the stated reason being in order that Africa might present a united front in the struggle against the ' injustice ' of the present distribution of seats. The emphasis on the unity of Africa was most welcome from that quarter.

In October 1962, Presidents Houphouet-Boigny, Modibo Keita, and Sekou Touré met together at Komogougou in Guinea for the first time since 1958 in order to exchange views on African and international problems. In March 1963, President Nkrumah dispatched top-ranking emissaries to all African leaders with proposals for African Unity for consideration at the Conference of Heads of State and Government which was due to be held in Addis Ababa in May of the same year.

It can therefore be seen that the inner logic of African Unity was itself driving the Heads of State and Government towards unity. Expressions of dissatisfaction with the existing groupings were common and frequent, and there was no doubt in the mind of those who were able to appreciate the dynamism of African change and the historical process which was rapidly unfolding itself, that the various African groupings would not survive the Addis Ababa Conference.

And so to the triumph of the Heads of State Conference at Addis Ababa in May 1963. Addis Ababa did not give all of us all we wanted although it gave us a great deal and promised us more. What it did give us was the Charter of the Organization of African Unity. The Charter shines more gloriously from month to month as it achieves coordinated action in more fields of human effort. Controversy and argument continue and will continue, as they must. But ' faithful are the wounds of a friend '. All African eyes are focused now ' on the highest goal . . . the hour strikes for Africa's quickened forward march '.

The July 1964 Cairo Conference of African Heads of State followed the London Conference of Commonwealth Prime Ministers in the dramatic, unexpected success of which Afro-Asian representatives played a distinguished part. In the Western world, London rather overshadowed Cairo. Yet Cairo will take a proud place in the unfolding story of the forward march of the African people.

It made a serious appraisal of the Organization of African Unity's successes in the fourteen months since Addis Ababa. It took a cool, hard look at our failures, asking honestly why our work had not been even more fruitful. Of course, there was hard-hitting ; African leaders are on truth-speaking terms with each other as they are with the citizens of their individual states. The Conference showed, in every debate, an eager, urgent interest in the question, where do we go from here ?

I have no doubt about the answer to the question. The African states have demonstrated their loyalty, on the great moral issues of the world, to the United Nations. They are pursuing loyally, and with single-minded purpose, the cause of non-alignment which is encouraging and enabling an increasing volume of world opinion to opt out of war, and of the economic rat race and political policies that provoke war. Now they must give fuller expression to their belief in themselves and their loyalty to each other by fashioning more powerful weapons of political unity.

Where do we go from here ?

We go on to the Union Government of Africa.

The Political Renaissance of Africa
A Charter for Union Government

The Organization of African Unity has grown in dimensions and influence, and further growth must be encouraged. The existing Charter of the Organization of African Unity under Article 20 provided for the setting up of an Economic and Social Commission ; an Educational and Cultural Commission ; a Health, Sanitation and Nutrition Commission ; a Defence Commission ; and a Scientific, Technical, and Research Commission. These Commissions have been working for several months and are now largely in possession of the facts on Africa in the respective fields. They are in a position to reveal the truth about the dead-wood of apparently non-viable economies bequeathed to us with independence by colonialism's haphazard and wasteful exploitation of our natural resources. They are in a position to expose our every weakness and our most urgent needs. They are in a position to floodlight the mighty strength which, if we cooperate efficiently, we can deploy to raise Africa quickly to give us a continental voice in world affairs.

All these Commissions, I hope and believe, will report to the next Conference of the Organization of African Unity. Their reports can and must spark off the dynamics of innovation and change. They can point only to a form of Union Government under which they can operate effectively.

Consider first the simplest, most obvious argument in favour of Union Government. A supreme requirement of every African state is, without exception, a fair price for its primary produce in the markets of the world. Until this is attained, we are denied both the means of securing a bare subsistence and the capital for social and economic development. The strong industrial powers are beginning to recognize this basic fact of economic life, but they will never yield to the persuasion of fact until the emerging countries combine with each other to create marketing organizations capable of meeting the industrial powers on equal terms. The other side of this medal reinforces the argument. The massive and growing productive power of the industrial nations is making emerging countries a necessary market for their goods. If they fail or refuse to pay us properly for our produce we cannot buy their goods; we shall return to the horrible pre-war practice of burning food and destroying goods of which millions of people are in need. Just as we cannot tolerate the industrial nations' monopoly control of our markets overseas, we dare not permit them to impose the toll of monopoly on the market we offer them. That way lies a widening of the already paralysing gap between the economies of the two worlds and the recurrence, everywhere, of the disasters of boom and slump and mass unemployment which modern men find abhorrent.

In this situation the small state is the helpless pawn and plaything of economic forces. Thus the continental direction of African resources is our only assurance of commercial justice and social stability; it is our one guarantee that the political power of colonialism which destroyed the integrity of our states will not be replaced by the economic might of an invisible empire of big business with a vested interest in balkanizing our states. Union Government is the only foolproof method of protecting our people against market manipulators who, in the past, have decided that men will eat or starve, live, or die.

Look, now, at another facet of the same problem.

Greatly though Africans welcome foreign investment – indeed, our prosperity and the prosperity of the nations whose viable customers we expect to become, requires that we offer a fair and secure return for capital, for entrepreneurial skill, and for industrial know-how – it is intolerable that an entire continent should be dependent upon the vagaries of speculation and the international money market for development finance. It is not only intolerable, it is ridiculous that emerging countries should be competing with each other for the favours of the international money market, pushing up, against each other, the price of these favours. A common African currency and continent-wide banking arrangements would strengthen our bargaining position, prevent the burden of usury from crippling our growth and, in addition, make possible an increasing contribution to capital growth from our own immediate resources.

None of this makes sense unless we forge the instruments of continental political influence and exercise that influence, not over the sovereign rights of states, but in the interests of all states. In plain words, our hopes and prospects are already blighted unless all the varied, passionate, and self-sacrificing efforts which all African states are exercising to lift up our people are given strong, clear political direction by a Union Government.

I am not here indulging in ' the fashionable idolatry of great states '. On the contrary, I would define the limits of this supra-sovereignty quite strictly. It must operate in defence to ensure our internal security and safeguard us from external interference. It must operate over the whole field of economic development. It must continue to operate in foreign policy where, already, our loyalty to the United Nations and to the principles of non-alignment is enhancing African prestige and influence everywhere. Our African leaders are endowed abundantly with what Lord Morley once described as ' the essential things in the statesman . . . strength of will, courage, massive ambition, passionate joy in the result '; these qualities they possess together with a humble care for human personality without which the glorious record of social improvement is turned into a void. And these qualities, now, must command our trust and our unity.

Within Africa itself Union Government, as I have tried to define it, would open up prospects as sparkling as our biggest diamond. Our development would be planned as an orderly whole. Industrial plants, for example, would be sited where the requisite raw materials are most abundant. Our extractive industries would be rationalized. We would attack the vampires of geography – the pests and diseases and erosion of our lands – where their defeat would yield the greatest gain to the greatest number. We would give the theory of comparative costs a fresh and meaningful application in Africa by establishing industries where climate, access to raw materials and available skills promise the best chance of success. We would apply, in up-to-date ways, the ancient principle that civilization follows the roadmaker, and the improvement in our communications would vastly increase the self-perpetuating internal trade which in turn would raise living standards and build up new reserves of enterprise. We would economize in some fields and thus have more to spend in others. We would command, as a continent, what no individual African state can command today – the magic of the computer and the most sophisticated modern machinery; and we would operate them where the able young men and women whose education we have made a high priority can make them most productive.

I believe, too, that continental planning would mitigate in developing Africa one of the most intractable problems of the non-Socialist countries of the west. This is the problem of inflation, of the falling value of money stimulated by the hypertrophy of selling and salesmanship. In America and Great Britain today men drive increasingly expensive motor cars along expensive new motorways at increasing speed to points of increasing traffic congestion, and the costs of travel and of distribution in these uncoordinated transport systems go up and up. It is a commonplace that it often costs as much to distribute the products of industry and to administer business as to produce the commodities and supply the goods and services that are in demand.

Nature in Africa is not niggardly. It is generous. Matched by the generosity of mind and spirit of African men and women, as I am certain it will be, nature can endow us with the bounty of plenty.

Union Government is our assurance of peace. It is our assurance of progress. It is our promise of early escape from poverty's prison. Union Government is our diamond of hope.

As the Commissions show, the Charter of the Organization of African Unity is not incidental in the history of Africa. It represents the reconciliation of several forces in Africa which were grouping for progress in the wrong conditions. This Charter was drawn up to satisfy a network of specific needs and to fulfil a complex of large purposes. For this reason, the Charter is founded upon a vision of a desirable future for Africa.

The Commissions have, however, almost completed their work ; but our great vision of a united Africa will remain paper-bound unless there can be added to it at this stage a realistic, positive, and clear statement of the means whereby the dream can be fully realized.

The apocalyptic vision is essential, for it is in relation to it that even the most carefully thought-out steps need to be examined. The time has come now for such a vision to be enshrined in a Charter of Union Government in high enough terms to command our intellectual, moral, and emotional allegiance. Such a Charter is now imperative. The Addis Ababa Conference ended the various groupings in Africa by launching the Organization of African Unity. Every member nation of the old groupings is a signatory to the Addis Ababa

Charter. All have sought faithfully to fulfil the obligations imposed upon them by that Charter.

The Cairo Conference, basing itself upon the unitary framework created by the Addis Ababa Conference, advanced to the recognition of the principle of a Union Government of Africa, a recognition of the necessity to put content in the framework successfully laid down by the Charter of the Organization of African Unity. This can be done by the Heads of States introducing and approving a Charter of a Union Government of Africa at their next conference.

Such a Charter must be based upon our irrevocable affirmation to consolidate the establishment and progress of the Organization of African Unity.

United in our common determination to enhance understanding among our peoples and cooperation between our states, as an elementary response to the aspiration of our people to solidarity, we must take the next fateful step – in such a way, however, that we protect the gains which we have already made. We must therefore at all costs avoid reopening the old wounds and the controversies which once divided us. We must also encourage every state to join a Union Government without delay in order to maintain the forward momentum of Africa.

We must also prevent the dissipation of those positive energies which have been inspired and awakened by the movement for African Unity. In this way, the Organization of African Unity will even now gear its deliberations to the theme of Union Government, to the definition with crystal clarity of its future role, and to harnessing its mighty strength in support of Union Government, and to the inevitable changes that must be made in our institutions if they are to meet the challenge of our changing times.

What I propose in all humility for consideration is the creation of a Charter of Union Government, which should be formulated in terms consistent with free and equal partnership, and this Charter should be signed by the Heads of State and Government at their next meeting. Thereafter, ratification can be debated in every Parliament and assembly in Africa, and the voice of the people may even be sought in referendums.

This democratic process is essential to the victory of the grand project, the grandest project, indeed, in the history of our continent.

The purposes of the Charter can only be the promotion of unity and solidarity of the member states of the Union ; the intensification and coordination of their efforts to achieve a better life in dignity and peace for the people of Africa. The Charter must outline the responsibilities of the future Union Government including internal security, external defence, general economic planning, foreign policy, and general federal legislation and administration.

Non-ratification should not mean a permanent exclusion of a member state of the Organization of African Unity from the Union Government. It is to be hoped however that all the independent states would ratify the Charter. The Charter could come into effect as usual at a designated time after two-thirds of the member states of the Organization of African Unity have ratified it.

Nevertheless, unanimity is not absolutely necessary for the success of the idea of Union Government. If any ten states agree to get together, they could deploy sufficient economic strength and political influence to bring the Union Government to birth. If the half-dozen or so economically advanced states ratify the Charter, a vigorous, healthy, and expanding future would be certain for the Union Government. Whatever the numbers ratifying the Charter, it could be described properly as the Charter of Union Government of the Organization of African Unity, and it would be registered with the Secretariat of the United Nations.

Thereafter, the ratifying countries would elect a committee to write the Constitution of the Union Government of Africa. And, let me repeat, the Constitution would be all-embracing, ever eager to gather within its fold all the children of our Continent.

CHAPTER THREE

ONE-PARTY DEMOCRACY

The one-party democratic state is not a subject of controversy in Africa. It is a matter of fact. It is a political expression of our African history and tradition, both of which are based upon a common allegiance to accepted purposes of society and to the basic principles of democratic centralism. African nationalism gave us the opportunity of rekindling our traditional social philosophy, and with it we fiercely and successfully opposed our colonial masters who proved to be powerless against it.

Twelve West African countries had achieved independence by 1961. Seven of them – Mauretania, Mali, Guinea, Ivory Coast, Upper Volta, Niger, and Dahomey – had no legal opposition at all. Four countries – Senegal, Sierra Leone, Ghana, and Togo – had one party in dominating strength.[1] Nigeria, alone, practised the Western, more particularly, the Westminster conception of government ; and in that great federation the results of local and regional elections during the past six years indicate an increasing control of each area by a single party.[2]

This trend towards the one-party state is continuous. Events, especially since 1962, suggest that most African countries are heading towards the formal creation of one-party democracies.

Addressing the July 1962 Conference of the Convention People's Party at Kumasi, President Nkrumah of Ghana said: ' We have stated often and made it clear that our objective is a one (party) state which gives equal opportunity to all the people and distinguishes citizens for merit and achievement but not on privilege.'

[1] I. Wallerstein, *West Africa*, 25 Nov. 1961.
[2] J. P. Mackintosh, ' Electoral Trends and the Tendency to a one-party system in Nigeria ' (1962), *Jour. of Commerce and Political Studies*, 194 at p. 207.

The Central African Republic, led by President David Dacko, adopted a one-party system in November of that same year.

Only in the 1962 Moroccan Constitution can I find provision for a different form of Government; Article 3 decrees that ' there shall be no single party Government in Morocco.'

In 1963 the Western Cameroun Legislative Assembly decided, by a large majority, to set up a single national Cameroun political party comprising all existing parties. The new Algerian Constitution legalized the one-party role of the F.L.N. (National Liberation Front), which is described as the ' inspiration of all political power '.

The interesting development of 1963 was President Nyerere's announcement in January of action towards statutory recognition of a one-party system in Tanganyika; interesting because it demonstrates that the trend is a response of African governments to the declared desires of African electorates.

In the 1960 election, the Tanganyika African National Union (TANU) was not opposed in 58 out of the 71 districts represented in the National Assembly. Of the 13 contested areas, TANU won 12. The solitary loss is said to have arisen because central party headquarters supported a candidate who did not come from the majority tribe in the area in question. ' Nyerere ', wrote Professor Margaret L. Bates[1], ' who had spoken sometime earlier of one-party democracy and its role in new states, now had very much a one-party country to govern '. In Tanganyika, as elsewhere in Africa, there is virtually no opposition to nationalism or to the nationalist party simply because such opposition is rejected by an overwhelming majority of electors.

This must be the explanation for the resort of intractable minority interests, which alas are frequently financed and directed from outside Africa, to conspiracy and subversion. These interests, finding themselves spurned by the majority of people, turn to crime, terrorism, and violence. The foreign agencies which support them do so in the hope of gain, in the hope of being able to return to the position where they can

[1] In *African One-Party States*, edited by Gwendolen M. Carter, Cornell University Press, 1962, p. 430.

intervene against our destiny of freedom and prosperity. These agencies, enjoying access to the press of their countries, inspire mendacious and irresponsible press features, whose aim is to frighten African leaders into embracing murders, into exposing themselves to assassins, and into jeopardizing the peace, safety, and security of our states.

How refreshingly different is the mood and spirit of inquirers who do not have to serve the whims of some British newspaper owner. For example, Lord Egremont, formerly John Wyndham, friend and confident of the former British Prime Minister, Harold Macmillan, wrote in 1964:

> The impressions I formed when I was in Ghana in 1960 were :
> 1. They valued European help both in administration and commerce.
> 2. They retained no feeling of attachment to Britain, no lingering loyalty, yet no hostility either. But –
> 3. Dr Nkrumah's party Press abused all ' colonial ' powers, including Britain, in the most violent terms.
> 4. Opinion in Ghana was scarcely disturbed at all by the suppression of the Opposition, the declining effectiveness of Parliament and the domination of all aspects of public life by a single Party. The view prevailed that strong government was, at any rate for a period, so essential for a State in the first stages of its independence as to outweigh the desirability of preserving to the full the rights and freedom of a democratic society.

Lord Egremont is altogether right in his impressions that we in Ghana value European help, both in administration and in commerce. Indeed such help, especially in administration, is not as significant today as it was in the earlier days of independence. We have already succeeded in establishing an African administration which is well known for its comprehensiveness and its efficiency. In Ghana we have no feeling of hostility towards Britain, although we are often led to wonder to what extent this piece of international decency is reciprocated. Our devotion to the ideals of international peace and world development has forced us into the stance of positive neutralism. Our loyalty is to social justice. Our party press lambasts colonialism, because colonialism is aggression. It is the forcible imposition of one people (indeed one race) upon another. Surely the British, who are so suspicious of everything alien, can appreciate our intense and deep-seated aversion to this most pernicious intrusion of the alien?

Lord Egremont was evidently an unbiased observer, but one must disagree with his choice of words on occasion. His view that a single party dominates all aspects of public life in Ghana is a valid one. It was so even before 1960 when he published his earlier impressions. Ghana was once a colony, and in the mobilization of popular forces against colonialism, no opposition can succeed. Even the opposition of the metropolitan power, having at its disposal the entire civil machinery, the civil service, the police, the church, commerce, the army both local and metropolitan – even this metropolitan opposition, powerfully endowed as it was, could not roll back the billows of nationalism, much less an anomalous and paradoxical, hackneyed and puny local opposition. The movement that directs the strategy of independence evidently enjoys the confidence and consent of the people at large. The Convention People's Party of Ghana has an enrolled membership of five million out of a total population of seven million. Obviously, not many adults are outside its following. With such stupendous backing, how could it avoid dominating all aspects of public life?

The Convention People's Party of Ghana has always presented to the people of Ghana mature, realistic, and promising manifestos, manifestos that have achieved an incredible amount for the people of Ghana. The people of Ghana spend a higher proportion of their income per annum on education than any other country in the world, including the United States, the U.S.S.R., and the People's Republic of China. Ghanaians enjoy completely free compulsory education for the first eight years. Books are provided free, as are uniforms in some areas. Ghana also has a six-year secondary-cum-sixth-form education in which books are supplied to pupils free, in which there is a large number of scholarships, in which non-resident fees are nominal and in which sixth-form education is entirely free. Ghanaians enjoy a university education, undergraduate and post-graduate, which is resident and entirely free. In addition Ghana has several thousand students overseas who are all maintained on comprehensive state grants. The cost of education to Ghana is enormous and heart-breaking; but the people of Ghana are blessed with a government, headed by Osagyefo Dr Kwame Nkrumah, which believes that, without education for all, social justice can never have a real meaning.

OUR PEOPLE'S PROGRESS

The Convention People's Party of Ghana insists however that its promises should not merely concern the future. Added to this tremendous educational structure is a successful mass education system of several years' standing, which has been much written about, much studied and often referred to as a model and revealing example.

The people of Ghana have a medical service which is virtually free, in that payment is in effect voluntary. The people of Ghana have up-to-date medical facilities even if the doctor-patient ratio is still one to ten thousand. Before independence only seven years ago, it was one to twenty-five thousand. The people of Ghana today enjoy a higher standard of living, for they have varied and high-level skills and have several industries. The people of Ghana have built one of the largest man-made harbours, railways, and towns, and are engaged on a hydro-electric project which will form the largest man-made lake in the world. The transformations which take place in Ghana today are so rapid that visiting Ghana in any two months is more like visiting two countries once than one country twice. Ghana's growing prosperity is obvious.

Within a period of thirteen years, the people of Ghana have enjoyed three national elections and two national referendums. Each time the people of Ghana have, in greater numbers and in a greater proportion, registered their support for the Convention People's Party. One supposes that each successive time the registered support for the Convention People's Party grows not merely on account of the piquancy of its manifesto, but because of its proven trustworthiness. The Convention

People's Party is ideologically positive and only such parties have credible manifestos ; only such parties can be regarded as intending to fulfil their promises.

The three elections were all supervised by representatives of the United Kingdom Government. At the last elections in 1956, the Convention People's Party was returned with 72 per cent of the seats. Later, many of the 28 per cent of the Opposition crossed the carpet to join the Government and almost caused a seating crisis ! So few were left that it was felt that it was more harmful to call them the Opposition than any other name. So they became the representatives of the minority and are that to this day.

When Lord Egremont therefore says that the opposition has been suppressed, one wonders which opposition he has in mind. No democratic opposition has been suppressed in Ghana. The Conservative Party of Britain knows very well that, the whip notwithstanding, it often has to cope with an internal opposition. Wherever there is discussion, disagreement is possible ; and some of the harshest critics of the policies of the Convention People's Party Government in Ghana have been not representatives of minorities, but members of the Government back-bench.

Hugh Gaitskell, after visiting Ghana in 1959, declared : ' It is not true that Ghana Opposition is barely allowed to exist. It is not well organized, and there is suspicion on all sides. I am sure that Dr Nkrumah wants to preserve Ghana on democratic lines.'[1]

There is, however, a certain opposition which has been suppressed in Ghana. This opposition is one which even in colonial days resorted to acts of terrorism, using dynamite, grenades, and rifles – the lunatic fringe of our society. The Government of Ghana is understandably opposed to terrorism and underworld politics.

Only an insincere Parliament can be ineffective. The Parliament of Ghana is in effect a Parliament of the Convention People's Party which like the Tanganyika African National Union holds almost all seats in Parliament. The Convention People's Party of Ghana is one of the great successful parties of

[1] *The Observer*, 24 May 1959.

the world, a historic party which is guided in all things by the welfare of the people. In what sense one may ask, can its legislative wing, its Parliament, decline without the Party itself declining ? Parliament in Ghana is more effective today than ever before, and is indeed seen by the people to be so. This is because, fully confident of the support of the people, it can without partisan considerations devote its total energies to the service of all.

The concern of Ghana has, right from the beginning, been to give a real content to the rights and freedoms of a democratic society, to create for the people the plenty without which personal and individual liberty is impossible.

Returning to Ghana in 1964, Lord Egremont saw nearing completion the mighty Akosombo Dam on the Volta which, in 1960, ' was represented by paper plans and two sticks in the ground : one on either side of the river between which it was proposed to build the dam. The sticks had gone now ; the dam was there.'

He also found at Tema, which in 1960 had been little more than a fishing village . . . one of the world's largest man-made harbours linked to the new town of Tema and the industrial and oil area to the east. It and the dam represent the purposeful beginning of the industrialization of Ghana.

' What we have in Ghana is about 6½ million of the most charming, gay, laughter-loving yet serious, courteous, highly educated people with the highest standard of living in West Africa, and much more potential wealth. Next to Lady Egremont and taking the stuffing out of stuffed shirts, my passion in life could well be Ghana.'[1]

Beyond all argument, however, I acclaim Lord Egremont as a perceptive critic who has grasped the basic reality that African political parties are neither for or against Westminster-style democracy. As Thomas Hodgkin has said these parties ' have to be understood as essentially African institutions . . . and in the context of the particular social systems in which they emerged. While they have borrowed techniques of organization and propaganda, as well as ideas, from Europe, America, and Asia, they have modified these to suit African purposes,

[1] *The Sunday Times*, 10 May 1964.

just as they have adapted " traditional " institutions and rituals to " modern " party political needs.'[1]

The failure of British commentators on Africa – even well-intentioned commentators like members of the Fabian Society – to understand the realities of African political life, was exposed brutally by Mr Frederic Mackarness Bennett, Conservative M.P. for Torquay, in a House of Commons debate on Malawi independence. Mr Bennett said :

' Having ruled with a sort of paternalistic authoritarianism primitive territories all over the world, we imagine that suddenly when we give them a sealed ballot-box they will adopt our system, and then we put up our hands in shocked horror when they find this difficult to do.

' That sort of attitude is humbug, whoever adopts it. There is no party point here. Members in all quarters of the House refer to the Westminster pattern. We give these people copies of Erskine May. We send out a mace, which is sometimes used to club the Speaker over the head. Having ruled them with an authoritarian rule, we give them a system of government in which they have had no practice at all, and then we express surprise when things turn out not as we would like them to do.'[2]

Happily, even the British government is beginning to recognize the facts of African life. It decided in May 1964 to legislate for the direct conversion of Northern Rhodesia, a dependency of the Crown, into the independent Republic of Zambia.

> The break with precedent [wrote *The Times*] essentially lies in creating an executive presidency for Zambia rather than a British cabinet system in which the functions of Head of State and Chief executive are separated. African leaders insist that this system is incomprehensible to the African masses who expect power and formal authority to coincide in one personality. Whether this is really true, either politically or anthropologically, the presidential system has been adopted in most African States, the significant exception being the one successful federation – Nigeria. On Zambia's independence day, Dr Kenneth Kaunda,

[1] Thomas Hodgkin in *African Political Parties*, Penguin, 1961, p. 169.
[2] Parliamentary Debates, 11 May 1964, Vol. 695, No. 107, Col. 81.

now Prime Minister, will receive broadly the extensive powers and prerogatives of the President of Tanganyika, though not those of the President of Ghana.[1]

We may now examine the affirmation that the one-party system is in accord with our African tradition.

In those African societies which had Chiefs, our traditional organizations reveal no formal and permanent opposition as such to the Chief of the state. More than one nominee usually contested the election of a Chief. The election over, all other campaigns ceased. The personal and private interests of every member of the community became secondary to the progress of the community or state. Any attempt by any citizen to disturb the political equilibrium of society was punished severely; so, too, was any effort to undermine state security and safety. This lack of a formal and permanent opposition, this absolute obedience to the law laid down by the Chief in Council had its roots in the family or clan, where the influence of the head was paramount over all the members.

Foreign critics of the traditional position of the Chief branded him as a tyrant, a despot, or a dictator. Such critics showed no understanding of the fact that the Chief governed with a Council of Elders, whose influence tempered the will of the ruler and was an effective barrier against the arbitrary use of power. No wise ruler would embark upon any important venture affecting his people unless and until it had been discussed and debated fully in Council.

Thus, to Africans, the Chief was not, and is not, regarded as a person who can enforce his personal will upon them, but only the will of the people. He is the living embodiment of their aims and aspirations, the axis of their political relationships, the symbol of their unity and tribal integrity. He is more than a secular ruler. His credentials, being derived from antiquity, are mystical.[2] Generalissimo of his people in time of war, he can be described in Western terms as a 'father figure'.

[1] *The Times*, 19 May 1964.
[2] M. Fortes and E. E. Evans Pritchard in *African Political Systems*, p. 16. (Oxford University Press for the International Institute of African Languages and Cultures, 1940.)

Yet the Chief who acts against the wishes of the citizens of his state could and can be destooled. No organized opposition group or party is necessary to initiate the process of destooling him. Charges can be preferred against him, and he in turn will be given an opportunity to defend himself. Indeed, the fresh air of criticism blows so freely in Africa that many countries including Ghana have passed laws to protect Chiefs against trivial and irresponsible complaints.

This traditional pattern is being preserved, even extended, in Africa today. The powers of the Chief are being assimilated to those of the President. Like Chiefs, Presidents can be destooled – through universal franchise and the ballot box.

African leaders have asserted often that the two-party or multi-party system is out of step with the needs of Africans at this stage of their revolution. Here and now, the imperative is to foster in every African country a unity of nationhood. Most of the ' opposition ' or ' alternative ' parties now existing are not and never were national organizations. They are groupings based upon local or tribal sentiment. They are, in truth, ' splinter groups ' encouraged, as a rule, by colonial interests eager to apply to African politics the old tactics of ' divide and rule '. Having imposed upon and having distorted our African tradition for too long, supreme objective – national unity, African unity, and an all-out united effort to raise living standards.

I find it impossible to believe that the giant task of African reconstruction, a task involving the peace and happiness of an entire continent, can be tackled competently without a coalescence of political parties just as the Western nations, when faced with the equivalent crisis of war, move swiftly and certainly towards coalition government.

MASTER-BUILDERS

The leader who inspired us to victory over Colonialism is regarded by Africans as the master builder of the new state, the architect of social and economic change, and the custodian of our social conscience. We expect him to be a soldier, a politician and a philosopher, to combine the qualities of a

Garibaldi, a Cavour, and a Mazzini in one person. He ensures in his declaration of fundamental rights a fair share to every citizen ' of the produce yielded by the development of the country '.[1] Any challenge to, or interruption of, the leader's constitutional powers is seen by the masses as a threat to their hopes for the future. It is the all-embracing nature of the single party that has made possible the creation of continuity by such leaders as Nkrumah in Ghana, Sekou Toure in Guinea, Nyerere in Tanzania, Kamuzu Banda in Malawi, Kenyatta in Kenya, Kenneth Kaunda in Zambia and, David Dacko in the Central African Republic.

Equally compelling is the fact that, unlike the capitalist democracies, we have no socially sundered communities in Africa, no native class interests to subserve. Thus we need not afford the luxury of an official opposition system which divides talented men and women into competing groups. And just as we cannot afford to waste talent, we dare not allow our grave, immediate problems to be obscured by the pursuit of Party advantage. The African M.P. must be free to support or criticize government policy according to the dictates of thought and conscience, not according to the cracking of any Party Whip.

An obvious result of strong, popular nationalist governments, as we have seen in the example of Tanzania, is that Parliamentary candidates are usually unopposed. Critics, ignoring the fact that such a result arises from the desires and requirements of African electors, argue that it makes nonsense of the ballot box, that it stamps the candidate as the agent of a dictator, and that it is part of the process of muzzling opposition. The answer is simple. In a British General Election, there are still a few candidates whose return to Parliament is unopposed. Before the rise of the Labour Party, these unopposed returns often exceeded 10 per cent of the total number of elected M.P.'s. In the 1918 General Election, there were 80 uncontested seats out of 706. In the seven General Elections held between the two world wars, the number of uncontested seats averaged more than 40. An official Conservative publication – *The Constitutional Year Book* – argued in 1933 that all the electors in constituencies represented by unopposed

[1] Preamble to the Ghana Constitution.

Tories could be assumed to support the Conservative Party !
They believed, then, in the one-party constituency although
they condemn, now, the one-party state ! Moreover, there are
still many ' blue-chip ' constituencies – at least half of all the
seats available come into this category, and are called ' safe '
Tory or ' safe ' Labour seats – in which one or other of the two
great parties commands a majority that is large and lasting.
In all these British seats, there are numerous applications and
nominations for election, and nomination is presumed to result
from a vigorous battle behind the scenes before a candidate is
chosen.   Exactly the same democratic process is pursued in
one-party states.   In Ghana, for example, two or more
candidates are nominated to fill a vacant seat in the Party.
Their claims and qualities are scrutinized as carefully and as
anxiously as elsewhere.

What is true within African states is true also of the relations
between African states.   In developing a basis for African
Unity – and many of the difficulties are an inheritance of
colonialism – we seek a democracy that is ' usable '.   Great
Britain, America, and West Germany were all on the run-up
to national elections during 1964.   According to the *New
Statesman*, this fact cast a cloud over world affairs for these
reasons :

> Just as Sir Alec Home is frozen in an absurd nuclear posture
> for electoral reasons and Dr Erhard makes speeches knocking the
> idea of a central European détente in order to strengthen his
> party's position, so President Johnson has to select his attitude
> towards Cuban trade with his election in mind.   In each of
> these cases it by no means follows that the political leaders are
> expressing the majority opinion of their electorates.   They
> certainly do not represent enlightened opinion.   Such, however,
> is the nature of the democratic system that no leader cares to
> risk an appeal to any emotion but vulgar patriotism.[1]

This cynicism does not yet impoverish our African political
life ; I hope it never will.   African leaders are on truth-
speaking terms with their own people – and, in the cause of
African unity, with each other.

[1] 15 May 1964.

As a friendly observer of the British scene, I note another example of cynicism of the multi-party system frequently exposed and criticized by political commentators in Britain. This is the tendency of the party in power, just prior to a General Election, to reduce taxes which they will almost certainly increase again as soon as the election has been won.

African leaders who indulged in this form of political bribery would not survive the wrath of the people even if their economies could survive the ordeal of being converted, for several months in every election year, into a plaything for vote-seeking politicians. And, naturally, African leaders wonder sometimes about the credentials of ' pork barrel ' politicians who love to lecture emerging countries on the true meaning of democracy.

A democracy that is ' usable ' in Africa is well illustrated in the new electoral procedure adopted by Guinea. There, we are told:[1] ' Almost all Guineans are members of the party which reaches through all levels of national life, from the supreme 15-member Political Bureau to the base committees. Before elections, individual electioneering is forbidden. Members of the Political Bureau supervise the nominations and check on the eligibility of the candidates.

' With the exception of the Political Bureau Deputies, who are chosen by that body itself to sit in the Assembly, each Region's nominations for the Assembly must be proposed by its Federal Bureau, the highest party body at regional level. They are then adopted at a special " Regional Congress " comprising representatives of the Federal Bureau and the Region " steering committees ". Candidates must be chosen from the outgoing Deputies, the members of the " Regional Congress " or " any militant cadres from another region whose political awareness, moral character, and talents are approved by the Regional Congress ". Finally, the list is elected by universal suffrage.'

In this experiment, which all Africans are watching with interest, President Sekou Touré is carrying the conception of ' democratic centralism ' – the party being the supreme organ

[1] S. Somerville on ' One-party Guinea votes on Sep. 28 ', E. African Standard, 21 Sep. 1963.

of the State – to the point where 'Authority rests not with the Government but with the people'. The Guinean example, he has stated, 'will shake the foundations of the old systems, for the people of Africa now know that the citizens of one of their own countries are able to express themselves freely, rejecting the idea of one man speaking for them, rejecting electoral campaigning and insisting on personally judging each man on his performance.'

The free flow of criticism and experiment within the one-party state, the vigorous, uninhibited debate within our Parliaments, the energetic effort to identify every elector with the state and all its activities – all this, in time, may give birth to opposition parties capable of operating constitutionally in our continent. If so, the process will be neither as prolonged nor as bloody as it has been in the countries of the West.

This principle has been expounded time and time again by African leaders. I cite Tom Mboya:

> Opposition parties must develop not because the textbooks say so but rather as a normal and natural process of the individual freedom of speech and freedom to criticize government and the right of a people to return a government of their choice by the use of the ballot-box . . . In practice when a country has just won its independence – (there will be room only) for a very weak and small opposition . . . at least in the initial period. Unless a split occurs in the ranks of the new nationalist government, this situation may continue for ten or even more years. This does not mean the abandonment of democracy but it is a situation which calls for great vigilance on the part of the people in respect of their individual freedom.[1]

Tom Mboya's clear projection of the political trend induced much heart-searching discussion among the loyal Kenya leaders of both parties: the Kenya African National Union, the governing group, and the Kenya African Democratic Union, the opposition group; and the desire of both groups to serve the public interest reached fulfilment on 10 November 1964, exactly eleven months after Independence. Then Ronald G. Ngala announced that KADU had been dissolved

[1] 'The Realities of African Independence' cited by Rita Hinden in Africa and Democracy', *Encounter* Pamphlet No. 8.

and that he and all members of the loyal opposition had joined the government party led by Jomo Kenyatta.

On crossing the floor of the House of Parliament, Mr Ngala said:

' We are joining the Government with no grudge or bitterness against Mzee or any leader in the Government, because we consider the cause of Kenya to be greater than any of our personal pride, gains or losses. This is one of the times that we must be prepared to sacrifice our political dignity for the peace and harmony of Kenya. We are joining forces *to build our country* and unify our social and political programmes. We shall endeavour to achieve free expression and true African democracy for our country.'

Men and women all over the world who have experienced Mzee Kenyatta's magic spell can well imagine with what generosity of mind and spirit he responded to Ronald Ngala's decision.

' I welcome our brothers wholeheartedly for realizing that Kenya needs a greater unity than we have had until now ', he declared. ' I regard this day as a great day, not for KANU but for the people of Kenya. Today is a great day and I hope now that we will work as one team and work in the spirit of Harambee to build the nation.'

The steps leading to this happy culmination are worth recording. They are a revelation of the true spirit of the democratic African revolution. I cite them from a fine article of historic importance contributed by John Dumoga to the *Daily Nation* on 11 December 1964.

When, in 1960, the British Government lifted its ban on nation-wide political parties, the political leaders who had stood united against colonialism parted company on the policies now to be pursued. The 1961 general elections resulted in stalemate. KANU won a majority in the Legislative Assembly, but refused to take office while Mr Kenyatta remained a prisoner of the colonial power. In April, KADU formed a minority government, in the words of Mr Ngala, to free Kenyatta.

Mzee was released in October, but KADU still rejected his overtures for Unity. Early in 1962 the first coalition government was formed with Mr Kenyatta and Mr Ngala as joint Ministers of State for Constitutional Affairs. The debate continued, however, and in 1963, KANU assumed the role of official opposition. Then came the General Election of May 1963, overwhelming victory for KANU and a mandate for Prime Minister Kenyatta to secure Independence with all possible speed.

On 21 August 1963, Prime Minister Kenyatta, in his capacity as President of KANU, made the decisive contribution to the great debate which, on both sides, had been conducted with dignity and a determination to serve faithfully the interests of the Motherland and Africa. Kenyatta's thesis made these points which, I suggest, clinch the argument for and about the one-party democratic state:

' We reject a blueprint of the Western model of a two-party system of government because we do not subscribe to the notion of the Government and the governed in opposition to one another, one clamouring for duties and the other for rights. . . .

' Through the historical process which has taken place since the last century, we find ourselves with myriad relevant grounds and conditions for a one-party state. It is inevitable. . . .

' In our particular situation, practice will have to precede theory. Should relevant grounds for a multi-party state evolve in the future, it is not the intention of my Government to block such a trend through prohibitive legislation.'

Who can doubt that the unity now prevailing in Kenya is the product of honest debate and an expression of the democratic process?

The late Dunduzu Chisiza of Malawi argued the wisdom of a national government to manage the affairs of an emergent African state during the first ten years, and U. Thant, Secretary-General of the United Nations, has summed up the problem admirably as follows:

It is a mistake to assume that the political institutions and forms of democracy in most of the newly independent countries will be of the same type as those prevailing in Britain, or that there will necessarily be two main parties competing against each other for the votes of the poeple.

The notion that democracy requires the existence of an organized opposition to the government of the day is not valid. Democracy requires only freedom for opposition, not necessarily its organized existence.

In many newly independent countries it is most unlikely that there will be a two-party system for many years to come. The nationalist movements are powerful indeed. They will control governments without there being any effective challenge to them from within. And any challenge from outside would only strengthen them.

Reporting the Secretary-General's speech *The Times* of 7 July 1962 added:

' As was the case in many European countries it might take some time before it would be possible for political opposition to be expressed in constitutional forms . . .'

Consider also the views of Julius Nyerere:

Now that the colonialists have gone, there is no remaining division between ' rulers ' and the ruled. There can, therefore, be only one reason for the formation of such parties in a country like ours – the desire to imitate the political structure of a totally dissimilar society. What is more, the desire to imitate where conditions are not suitable for imitation can easily lead us into trouble. To try and import the idea of a Parliamentary opposition into Africa may very likely lead to violence – because the opposition parties will tend to be regarded as traitors by the majority of our people – or at best it will lead to the trivial manoeuvrings of ' opposing ' groups whose time is spent in the inflation of artificial differences.

There, concisely argued, is the case for Africans refusing to ape Western forms of government, willing though we are to learn from them. We must be true to our African personality, to the needs and desires of our own people. We owe nothing to the example of former Colonial administrations; they banished or imprisoned every African freedom fighter, including many of our Chiefs. Time and time again, British governments have been forced to hand over power – in Ireland, India, and Africa – to men they had outlawed. When the Convention People's Party began to demand positive action in Ghana, it was virtually proscribed. Dr Nkrumah its leader, was held in prison until the very day when, by their vote, the people of Ghana decided for themselves what was good for their country. A look at South Africa gives no support to the suggestion that organized opposition is a factor in liberalizing a régime. Elected opposition does not stop Dr Verwoerd from oppressing Africans. In the debate on the disreputable ' 90 days without trial Bill ' the Leader of the Opposition announced his support for the Bill!

Opposition at Westminster is neither created nor sustained by statute. According to *The Law of the Constitution*[1] by Sir Ivor Jennings, government in Britain is possible without opposition, opposition being simply one of the many conventions and usages that have grown up and around the British Constitution. The theory of organized opposition is not even hallowed by age.

When the ancient Greeks gathered to discuss the affairs of the country in the *agora*, or market place, they were performing the same function which African Chiefs perform to this day. They were arguing about issues of importance to the nation. Only when a decision was reached and ratified by a large majority of those assembled did it acquire the authority of law. The Germans once had an amusing but no less democratic method of deciding important public questions. They called all the members of the community to a drinking feast, and while the flagon flew ideas were exchanged and opinions debated far into the night. Wise men circulated among the revellers, noting what was being said or, like the Prime Minister at a British Cabinet meeting, ' collecting the voices '. Next day, reports were submitted to those holding responsible positions in the community, and so emerged the final decision. The ancient Germans acted on the principle that in wine is truth. In the old Gaelic world, the method of canvassing public opinion was similar – and democratic.

Africans, certainly, are not alone in wishing to retain their traditional ideas of democracy, giving them expression in modern form. What is more, Africans are not at all disturbed when told that their conventions and usages find few or no parallels in the West. Their thesis is that the one-party system

[1] 3rd Edition, p. 90.

is compatible with democratic practice in Africa. And a million proofs are available to the clear-eyed observer. Our vastly accelerated progress in education, health, and industrialization since the end of Colonialism are among these proofs. So is the fast growth of communication and transport within and between African states. Perhaps most decisive is the evidence of the increasing participation of individual African citizens in every aspect of the business of governing themselves.

My personal view is this : One-party democracy, already rich in achievement in many African states, has an even more dynamic role in the future of the Continent. It will grow, inevitably, into a Continental mass party embracing all Africans – perhaps under the name of the African People's Party – and comprising all African states. And it will provide the unshakeable foundation of the Union Government of Africa.

Ghanaians, especially, find their democratic faith fortified by an event in their recent history. Dr Nkrumah, addressing the National Assembly on 2 October 1962, referred to a motion congratulating him on his escape from the bomb attack on his life at Kulungugu and expressing a popular and unanimous wish that he should continue in office as President for the remainder of his life.

In an atmosphere charged with deep emotion, Dr Kwame Nkrumah told his fellow countrymen :

> I thank you for your motion, which is a mark of the confidence you have in me, and a unanimous expression of solidarity behind my person and office.
>
> I would, however, remind you . . . that we have adopted a People's Democracy in which the sovereign will of the people is exercised through Parliament, a President and a Party. We are guided by a unique Republican Constitution which states quite clearly that elections for the office of President shall be held once every five years.
>
> It is essential that the people shall freely exercise their sacred right and duty of self-expression through voting ; that once every five years they shall have the opportunity to renew their faith and confidence in the Party and its leader.

These are the authentic accents of democracy.

CHAPTER FOUR

CENTRALISM : THE DYNAMIC OF DEMOCRACY

A distinguished American scholar has acknowledged that ' in Africa today . . . peoples, parties, and Leaders are experimenting with new political forms which are influenced strongly, either positively or negatively, by their experience with Western-type institutions but are sufficiently distinctive to be worthy of fresh standards of evaluation.'[1]

Though Professor Carter's observation is apt, it is inadequate. The new political forms in question are not distinguished by the fact that they are influenced strongly by our experience of Western-type institutions ; rather they are institutional summaries of our diverse political experiences. Western influence there needs to be, for our experience of the Western world has launched us beyond the point of no return into modern times. Modern times with all their complexities call for suitable machinery for national administration. The only institutions which are calculated to suit modern needs and of which we have some experience, are those which are usually called Western, but which are in fact to be found all over the world. In Africa, we have taken over aspects of Western political institutions, but we have done so rationally.

Though the Western institutions which we are familiar with are in a sense modern, they nevertheless have certain shortcomings in the context of Africa. They do not meet the democratic standards which Africa accepts, for they do not guarantee for every individual that continuing right which is his to have a say in the affairs of state. We in Africa evolved centuries ago a method of political discussion which assures to the individual full opportunities for exercising this right.

[1] Gwendolen M. Carter, editor, in her introduction to *African One-Party States*, Cornell University Press, 1962, p. vi.

This method is at the centre of democratic centralism. Democratic centralism in Africa today was pioneered by President Sekou Touré, the distinguished, thrusting leader of the Republic of Guinea.

Three vital aims animate democratic centralism. They are to ensure, at leadership level, a full understanding of public opinion ; to encourage political awareness throughout the community so that varied views will be voiced ; and to give elbow-room to what is known, in Western terms, as ' loyal opposition '. This inter-action between government and opposition implies an inner unity of purpose. It became institutionalized long ago in the democracies of the West ; so institutionalized that it is taken for granted by electors in Great Britain who do not recognize that democracy can operate in many other ways. I hope to convince such electors that democratic centralism, in relation to the one-party democratic state, is Africa's answer to the problem posed by Professor Carter :

' *The role of the loyal opposition is a difficult one to play. No party in newly independent Africa has yet accepted its discipline.*'[1]

The idea of democratic centralism had a modest beginning. It was a method of organizing the mass vote. After its adoption by the *Parti democratique de Guinée*, it was copied as an electoral device by most of the French-speaking communities of Sub-Saharan Africa. In this, its most simple form, it turns the whole country into an electoral district within which the winning party takes all the seats. It is like the block vote system, which is accepted and defended by the two major British parties in preference to proportional representation as demanded by the Liberal Party. It is fair enough to remind readers that in the 1924 General Election the Conservative Party captured well under eight million of the sixteen-and-a-half million votes cast, yet obtained two out of every three Parliamentary seats, and in 1935, with only a little more than 50 per cent of the votes cast, they and their ' National ' allies, nevertheless captured over 69 per cent of the seats. In both cases the Conservatives were able to operate like the government of a one-party state through their commanding

[1] Carter, *op. cit.*, p. 8.

majority in the House. Naturally, they rejoiced in these results! The significance of these British results, however, is grave for democracy. For one thing, a political party supported by less than half of the electorate understood that it had been given the right to impose its ideas upon the whole nation; i.e. carry out a political programme of action against which more than half of the electorate must be taken to have voted. For another, the pattern of the polling shows that political discussion was incomplete. The method of political discussion in the Western democracies is such that, by election day itself, it is unlikely that a national concensus of opinion will have been reached.

The block vote works rather differently in French-speaking West Africa, for there no group can rule a nation on less than half the national suffrage. The winning party, to govern, must poll at least 51 per cent of the votes cast, and it is desirable for it to poll upwards of 91 per cent. A poll of 91 per cent is an unmistakable testimony of the moral right to rule. A ruling party polling 91 per cent obviously has better founded authority than one which polls only 48 per cent. A vote of 91 per cent demonstrates the firm national basis of a ruling party. African politicians rejoice in such a result.

A glance at Guinea's post-war history will illuminate the growth and development of democratic centralism.

Sekou Touré, Secretary-General of the PDG, was also prominent in the *Rassemblement Democratique Africain*, which in the mood of surging nationalism agitated for equal rights with those of the citizens of Metropolitan France. Literally all the leaders of the parties comprising the RDA, including Touré, repudiated the advice of the then powerful French Communist Party that change in Africa must await the victory of the proletariat in France. Where Touré disagreed with some of his colleagues – and in this he was supported by the younger generation in Guinea and throughout French Africa – was in his demand for a relationship with Paris founded upon equality *and* independence. In pursuit of this policy, he made the PDG a spearhead of the nationalist movement and rescued it from the minor role of a vote-getting machine which, in his own words, ' crumbled under the mutually opposing interests of its own leaders ' immediately the ballot boxes were closed. The rise of the PDG to the stature of an alternative government meant vigorous exposure of the campaign conducted by the administration and the salaried *chefs de canton* against his party, especially in rural areas. It required that political organization be taken out of the hands of the intellectuals, usually minor civil servants, who were in politics to serve their own interests rather than the needs of the peasant masses. Above all, it demanded strong, intimate and continuing contact between the active party members and the people.

Touré harnessed the growing power of trade unionism to his cause. He identified himself with the 67-days' strike which, in 1953, won the 40-hour week. He aroused the political consciousness of the nation. He unified the traditional authority of the more progressive chiefs with the popular movement. He attracted millions all over French Africa to the cause of independence as an assertion of African Personality and dignity.

By mid-1957, the PDG, with Touré a member of the Council of Ministers, was poised to meet the challenge which, on 28 September 1958, faced Guineans called upon to vote *Oui* or *Non* to the constitution of the Fifth French Republic. The Franco-African Community projected by General de Gaulle, Touré argued, did not offer real independence to its African members. Its real aim was to break up the old federation of French West Africa and French Equatorial Africa and obstruct any future union of Africa.

Let me quote Touré's own statement on the position as he saw it. ' The *loi cadre* by dividing the federation into separately administered territories, by refusing even to consider a co-ordinating government among the territories, sowed the seed in Africa of the break-up of the federation. And it was not by chance that French West Africa was given eight autonomous governments instead of a single one. It was part of a nefarious scheme to continue metropolitan control over under-developed but potentially rich territories. It was to perpetuate colonialism in less apparent but nonetheless efficient form, in the final analysis to continue the exploitation of the men and riches of

Africa, who were to be rendered the more vulnerable by this " balkanization ".[1]

TOURÉ AND THE GENERAL

On 25 August 1958, General de Gaulle made a personal visit to Conakry to rally support for the Referendum. Touré announced, briefly, the conditions upon which he would ask Guineans to vote Yes : independence and juridical equality must be recognized : Guinea should have a voice in the Community's affairs and freedom to withdraw from the Community. The French President replied in accents that shattered the faith of many Africans in his promise of liberation : ' I say here even more loudly than I have elsewhere that independence is up to Guinea. It can have it on 28 September by voting " No " to the proposal, and I guarantee the Métropole will make no objection. There will, of course, be some consequences for Guinea, but there will be no obstacles in the way . . . If Guinea says " yes " – that is, if it freely, spontaneously, of its own accord accepts the constitution – and if France on its side says " yes ", then the African territories and the Métropole can work together for mutual profit.'

The chips were down. The French administration began to apply pressure on the people for an affirmative vote. They poured millions of ' propaganda ' francs into Guinea ; Touré advised his militants (i.e. party organizers and local leaders) to take whatever cash was offered for their franchise and vote ' No '. French paratroops were brought in ' to maintain order '. A territorial conference of the PDG in September decided that, in view of the choice offered by de Gaulle, ' no dependent people would hesitate for a moment between independence and the proposed Community '. The administration being responsible for counting the votes, nothing could obscure the meaning of the result : ' No ' 1,130,292 ; ' Yes ' 56,959 ; spoiled or blank ballots, 12,920. Among the eight territories of French West Africa, Guinea stood alone.

President de Gaulle literally rushed to recognize the *de*

---

[1] *Experience* p. 168, cited in Carter, *op. cit.*, section on Guinea by Prof. L. Gray-Cowan, p. 164.

facto INDEPENDENCE of Guinea, and to tell it that it was cut off immediately from the Community and that French administration, and that economic assistance had ended. The custodians of law and order were withdrawn. Administrators and technicians, under agreement to remain at their post for a period of twelve months, left at once and in large numbers, after having destroyed vital files and dismantled communications in order to aggravate the problems of the new régime. French teachers en route by ship for the opening of the new school year in Guinea were halted at Dakar. Guinean students at schools in Dakar and Bamako on scholarships valid until the end of the year were dismissed immediately. The French Government made *de jure* recognition impossible, first by making it contingent upon negotiation of an agreement on Guinean membership of the franc zone, then by imposing conditions which any sovereign power was bound to reject. Guinea's request for ' association ' under the terms of Section XIII of the Constitution of the Fifth Republic was ignored.

Happily, France underestimated the courage and pride of the great grandson of Almany Samory Touré, last of the nineteenth-century Sudanese conquerors, and fighting opponent of French hegemony in Guinea. His name lives on in local song and story. Now, led by Sekou Touré, ordinary men and women in thousands of village and urban groups and committees were to write a new saga of trial and triumph.

There was no looting, no disorder, no violence. There were no weak brethren to become the tools of traitors. The people accepted gaily the declaration of independence on 2 October 1958. They had entered the political kingdom. In human affairs in time of stress, the lie runs miles before truth gets its boots on. Here, the boot of truth was in the lie's backside before it could make a start. The natural dignity of comrades prevailed above all dividing and corrupting influences. Democratic centralism had produced democratic discipline.

Meanwhile, Guinea strode proudly across the international scene. Her new government was recognized at once by near neighbours, Liberia and Ghana. Ghana gave, a little later, the practical aid of a £G10 million loan. Russia and the

Eastern bloc soon followed suit. On 30 October, Great Britain, in face of French disapproval, became the first of the NATO countries to establish diplomatic relations. By the end of the year, sixty countries, including China and a rather reluctant America, had welcomed the new state into the diplomatic family of nations. Guinea was received into membership of United Nations on 13 December, only France abstaining from voting in the General Assembly. At last, on 7 January 1959, France signed a protocol covering technical aid and cultural relations. Early in that New Year, Touré had cleared the decks for action on mass education, the conversion of the economy from the colonial pattern, the improvement of agriculture, and the fulfilment of Guinea's revolution by an unceasing effort to make his party a faithful reflection of the will of the people.

I have described, in the previous chapter, how in Guinea people are elected to responsible positions in conducting the business of the state. Before examining the structure of the Party, let me make clear this important point : my friend Sekou Touré does not regard Guinea as a single-party state. His experiment seeks to make the PDG representative of the whole state, and of the interests of every individual man and woman in the state. This distinction is a most important one, and once it is made it quickly becomes clear why African societies are rejecting the party system of Government in favour of the national system. According to us, the ideal, could it be attained, would be for all of us to be in the Government. This would be true self-government.

In practice, however, society today is too large, and is too complex, for this kind of literal self-government. Representative government thus becomes the one practical approximation to literal self-government. Under a party system of Government, however, it is almost impossible to achieve representative government. In European political theory, a party can only represent a section of the nation. This immediately perverts the intention of representative government, which is to be representative of society as a whole, and not just of one section. This is what cannot be achieved in a party system of Government. It is obvious that, in this sense, a multi-party system is incapable of offering representative government except in the form of a national coalition.

In the one-party states of Africa, however, we have no parties in the normal sense. The national organization which we call parties are not built around sectional interests, but are rather an administrative organization of society for organizing and pursuing its general interests, and for creating and maintaining the kind of state in which legitimate individual interests can thrive. In Guinea, as in Ghana, the party does not merely make it possible for a government to be elected to office. The régime is the party, and the party is the organization of the people into a political body. Says Touré: ' All our people are mobilized in the ranks of the PDG . . . the common will derives not from the summit, but from the base of the popular will. Authority rests not with the government but with the people.' In the effort to expand national unity and release the dynamic of democracy for national progress, the PDG cannot be the instrument of any one class, any one social section. Its supreme task is to be in touch with all the people all the time.

The basis of the popular will resides in the PDG's more than seven thousand village and urban committees. They provide ' the point of articulation between the party and the mass of the Guinean population.'[1] Their task is to organize support and implement the decisions made by the party as a whole. Village meetings are held at least once a week, on the same day, at the same hour, in the market place. They discuss village, regional, and national affairs. Village executive committees are elected once a year by the party members who in theory, and largely in practice, are all eligible voters in the community. An executive includes four men, the three women officers of the local women's group, two representatives of the youth group, and the mayor of the village.

COLLECTIVE DECISIONS

As Professor L. Cowan Gray points out: '. . . the *comité de village* . . . is in essence the traditional village council meeting. Decisions of the *comité de village* are arrived at in African

[1] Carter, *op. cit.*, p. 179.

fashion – that is, by common agreement, after lengthy discussion in which all may, and do, participate and at the end of
which no dissident minority elements remain. In such
meetings the emphasis is on collective decision, not on majority
vote. Once a decision has been made, however, all participants
bear equally the burden of its consequences since each feels that
he had a share in making it.'[1] Professor Gray makes plain the
connection between the modern political life of Guinea and
traditional African customs. Democratic centralism in Africa
is fundamentally the reiteration of traditional African democracy in modern circumstances. Equally important is the
fact that political discussion at the basic level in Guinea aims
not at a majority decision but at a collective one with everyone
participating in it, and morally binding to an equal degree
on all.

Above the village committee is the Directing Committee,
holding two sessional congresses annually in each of the 43
sections into which the country is divided. The Directing
Committee Executive, of whom two are women and two
chief officers of the regional youth organizations, is elected
from the village groups. The General Secretary is responsible
to the *Bureau Politique* which is the highest authority in the
Party and is its national headquarters. Every one of the
fifteen members is assigned a specific duty relating to political
and economic affairs, propaganda, organization, and finance.
They initiate working sub-committees, on to which non-
elected persons with specialized knowledge can be co-opted, to
study and report upon the problems submitted by the villages.

A permanent official receives *mots d'ordre* from the Political
Bureau. These circulars deal with questions of national policy
and action; such questions, for example, as family allowances,
respect for religious convictions, the responsibilities of trade
unions, aspects of mass education, and even the developing
role of the Directing Committee itself. The *mots d'ordre* are
then distributed to the villages for debate and action. In this
way, the semi-annual section meetings provide a vital and
vitalizing personal link between the membership and the
Political Bureau.

[1] *Ibid.*, p. 226.

Into this deep vertical structure there is inserted a horizontal organization in the form of six-monthly regional conferences of all the *Comités Directeurs* of the sections within a single administrative region. Party officers are joined by delegates from the village committees, the *commandant de région*, administrative officials, managers of regional co-operative societies, trade union leaders, and the regional military commanders. The aim is two-fold: to enable administration and party to meet at an administrative rather than at a party level; and to bring the regional section committees together. Similar meetings of delegates from the section and of nation party leaders are held annually.

With a political system designed to ensure that the popular will animates all social, political and economic, activity, the Political Bureau, the final decision-making authority, reflects all aspects of the party organization, and is the focus of power both in the party and the nation. Its policy, explained in every detail and debated, pro and con, by literally every citizen, cannot be opposed when embodied in act or decision. In this way, something else is also achieved. Communications in Africa are still inadequate. Furthermore, the administrative language of African societies is almost always other than the languages of most Africans. There can therefore be posed in an acute manner the real and dangerous problem of a government pursuing policies which have not been well understood by the populace. The dangers of this are two-fold: first, groups of individuals may arise who oppose national policies not because of any objective drawbacks about them, but because their full meaning and significance has not been grasped; second, the complete dynamic commitment to policies required in a growing country will not be forthcoming when people have been prevented by lack of understanding from grasping policies fully. Understanding must precede creative labour. These two dangers are obviated by the full and basic discussion which every *mot d'ordre* undergoes before it is implemented. In this way also the axis of national development comes to lie in every individual, and none can have that negative attitude towards policies which is so easily generated in a multi-party system. In the multi-party system, policies can very easily seem to be not national policies to be embraced by all citizens, but rather party and sectional ones. Surely one can learn a lesson from the negative difficulties which the programmes of the 1945–51 Labour Government of Britain attracted.

Here, in such a system as that of Guinea, I want to repeat, is the essence of democratic centralism. Policy is debated fully throughout the Party. Criticism and free expression are encouraged everywhere within the Party. All voices having been heard, the conclusions reached are accepted by the entire membership.

' Human government is either based on discussion or on force. This distinction is more fundamental than any classification based on differences of form, as, for instance, monarchy or republicanism, democracy or oligarchy.' This proposition, stated by a prominent British Conservative and Lawyer, the Rt. Hon. Quintin Hogg, M.P., will be accepted readily by most political theorists. Mr Hogg, writing in *The Purpose of Parliament*,[1] develops the argument as follows :

> Of course all governments are to some extent a mixture of the two principles. No country is wholly governed by discussion. Human government is by its very nature compulsive and proceeds in the name of authority to coerce those who will not submit to law. Nor is any country wholly ruled by force. Human action is by its very nature voluntary and springs from reason by means of an act of will. But the essence of a despotism is that discussion is tolerated only when it is unavoidable ; of free government, that discussion is a right and the willing compliance of all, a conscious objective . . . The right to talk, to reason with Government before compulsion is brought to bear, is the foundation on which the whole of Parliamentary Government is built.

So too with democratic centralism, whatever form it takes in our varied African societies. Discussion is a right of all. Willing compliance in discussion and acceptance of the decisions arising from discussion and debate are fundamental to our free assemblies, from the meetings in the village market place to the great gatherings of our Parliaments and the conference of our Heads of State and Government.

[1] Quintin Hogg, *The Purpose of Parliament*, Blandford Press, 1947, pp. 2–3

The Political Bureau has seventeen members, nine of them Ministers of the Government, and the others all holding important positions such as the Presidency of the National Assembly, the Headship of the Armed Forces, and the Chief Inspectorate of Education.   Government, from Assembly to Cabinet, might be described as the administrative limb of the party in the conduct of the nation's business.

Every three years, the PDG holds its national conference. It elects the national executive, decides over-all policy for the forthcoming triennium and, since the work of government and party is so closely inter-linked, listens to what is in effect, a state of the nation message from Sekou Touré.   As Secretary-General of the Party and President of the Republic, Sekou Touré presents a *rapport moral* in which he expounds the political theory that gives meaning and coherence to party policy. These reports are always exciting and they are expressed in felicitous language.   They make a valuable and ever-growing contribution to political thought and philosophy in Africa and, indeed, in the world.

Here again one can see reason for the importance of ideology in the political life of Africa.   Ideological expositions in Africa, such as that which *Consciencism*[1] so notably presents, give the theoretical basis of national programmes.   African society is a self-conscious society.   We not only want development, we also know why we want development, what kind of development will satisfy our demands and how we shall attain that development.   Thus, in *Consciencism*, President Nkrumah writes :

> What is called for as a first step is a body of connected thought which will determine the general nature of our action in unifying the society which we have inherited, this unification to take account, at all times, of the elevated ideals underlying the traditional African society.   Social revolution must therefore have, standing firmly behind it, an intellectual revolution, a revolution in which our thinking and philosophy are directed towards the redemption of our society.   Our philosophy must find its weapons in the environment and living conditions of the African people.   It is from those conditions that the intellectual

[1] Kwame Nkrumah, *Consciencism*, Heinemann, 1964, p. 78.

content of our philosophy must be created. The emancipation of the African continent is the emancipation of man. This requires two aims : first, the restitution of the egalitarianism of human society, and, second, the logistic mobilization of all our resources towards the attainment of that restitution.

Now the democratic forms I have tried to describe in broad outline, are unknown to Western countries. I am willing to admit that they might be unsuitable in Western conditions, although I would place no ban upon their export ! They are not intended for a civilization which is already industrialized, and they will change and diversify under the impact of industrialization in Africa. But they are necessary today in order to preserve democracy while we seek industrial development. What must be understood is that the instruments of democracy are being forged, amid all the pressures of time and of Africa's enemies, to meet the needs of an under-developed country dedicated to freedom and to its own ideals of healthy, happy, and progressive human society. Democratic centralism, although based upon tradition, is far from being tradition-bound and inward-looking. Indeed, it has taught Guineans to equate their own freedom with the freedom and unity of all Africa. One result is that Guinea is the first French-speaking country to make English a second language in its schools in order to facilitate communication with fellow Africans and the West. Action of this nature, I suggest, is much more important to the future of Africa and men the world over than is the slavish copying of western-style forms of government and law.

Meanwhile, within the African continent, the theory and practice of democratic centralism attracts increasing attention. There is some evidence to support the view that, with an entire nation involved directly in the political process, the threat offered to the security of the state by internal and external enemies is greatly reduced. No colonial administration ever encouraged communication among ordinary people in Africa. Communication, made easy in the West by universal education and newspapers, has always been difficult to develop and sustain. With the price of newsprint and the cost of its haul from overseas at prohibitive rates during the last twenty-five years, and with circulations restricted by illiteracy, there has never been anything resembling a mass-selling popular Press in the continent. As things are now, any African states, offered the choice of importing expensive newsprint or the books required for millions of eager students, would certainly choose books. Democratic centralism, however, has solved this problem. It offers an effective medium of communication without which there can be no democracy whatever. To that medium, the new prospects of radio and television and, in Guinea, the Party's tri-weekly newspaper, *Horoya* (Dignity), are valuable additions.

Democratic centralism has also given birth to the most original expression of dynamic democracy ever seen in Africa or anywhere else. This, in Guinea, is *investissement humain*, or voluntary labour, or as we Ghanaians call it, community development. The idea was magically simple ; the human energy generated by the national effort put into the Referendum victory could and should be channelled into producing some concrete results of independence of which the people would be proud. *Investissement humain* would promote a feeling of individual responsibility towards the community and ' a love of the value of work for its own sake '. It would demonstrate ' the pre-eminence of constructive action over verbal wrangling '. The third party congress, in June 1958, translated the idea into a programme. Details of projects were left to the initiative of village and section committees. For some plans the government offered assistance in providing materials ; for all plans the public supplied voluntary labour. Only meagre skills were available, especially in rural areas where, also, only limited time could be spared from tending crops and cattle. The nation, however, took positive action. In many places people laboured under floodlights when their normal day's work was done. Already, in 1959, Sekou Touré was able to announce that 5,035 miles of road, 33 schools, 672 bridges, and 15 mosques had been built, and that schemes based upon Guinea's example had been launched in Mali, Senegal, and Togo. And the grand idea, now under observation by some of the world's leading sociologists, goes marching on.

I testify, gladly and proudly, to the value of community development in my own country, Ghana. It has created many amenities including schools, roads, and health clinics and has thus improved the quality of life even in our remotest villages. It has provided a variety of public buildings, from lavatories and health dispensaries to halls and community centres, where great campaigns for better nutrition and the welfare of our children are carried on. In short, community development has added significantly to the impressive infrastructure of public services which, since independence, has changed the face of Ghana; so significantly that a distinctive place has been defined for it in our £G1,016 million Seven Year Development Plan. Of the 'private investment' in the Plan worth £G540 million, 'direct labour investment' is expected to provide physical assets to the value of £G100 million, and is to be extended to urban areas.

In Ghana, as in Guinea, as indeed in other African States, we foster the rights of the individual party member. Every member is entitled and expected to attend party meetings, to express his views freely upon all matters that arise for discussion, and to vote according to his conviction. He has the right to elect and to be elected to party bodies, and to address any question or statement to any party body, including the National Executive and the Central Committee. If a party member desires to contest a decision of his Branch Party, he can carry his appeal right up to the Central Committee and to the Leader of the party in person. In other words, like a member of a family, he has access to the Head of the House. He has still a final 'court of appeal' – to the National Delegates Conference of the Party.

A similar process leads to decisions on all important questions of policy. Discussion begins at Branch level. The arguments, pro and con, move on to the District Executive Committees of the Party, then to the Regional Executive Committees, and from there to the National Executive and the Central Committee. Next the Cabinet gives assent, probably with some modifications and interpretations to ensure the fullest possible concensus of party opinion. Finally, in accordance with our African tradition that, all voices having been heard, the entire family of the nation will be faithful to the decision made, the President makes a proclamation.

This is our African conception of democracy. Ours is a human, warm, vital democracy, great in achievement and greater still in promise.

CHAPTER FIVE

NKRUMAH: ONE IN A MILLION

Certainly, Dr Nkrumah is a man in a million. He is a man who was bitten once by an idea, and has since then devoted his whole energy and life to that cause – the cause of the African and the idea of a regenerated, prosperous, happy, and effective African society. Dr Nkrumah is also a man of millions. Millions all over Africa and the world admire his striking achievements in diverse fields, his achievements in the field of letters, thought, and political strategy and action. Millions admire those achievements which have also destroyed for ever the mortifying colonialist fiction of African inferiority. People all over the continent see in him the flesh and blood of the African Personality, a vision which gives them inspiration, ambition, and the self-confidence necessary for fulfilling both. Dr Nkrumah has met many thousands of his fellow citizens face to face – in the day-by-day struggle of political life and affairs in the market place, and in the dance. Millions know that this man understands the African heart throb and, with a poet's intuition, transmutes it into a social and personal ideal.

Some of us quite early in our association with Osagyefo – the word means ' Victorious Leader ' – grasped the essential meaning of his power: this man cannot be separated from the African masses. He himself says that the masses are his father and mother, the origin of his strength and sustenance. He is of them, and with them and for them. I smile when I recollect the fatuous criticism, inevitable during the adolescence of a new political party, that our leader was too close to the people, that he identified himself too intimately with the meek and humble. He, with his adored and adoring mother, kept open house in Accra for all who needed help, or advice, or the opportunity to clarify their own thought by talking to a sympathetic audience. At our great Party meetings and rallies he enjoyed most, and still enjoys, sharing a simple meal with the rank and file, exchanging experiences, ideas, jokes, as one of themselves. In criticizing this perfect identification with the people, some men showed their complete ignorance of the one valid purpose of political liberation – that the people might be more effectively and more justly served.

Soon we understood that Osagyefo was better informed about the ebb and flow of Party opinion than any of us. Soon too Osagyefo became recognized as the authentic African voice crying in the colonial wilderness for his people, a modern African political leader moulded in the great tradition of good chieftainship – the tradition of face-to-face relations between chief, or leader, and people. The West, where politics are a reflection of class interests, seldom produces a prototype and cannot be expected to understand a way of life so different from its own. One hopes and prays, however, that the West can learn that a tradition is not inferior because it is different. The values of African tradition, in their own environment, are real and proud and lasting.

Politics is many things. It is in one of its aspects the art of managing a society solely for the interests of society. This is a conception presupposed by the continuance of the African society. Hence the necessity for the continual confrontation of leader and people.

In practical terms, this confrontation of leader and people can never be clouded by the vague generalities of the political mountebank and the mere seeker after power. It is direct, simple, and intimate. It is the communication of social truth. The people are the source of all social power, and their interests the source of all principles of social action. Through confrontation of leader and people, the interests are clarified and the principles are confirmed. No African today asks the question that plagues every politician in Western societies: Is anybody listening? In the ferment and fervour of modern Africa, everybody is listening, and only the message of social truth can be heard permanently and gladly. To the expression of this form of leadership, Nkrumah brings many individual and relevant qualities. He has vast learning and acute awareness of the movement of thought and intellect in many fields of knowledge. He has deep respect for ordinary men and women and from this respect there flows a noble scorn for colonialism and racialism. He has the gift of pungent, amusing speech which we Africans describe in a typical saying: 'His sling has many witty stones'.

The former Governor of James Fort Prison, where Osagyefo was held, has testified to yet another of Osagyefo's vital qualities – his redoubtable courage.[1] When he was arrested in 1950, following the launching of his Positive Action campaign, the prison warders were being incited to beat him up. The prison Governor intervened to prevent what promised to be a murderous assault. He found Nkrumah calm and unafraid, the one relaxed person in a storm of rage and threat and passion. During fourteen months' imprisonment – Osagyefo was released only when the voters of Accra Central elected him a member of the National Assembly by the largest poll ever recorded – he conquered all the horror and indignity of living in an overcrowded, filthy cell by his cheerfulness, optimism, asceticism, and unflagging energy. He continued to direct the massive political campaign still raging outside, giving orders, writing manifestoes and messages on the meagre ration of toilet paper and getting them smuggled out under the noses of his jailers. I myself, with some Party friends, was visiting his home in Lagostown, Accra, on the night it was dynamited. On the first explosion, we all ran towards the house shouting, 'Come out, Kwame! We'll look after Mother.' Back came the calm reply : 'No! This is our home, and here we stay !'

Osagyefo's political colleagues are reminded constantly of his amazing flair for principle. He has a sharp, clear mind possessing a tenacious memory for details, and an analytical intelligence for sorting them out. He quickly grasps the essentials of the subject under debate. Just as quickly, he relates them to basic political principles and expounds his argument in terms which bring light and understanding to everyone. Crises, common enough in all political parties and inevitable in times of social upheaval, stimulate his rare foresight and call forth his ability to allay fear, destroy doubt and point the way to action.

This flair distinguishes all Nkrumah's political tactics. I

[1] In *The Proud African*, a B.B.C. TV Programme, 4 June 1963.

recall when the fading Opposition sought to embarrass the Government by proposing a motion endorsing the leader's own demand for Self-Government Now. Naturally, the move excited glee among our enemies. Nkrumah's reaction was characteristically subtle. He offered to co-operate in passing the Opposition resolution on condition that they would endorse the policy of Positive Action Now by challenging the Colonial administration and risking imprisonment if Independence was refused. The Opposition had second thoughts and characteristically preferred to stay out of the Colonial jails even at the cost of sacrificing the chance of national independence !

During a very full and relentless life as political leader, statesman, and philosopher, Osagyefo has found time to create a distinguished record of authorship, including his widely read autobiography. Nevertheless, a swift look at the experiences which moulded this man, seen through the eyes of a loyal supporter, might be valuable to the readers of this book.

MASTER AND PUPIL

Nkrumah was born, in very humble circumstances at Nkroful, a small village in Nzima. The earliest influence in his life has been the most enduring, that of his mother. She wrested out of poor conditions a happy boyhood for her only child, giving him the security of love, serenity, and a sense of gaiety, besides encouraging his ambition for education.

When the young Kwame entered the Prince of Wales's College at Achimota, he found his first political hero in Dr Kwegyir Aggrey, then Assistant Vice-Principal. Aggrey's vast scholarship was inspired by a fine idealism. A great patriot and lover of Africa, he was also a fierce opponent of racialism in the very place from which Africans had been transported as slaves to the New World. Aggrey's idealism stimulated in his pupil the resolve to become a teacher and the determination to seek his further education in America, which he hoped to find free from the trappings and prejudices of Colonialism.

This adventurous leap into a larger life became something bigger and more arduous than the realization of an adolescent dream. Nkrumah's experiences turned it into a long period of preparation for the giant's task of liberating the Gold Coast, now the country of Ghana. In Philadelphia he made a survey of the religious, social, and economic position of the black man. The facts shocked him. 'When I compared this racial segregation with the modernity and advancement of the country,' he has written, 'it made my heart sink.' Osagyefo was beholding and indeed experiencing the traumatic reality of widespread public squalor amidst the private affluence of a few. He had to earn the daily crust during most of the years he lived in America, and found that the only means of earning it open to him were the menial jobs in slum workshops that alone were available to a coloured man. Nkrumah's self reliance, personal pride and depth of character were revealed in the patience with which he bore the rebuffs and difficulties arising from his lack of money. After nights of sleeping under the stars (and there were many such nights) he was still able to laugh and joke with his friends. He treated time as a miser treats gold. He treated it as a businessman treats capital. He deployed it with circumspection and effectiveness, acquiring knowledge, reflecting on its application, and imparting it as a university lecturer. He had a genius for selecting the most important tasks to hand and devoting all his hard-pressed time to discharging them. He must have wondered often where he would sleep. We, looking at his record, wonder if he ever did sleep ! To most of us cast in earthly mould, such a life would have been intolerable after two or three months. Not so Nkrumah. His asceticism and mysticism – characteristic of the greatest Africans in the dawn of civilization, and among the qualities with which his life in Nkroful had endowed him – were proof against loneliness and poverty and the thousand petty, pitiless persecutions which dog the lives of our people.

While at the University of Pennsylvania, Nkrumah founded the African Students' Association of America and Canada. Later, he organized the publication of its official organ, the *African Interpreter,* in order to give his fellows faith in themselves as members of the human race. What hope for the future this journal fed to many an African can only be imagined by those who have never felt the lash of racial discrimination. Africans in America are not treated as full citizens unless, of course, they excel in sport, when they are acclaimed and expected to carry the Stars and Stripes around the world, though they themselves are more familiar with the stripes than with the stars ! This is chauvinism reduced to absurdity ; for black men, a hurtful and humiliating absurdity.

After nine hard years in America, Nkrumah came to London. There he found a modest lodging in Tufnell Park, gathering around him dear friends in the late George Padmore, whose work has been commemorated worthily in Accra; T. R. Makonnen, now active in Ghana; and Peter Abrahams, the distinguished South African writer. Together, this team initiated the sixth in the series of Pan African Congresses, at the first of which, held in 1900, the late W. E. B. DuBois uttered a challenge which, only now, is penetrating the consciousness of the Western World. ' The problem of the twentieth century ', declared the great Africanist who later became a citizen of Ghana, ' is the problem of the colour line – the relation of the darker to the lighter races of men in Asia and Africa, in America and the islands of the sea.' This challenge has been fittingly taken up by Nkrumah.

This sixth Pan African Congress was held in Manchester under the joint Chairmanship of Dr DuBois and of Dr Peter Milliard of British Guiana in 1945. The new generation of African leaders were there: Kenyatta from Kenya, Akintola from Nigeria, Johnson from Sierra Leone. A Labour Government had taken power in Great Britain and was giving encouragement to the campaign for Indian freedom. Ideas of world unity were in the air – had not mankind just emerged victorious from a war provoked by Nazi racialism? Thus spoke Africa: ' We demand . . . autonomy and independence so far, and no further than it is possible in this One World for groups and peoples to rule themselves subject to inevitable world unity and federation.' And to make the demand ring loud and clear, Africa also declared: '. . . if the Western World is still determined to rule mankind by force, then Africans, *as a last resort*, may have to appeal to force in the effort to achieve freedom.'

Nkrumah returned to London, to the hard grind of organization and propaganda pursued relentlessly, despite a hampering lack of funds. He made fresh and fruitful contacts with men like Mr Fenner Brockway. He formed the Coloured Workers' Association, which still does good work for immigrants, and forged strong links of unity with Indian and West Indian men and women. He visited Paris to meet the African members of the French National Assembly, and to outline his proposals for a Union of West African Socialist Republics as a big step towards African Unity. Everything was sacrificed for the great cause. While retaining studious habits and discipline, Nkrumah gave up the prospects of an exciting and secure life as a teacher and lecturer, interrupted once before in America. Even romance was eschewed ; all who understand the test of renunciation of the natural joys of life in the interest of others now rejoice that Osagyefo is happily married and a father. Above all, he was vigilant to protect his organization from the eroding influence of 'sympathizers' who sought merely to preserve 'the temples of their gods' by blunting his purposes while pretending to support them, or who, in his own graphic words, ran with the hare and hunted with the hounds. He was not deceived even by those soldiers without swords dressed in the cloak of religion.

RETURN TO THE GOLD COAST

He was invited to return to the Gold Coast as General Secretary of the United Gold Coast Convention, a political organization seeking independence 'in the shortest possible time'. In December 1947, after twelve years' absence, Nkrumah breathed the African air again. Alas, he found the U.G.C.C. slow in converting the African air into freedom's air, 'probably', he has written, 'because it was composed mainly of business and professional men, especially lawyers.' Yet a lively sense of political awareness was evident. The country was in the grip of economic crisis, with ex-servicemen its hardest hit victims. There were demonstrations by Accra housewives against the high and soaring cost of living which at the same time brought no increase in public services. The constitutional reform of 1944 which permitted the appointment of Africans to the Executive Council had failed to ease the social unrest. Before long the Colonial administration began putting him ' on the run ', and, partly because of its anti-Nkrumah activities, the message of independence and African Unity was dominating Gold Coast politics.

Nkrumah had brought the spirit of the struggle for freedom into the heart and mind of his beloved homeland.

' Seek ye first the political kingdom.' This, the vital principle of democratic change, was enunciated vigorously in the campaign that inspired the Chartist Movement in England over a century ago; the campaign for political freedom as the first, essential step towards economic emancipation. In this statement we also have a crystallization of a deep truth of political transformation. Peaceful change is the only kind of change which can preserve the most that is worthwhile in a changing society. Violent change destroys many grains along with the chaff. In the context of a not fully developed society, the loss of too many grains can become too major a setback. At the same time, it is only with the guarantee of political supremacy that an agent of change can get the best of both worlds – the old and the new. With political supremacy, an agent such as the Convention People's Party of Ghana can bring about peaceful social changes, and at the same time ensure that none of the features preserved from the old society should turn out to be reactionary and negative. Only a party charged and vibrating with a revolutionary ideology can bring off this supreme feat. And such is the Convention People's Party of Ghana. Translating the principle of the supremacy of political action into the terms that set Africa alight, Nkrumah was asserting also the faith from which he has never deviated, whether in pursuit of freedom for every individual in Ghana or in the cause of United Africa. Indeed, a study of Osagyefo's speeches reveals two of the profound qualities, stemming from this faith in political action, which characterize his leadership. They are his honest consistency and his capacity to prepare public opinion for every advance in the development of his policy.

Always and everywhere, for example, he has attacked the twin-headed evil of bribery and corruption. Power to manage, or mismanage, our own affairs will involve us in mistakes, but mistakes which are ours can be positive and teach us how to do better and be more successfully self-reliant; mistakes arising from bribery and corruption however are criminal and must be treated as crimes, for they are purely negative, and destructive, in the short and long run, of the general welfare. One of his earliest speeches after his return to the Gold Coast was on the subject of 'The True National'. He described such a man as 'morally strong, skilled in action, honest, free from bribery and corruption'. He was to repeat the theme again and again in the years that followed. Soon after his election to the Legislative Assembly, he warned Party members:

'Bribery and corruption, both moral and factual, have eaten into the whole fabric of our society and these must be stamped out if we are to achieve any progress. Our election to the Assembly shows that the public has confidence in the integrity of the Party, and that we will not stoop low to contaminate ourselves with bribery and corruption at the expense of the people.'

In his 1955 oration on the Twelfth of July – always a notable anniversary celebration of the founding of the Convention People's Party – he supported a moving affirmation of his belief that ' it is the peaceful means that endure ; the gains of violence are transient ; the fruits of patience are imperishable ' with this invocation : ' Let us move forward together to build up a new Ghana – strong, clean, incorruptible, virile, and cohesive, as a symbol of emulation for the rest of Africa. I have never ceased to condemn bribery and corruption and I have warned that anybody, no matter his rank and office in the Party, who shall be found indulging in these vices shall be immediately exposed and punished.'

At the 1957 Easter Conference of the Party, just before the coming of independence, he referred to a nation-wide campaign to stamp out venality, and reminded his hearers of his plea of 1951 that Leaders, Assemblymen, and Ministers must not be spoiled by the sweets of office, and reiterated his view : ' I have always considered that bribery and corruption are social evils which must be completely uprooted from our social fabric, and I am determined to see that these evils are rooted out.'

This theme was the subject of the first of his dramatic Dawn

Broadcasts which have become as popular and important in Ghana as the late President Roosevelt's fireside chats on radio were in pre-war America.

Racialism, tribalism, and violence aroused his contempt, for they are all unethical and are founded on arbitrariness and selfishness. In a New Year Broadcast at the end of 1955, he insisted, not for the first time :

> Racialism and tribalism and violence must cease to be political factors in our national life. Violence must be completely rejected as an instrument of policy. I make this appeal not only for the happiness and well-being of our country. I would like every citizen in the Gold Coast – on the Coast, in Ashanti, in the Northern Territories – to remember that the hopes of millions of Africans living in our great Continent are pinned upon our experiment here. They want us to prove by our performance that we can peaceably and responsibly, with give and take and fairplay, manage our own domestic affairs.

Few men in Africa understand more surely the motives of the human heart and, in abolishing ' ritual murder ', as independent India has abolished ' ritual suicide ', Nkrumah appreciated the desire of the bereaved to provide companionship for their beloved dead beyond the grave. Ritual murder, however, had degenerated into a symbol of the unenlightened past, and was widely recognized as such. Like oath-swearing – a ' decadent tyranny ' – it was among the outworn traditions which enemies of the new society exploited blatantly ; these traditions had to go.

Always the Leadership sought, by inspiration, education, and legislation, to improve the quality of relationships in the private home and to raise new standards of probity in public life.

On another very practical question which provokes controversy in highly sophisticated societies – the question of foreign investment – Nkrumah has revealed again his amazing influence on the climate of opinion.

As long ago as March 1954, he offered assurances to overseas investors, ' thinking hard about the wisdom of putting their money into industry in the Gold Coast '. A speech in the Legislative Assembly then promised fair compensation in the event of the nationalization of any particular industry. While advising Ghanaians that ' a democratic Ghana should not develop a propensity for the consumption of foreign capital, except what is absolutely necessary ', and rejoicing that ' we can stand on our own feet ', he constantly underlined the need to encourage foreign investment. In a noteworthy eve-of-Independence address, with the eyes of the world on Ghana, he made these important points :

1. We ' did not seek continuing aid as a gift from the richer members of the Commonwealth. When spending £124 million during the course of our Five Year Development Plan we had received £1½ million in aid from Colonial Development and Welfare Funds. It was not a large proportion and we had in return made our contribution to the gold and dollar resources of the sterling area. The Gold Coast has contributed, on the average, 25 per cent of the net dollar earning of the British Colonial territories and taking into account our contribution of around £9 million a year in gold, in the five years from 1951 to 1955 in which the Convention People's Party have been in power, the Gold Coast contributed a net positive balance of £153 million to the gold and dollar reserves of the sterling area.'

2. Ghana would reconsider commercial and company law and fiscal policy which, while ensuring that ' no foreign cartel or trust is allowed to dominate the economy of the country ', would provide conditions attractive for investors.

3. ' While it is important for us to attract private investment, it is equally important that we prove ourselves credit-worthy to national and international financial organizations.'

In July 1957, opening the Bank of Ghana, Osagyefo summed up his long opinion-forming dialogue with the nation in these words :

'. . . it would be ungenerous if we did not acknowledge the great value to Ghana of the investment already made here by foreign companies and individuals. It is the intention of my Government, and the wish of the country, to do all we can to encourage such investments, to protect the interests of those who have already invested and to attract new investors.'

' No man is an island ', and no nation today can live and

grow in ' splendid isolation '. It was in full realization of the need for co-operation with others that Ghana, in the Capital Investment Act of 1963, presented a clearly drawn economic map defining the place of private investment, both foreign and local, in its expanding economy.

The aim of the Act is ' to encourage the investment of foreign capital and other purposes connected therewith '. A Capital Investment Board, set up to administer the Act, includes a representative of the Bank of Ghana, the Official Head of the Ministry responsible for Finance, the Official Head of the Ministry responsible for Industries and the Managing Director of the National Investment Bank.

Here are the guarantees offered to the foreign investor in Ghana : No investment shall be subject to expropriation by the Government. If exceptional circumstances arise and an approved project is taken over in the public interest, fair compensation will be paid in the currency in which the investment was originally made. Any dispute about compensation will be referred to an arbitration of the parties and, if that fails, to the arbitration of the International Bank for Reconstruction and Development. Capital can be remitted to the country of origin in the event of sale or liquidation. Profits can be transferred to the country of origin without restriction, after due payment of taxes. Payments in respect of principal, interest and other financial charges are also permitted. Reasonable facilities are available to enable expatriate personnel to ' send home ' money for family and personal purposes.

In addition to these eminently fair conditions, foreign investors are offered substantial incentives. An approved enterprise can obtain a ' tax holiday ' for five years beginning from the date of going into production; in special cases, this exemption from payment of income tax may be extended to ten years. Capital allowances are generous. Investment on scientific research is deducted from income at the rate of 20 per cent per annum for five years. The incidence of double taxation is minimized. Foreign investors, too, can obtain exemption from indirect taxes and deferment of registration fees and stamp duty on capital. Warehouses, factories, and workshops are free from property taxes and local rates – in British terms, they are ' de-rated ' – for five years.

The foreign investor may search far and wide without finding a finer opportunity for participation in the economic growth of a stable, developing economy.

In Ghana political policies always have a reference to the welfare of the people. It has been pointed out that one way of ensuring this reference is through the confrontation of leader with people. This however does not make fully explicit the significant political fact that policies of a political nature attain their birth and growth in a political gold-fish bowl – transparent for everyone to see what goes on. No political policies in Ghana can be secretly conceived and secretly adopted. The political autonomy of the people also ensures for them the right to put forward policies of a political nature for logistic consideration. Nevertheless, even the best conceived policies and the most democratically decided ones can be vitiated by the corruption of individuals. Consequently, in Ghana, to the extent that human wisdom and wariness can ordain, affairs of state are entrusted to men with transparent glass pockets. The result is that Ghana makes it as difficult as it is perilous for individuals to divert to their own use resources meant for the public welfare.

' NKRUMAHISM '

Nkrumahism is the name given to the body of doctrine preached and practised by Osagyefo in and for Ghana, in and for Africa. Some aspects of the doctrine are applied in every independent African state. Other aspects have enjoyed a distinctive, even decisive, impact in Africa and in the arena of world debate through Nkrumah's subtle advocacy and powerful example.

Let me cite, as an instance, the idea of African Unity, or Pan-Africanism, about which I have written elsewhere in this book. It became a dream of young Nkrumah, as it had been a dream of many other notable Africans, soon after his American experiences had begun to broaden his outlook and deepen his thought. Nkrumah, even then, was a man who 'dreamt his dream and refused to dream it was a dream'. He made it a vital inspiration in the Convention People's Party's bid for political power in Ghana. It remains a supreme motive in the exercise of political power. Thus Article 13 of the Ghana Constitution affirms: 'that the Union of Africa should be striven for by every lawful means and, when attained, should be faithfully preserved: that the independence of Ghana should not be surrendered or diminished on any grounds other than the furtherance of African Unity'. This article has since been written into the constitutions of several states. In due course, it will become an article of faith in all African states. Ghana, says the Seven-Year Development Plan launched successfully in 1964, 'will be an asset to Africa and a force for the liberation and Unity of the Continent in proportion to the strength of her economy'.

This exciting conception of Union Government for Africa has still to don achievement's crown. Yet it took a long step towards realization in May 1963, when thirty-two Independent African States, all but two of them former colonies, met at Addis Ababa, accepted a Charter of African Unity and created an Organization for African Unity. Already O.A.U. has scored important successes; it adds to these successes with growing confidence and at increasing speed. Basic to this conception is the assertion of the African Personality.

Wherever people are made economic and political aliens in their own land, the slave masters, slave traders or colonial powers – call them what you will – deprive the local societies of any future. They do more. They deprive the conquered societies of their past. This denial of a nation's history is an essential technique in the pursuit and maintenance of alien power – although it failed in many parts of Africa even when backed by overwhelming military force – and it salves the conscience of the slave trader and slave master. Thus the assertion of a national personality is a restoration of history, of dignity and of personality to the once subject people, and a defence against neo-colonialism with its propaganda that colonialism was a 'a vision splendid' inspired, not by greed and grab, but by Christianity, Puritanism, sacrifice and noble enterprise. To Nkrumah, Africa is not an annexe of Europe, and African history is not an incidental outcrop of European capitalism; and in *Consciencism* – which he sub-titles as ' philosophy and ideology for de-colonization and development with particular reference to the African revolution ' – he advances this theme with intellectual vigour and persuasive argument.

' The history of Africa, as presented by European scholars', he writes,

> has been encumbered with malicious myths. It was even denied that we were a historical people. It was said that whereas other continents had shaped history, and determined its course, Africa had stood still, held down by inertia ; that Africa was only propelled into history by the European contact. African history was therefore presented as an extension of European history. . . . In presenting the history of Africa as the history of the collapse of our traditional societies in the presence of the European advent, colonialism and imperialism employed their account of African history and anthropology as an instrument of their oppressive ideology.[1]

Nkrumah deals with the political facets of this imperialistic ideology.

> Earlier on, such disparaging accounts had been given of African society and culture as to appear to justify slavery, and slavery, posed against these accounts, seemed a positive deliverance of our ancestors. When the slave trade and slavery became illegal, the experts on Africa yielded to the new wind of change, and now began to present African culture and society as being so rudimentary and primitive that colonialism was a duty of Christianity and civilization. Even if we were no longer, on the evidence of the shape of our skulls, regarded as the missing link, unblessed with the arts of good government, material and spiritual progress, we were still regarded as representing the infancy of mankind. Our highly sophisticated culture was said to be simple and paralysed by inertia, and we had to be encumbered with tutelage. And this tutelage, it was thought, could only be implemented if we were first subjugated politically.[2]

Finally, Nkrumah explains how ideological error about the past can lead to misrepresentation of Africa today.

[1] *Consciencism*, p. 62.   [2] *Ibid.*, pp. 62–63.

The history of a nation is, unfortunately, too easily written as the history of its dominant class. But if the history of a nation, or a people, cannot be found in the history of a class, how much less can the history of a continent be found in what is not even a part of it – Europe. Africa cannot be validly treated as merely the space in which Europe swelled up. If African history is interpreted in terms of the interests of European merchandise and capital, missionaries and administrators, it is no wonder that African nationalism is in the form it takes regarded as a perversion and neo-colonialism as a virtue.[1]

Nkrumahism, in this aspect of restoring self-confidence and faith in the national being, is the dynamic of Africa's modern poets and artists, scientists and sociologists, creative workers in every field of human endeavour. The dynamic is given practical direction by the Ghana Government's encouragement of the study and writing of African history, folklore, dance, and music, and by the Ghana Academy of Sciences of which the Duke of Edinburgh was President for two years, and is now patron.

Osagyefo postulates the view that ' philosophy always arose from a social milieu, and that a social contention is always present in it either explicitly or implicitly. Social milieu affects the content of philosophy, and the content of philosophy seeks to affect social milieu, either by confirming or opposing it '.[2] He goes on to endorse Mazzini's famous dictum:

> Every true revolution is a programme ; and derived from a new, general, positive, and organic principle. The first thing necessary is to accept that principle. Its development must then be confined to men who are believers in it, and emancipated from every tie or connection with any principle of an opposite nature.[3]

Dr Nkrumah continues, ' The statement, elucidation, and theoretical defence of such a principle will collectively form a philosophy. Hence philosophy admits of being an instrument of ideology.'[4]

For Osagyefo morality is no less pervasive than ideology,

[1] *Ibid.*, p. 63.
[2] *Ibid.*, p. 56.
[3] *Ibid.*, p. 56.
[4] *Ibid.*, p. 56.

' a network of principles and rules for the guidance and appraisal of conduct '.   Such rules are not explicit.

> Very often we are quite definite about the moral quality of an act, but even when we are so definite, we are not necessarily ready with the reasons for this decision or opinion. It is not to be inferred from any such reticence, however, that there are no such reasons. We share within the same society a body of moral principles and rules garnered from our own experience and that of our forebears. The principles directing these experiences give us skill in forming moral opinions without our having to be articulate about the sources of the judgements . . . Just as a morality guides and seeks to connect the actions of millions of persons, so an ideology aims at uniting the actions of millions towards specific and definite goals, notwithstanding that an ideology can be largely implicit.[1]

In ' practicalizing ' his philosophy in subsequent passages in Chapter 3 of *Consciencism*, Osagyefo relates it to the sanctions that enable all communities to obtain conformity to their ' permissible ranges of conduct ', including the instruments of ' coercion ' like ' the sermon in the pulpit, the pressures of trade unionism, the opprobrium inflicted by the press, the ridicule of friends, the ostracism of colleagues ; the sneer, the snub and countless other devices . . . by means of which societies . . . achieve and preserve unity '. ' The individual,' he insists, ' is not an anarchic unit. He lives in orderly surroundings and the achievement of orderly surroundings calls for methods both explicit and subtle.' Thus the law, with its executive arms, for example, ' must be inspired at every level by the ideals of its society ' – as, indeed, they can be identified most readily by the fact that they escape the wild and woolly criticisms of one-party democratic states so common in the newspapers of the West ! Nevertheless, as Osagyefo points out, ' the traditional face of Africa included an attitude towards man which can only be described, in its social manifestation, as being socialist. This arises from the fact that man is regarded in Africa as primarily a spiritual being, a being endowed originally with a certain inward dignity, integrity and

[1] *Ibid.*, p. 58.

value. It stands refreshingly opposed to the Christian idea of original sin and degradation of man.'

So emerges the theme which I have sought to explain in my description of the one-party democratic state, and which Western commentators on Africa have misunderstood so lamentably : the theoretical basis of African communalism ' expressed itself on the social level in terms of institutions such as the clan, underlining the initial equality of all and the responsibility of many for one '. The conclusion is drawn, clearly, in *Consciencism*.[1]

> In this social situation, it was impossible for classes of a Marxian kind to arise. By a Marxian kind of class, I mean one which has a place in horizontal social stratification. Here classes are related in such a way that there is a disproportion of economic and political power between them. In such a society there exist classes which are crushed, lacerated, and ground down by the encumbrance of exploitation. One class sits upon the neck of another. In this sense, there were no classes in traditional African society. In the traditional African society, no sectional interest could be regarded as supreme ; nor did legislative and executive power aid the interests of any particular group. The welfare of the people was supreme.

These were the traditions challenged, distorted, and all but destroyed by Colonialism.

Colonialism never established anything remotely approaching a universal system of education in Africa. Instead, it created a small African cadre, seeking to Europeanize these young people and to associate them so closely with the colonial power that they were divorced from their own society. Merchants, traders, lawyers, doctors, politicians, and trade union leaders tended, under patronage, to coalesce into a type of African middle-class, quite alien to the African tradition. Now, with the collapse of colonialism, a new harmony must be developed, ' a harmony that will allow the combined presence of traditional Africa, Islamic Africa, and Euro-Christian Africa, so that this presence is in tune with the original humanist principles underlying African Society '.[2] The philosophical

[1] *Ibid.*, p. 69.   [2] *Ibid.*, p. 70.

expression of this ideological harmony is what Osagyefo calls philosophical consciencism. Throughout a book covering every phase of philosophical history and debate, there is sustained the dialectical idea of the possibility of the creation of a new whole from forces opposed to one another, and the basic Marxian argument that 'it is materialism that ensures the only effective transformation of nature, and socialism that derives the highest development from this transformation'.[1]

POSITIVE ACTION NOW

Perhaps the most distinctive, as it is the most potent, weapon in the armoury of Nkrumahism, is known popularly and exactly as 'Positive Action'. The strategy of positive action is to win political power and to preserve and expand it in the aftermath of social revolutionary change. *Consciencism* distinguishes the difference between positive action and negative action. The one represents 'the sum of those forces seeking social justice in terms of the destruction of oligarchic exploitation and oppression'.[2] The other represents 'the sum of those forces tending to prolong colonial subjugation and exploitation. Positive action is revolutionary and negative action is reactionary. . . . Neo-colonialism is negative action playing possum.'[3]

The slogan 'Positive Action Now' supplanted pleas for independence in the shortest possible time on the eve of political change in Ghana. It circumvented the policy of containment which, by means of endless conferences and long-drawn-out reformist measures, would have delayed the process of change. It continues to fortify the young revolution against inevitable attempts to foment discontent and disunity, and against all schemes and stratagems to spoil the people's victory. Positive action must acquire survival value if neo-colonialism is not to become a greater danger to independent countries than the cruel colonialism from which they have escaped. Neo-colonialism can invade the citadels of political power

[1] *Ibid.*, p. 77.
[2] *Ibid.*, p. 99.
[3] *Ibid.*, pp. 99–100.

through economic penetration, by corrupting the new leaders, by compromising what does not admit of compromise – the true welfare of the nation. Thus positive action must be supported by a mass party, complete with its instruments of education and instruction, and realizing in an ever-increasing degree the spiritual and social value of the African Personality. In African conditions, only positive action against neo-colonialism can ensure for every man and woman the promise of Ghana's Constitution – a voice in the affairs of State, a fair share in the productivity of the State, and the peace and stability in which the better life can be enjoyed.

Of course, the theory and practice of positive action arouse criticism, often spiteful, from the defeated enemy and from overseas observers who dodge the responsibility of understanding it. In Africa, however, positive action has become the watchword of the people, especially of the young people.

In South Africa, the literate young African is sustained and inspired by ' overall African progress ' and the leadership of Nkrumah.[1] As soon as one sets foot in Africa, Mr Geoffrey Taylor has recorded in the *Guardian*, ' one is reminded that the strongest nationalists, those who question most loudly the universal application of Western institutions, are the men most concerned to maintain high standards of incorruptible administration '.

' It is among such men,' Mr Taylor continues, ' that one will find the admirers of Nkrumah . . . it is Nkrumah, these men will say, who is trying to pull Africa to its senses. Leadership is what Africa needs, they say, even if it is ruthless.'[2]

Salute Nkrumah, philosopher and practical politician !

Let me conclude this chapter by discussing what Nkrumahism means to me as a Ghanaian and a politician trying to translate policies into everyday practice.

Nkrumahism and African nationalism are synonymous. I know that, in the West, nationalism is suspect. A noble word

[1] E. A. Brett, Institute of Commonwealth Studies, London University, in New Society, 28 Nov. 1963. Report on an opinion survey in South Africa.

[2] 20 February 1964.

has been corrupted by Nazi aggrandizement and Fascist terror. Not so in Africa. Nationalism is the wind of change, the source of the unity which broke the colonial yoke. It is the inspiration of a United Africa which, in bringing fellowship and prosperity to our continent, will contribute greatly to peace and friendship all over the world. It also ensures, by restoring the African Personality, the revival of one of the most civilizing cultures known to history.

Colonialists neither sought to preserve Africa's cultural heritage nor to assimilate themselves to our customs and social behaviour. On the contrary. Their aim was to force Africans to conform to alien rule and government and administration, as though we were an immigrant minority in our native land. Imperialism is an impertinence as well as a crime. Military occupation of our countries was followed by an attempt at psychological occupation of our minds, at creating a ' colonial mentality ' belittling the national language, dress, and manners. Of course, this vulgar psychological offensive, which was not confined to Africa, scored miserable victories all over the world; it still scores them. Imitators of the ruling power change their names in the hope of hiding their national identity. They copy alien styles of dress and manners and ape the silly snobberies of their masters. They cultivate the ' wit that can creep and pride that licks the dust '. They are the ' so very 'umble ' Uriah Heeps of society, half human, neither flesh, nor fowl nor good red herring.

Nationalism recaptures and breathes life into all that is best in African culture and tradition. It stimulates us to build modern roads and factories, and to use modern machinery. But nobody anywhere wears electric bulbs on their heads and dresses up in motor cars! Motor and electricity are among the physical amenities of life. They do not serve the spiritual needs of man. They light no lamps within the brain. They are no substitute for a people's poetry and language. To draw heaven and earth together in imagination – that is the rare privilege of the philosopher-poet, like the tentmaker, Omar Khayyam, whose *Rubáiyát*, written in the language still spoken by a large percentage of Africans, has held the world in thrall for eight centuries.

You remember this:

> *A Book of Verses underneath the Bough,*
> *A Jug of Wine, a Loaf of Bread – and Thou*
> *Beside me singing in the Wilderness –*
> *Oh, Wilderness were Paradise enow!*

And this:

> *For some we loved, the loveliest and the best*
> *That from this Vintage rolling Time hath prest,*
> *Have drunk their Cup a round or two before,*
> *And one by one crept silently to rest.*

All of us have re-echoed this:

> *Myself when young did eagerly frequent*
> *Doctor and Saint, and heard great argument*
> *About it and About; but evermore*
> *Came out by the same door wherein I went.*

And, too:

> *The moving finger writes; and having writ*
> *Moves on: nor all your Piety nor Wit*
> *Shall lure it back to cancel half a line,*
> *Nor all your Tears wash out a Word of it.*

Now listen to the voice of Youth everlasting:

> *Ah Love! could you and I with Him conspire*
> *To grasp this sorry Scheme of Things entire,*
> *Would not we shatter it to bits – and then*
> *Re-mould it nearer to the Heart's Desire.*

A world of wonder and wondering, of regret and hope –
all is captured in simple language that has uplifted the hearts
and inspired the minds of countless millions of human beings,
and will do so until the end of time.[1]

When my fellow citizens can read the scholars and poets of
the ancient Kingdom of Ghana, they will read them gladly
in fast flying jets and in modern homes, as well as in the shade

[1] The English renderings are by Edward Fitzgerald, edited by W. Aldis
Wright in *Rubaiyat of Omar Khayyam*, Macmillan, 1949.

of the palm tree; and, as they do today, the young students of Accra will memorize their verses to the exhilarating accompaniment of surf and breeze on our beautiful beaches. G. K. Chesterton, humanist and wit, sought to excite the English about ' the poetry of the commonplace '. Much of the commonplace in Africa *is* poetry – men and women going about their daily tasks dressed in the dignity of their national costumes. Witness, also, the arresting grace of the Arab in his flowing robes. If, farther south, clothing is scanty, there is good reason for that, too. The sun fashions strange costumes everywhere. I fancy the Mediterranean sea-board would be an eye-opener to most Africans South of the Sahara, especially during the summer months! So would the ladies of London and New York in a heat wave.

Dr Nkrumah is a distinguished Marxian scholar who regards Marxism not as a dogma, but as a guide to action. He endorses Frederick Engels's repudiation of those theorists who, by claiming that the economic element is the *only* determining element in history, convert into a meaningless phrase this basic proposition:

' According to the materialist conception of history, the *ultimately* determining element in history is the production and reproduction of real life.'[1]

Nkrumahism relates socialist philosophy to Pan-Africanism, to the total liberation of the African States, and to the political economic, and social unity which, as I see it, is the essential prerequisite of a United States of Africa. It does not place everything African above the rest of the world. It is rather a balancing of the world through the salvation and regeneration of African society. It seeks the application in practical terms of the principles of the Atlantic Charter of August 1941. That Charter was the blueprint for the United Nations, the work of President Roosevelt and Prime Minister Churchill. The principle which, despite many successes in other areas of action, the United Nations has failed most signally to apply is that there should be ' access on equal terms of all people to the trade and raw materials of the world '.

---

[1] Letter from Engels to J. Block, London, 21–22 September 1890 : Quoted in *Consciencism*, p. vi.

Gold from Africa provides the basis of countless financial transactions throughout the world ; it benefits people overseas, and whites in Africa, but not Africans in Africa. Diamonds from Africa are much more than a decoration in the hair, on the bosoms and fingers, and in the ears of rich women. They are essential to many industrial processes. Yet Africans are expected to be grateful mendicants bowing and scraping before their rich exploiters. Sugar and cocoa from under-developed countries are the raw materials of many important foodstuffs and luxury products. In 1964, British processors of cocoa and chocolate were boasting record profits and the British Treasury benefited from a recently imposed purchase-tax on these commodities. Yet sugar growers and cocoa farmers received lower prices than for many years previously. In short, the market economies of the great industrial countries buy cheap from Africa, sell dear to Africa the industrial goods we need, and think we should welcome as an act of generosity the return to us of a tiny portion of their loot in the form of financial aid !

The mal-distribution of wealth within modern industrial states causes social unrest and is recognized as an incitement to revolution. In exactly the same way, the refusal and failure to distribute the product of the world's economic activities between states precipitates poverty in Africa, Asia, and South America and is the source of menacing tension between the nations. The facts are stark and frightening. Over two-thirds of the world's real income goes to one-sixth of the world's inhabitants. One-tenth of the world's real income is distributed over one-half of all God's children. In 1961–2, Africa's exports increased 3 per cent, and her imports fell 3 per cent. Nevertheless, the terms of trade worsened for Africa because the average unit value of exports to the speculative market economies of the West fell by 1 per cent. This imbalance in world economic conditions is creating, in the words of a distinguished American expert, a ' law of cumulative inequality ' – as the rich countries get richer, the poor countries get poorer.[1] To quote the *Guardian* correspondent again, the under-developed countries are ' financing the galloping

[1] Evan Luard in *Nationality and Wealth*.

affluence of the West '.[1] *The Economist* (London) has summed up the situation in a sentence : ' With the division of wealth in the world coinciding with the division of colour, we could be living close to something like a white man's 1789.'[2]

ECONOMIC BASTILLE

Nkrumahism prepares for the peaceful demolition of this economic Bastille by postulating economic unity in Africa and an African Common Market. It protects Africans against the beguilements of membership of the European Common Market without any policy-making voice in that organization by warning them of the dangers of neo-colonialism ; in plain words, the imperialistic economic penetration which would mock their hard-won independence and turn them into economic dependencies of the West forever.

Please do not arraign me as an opponent of aid for emerging nations. Mighty efforts of thought and great generosity of heart have gone into plans to assist us. What I am saying is that aid with strings is abhorrent, that aid as a substitute for economic justice is no solution to the deepening world crisis.

Equally abhorrent is the use of economic sanctions by modern states against emerging countries like Cuba. This policy turns economic power into a tryranny on the international scale. All history tells that when poor, proud nations resist, the tyrants turn to other methods, including murder. Adieu, Lumumba, whose beloved Congo suffered these abominations for many years before his death.

Meantime, in Ghana, Nkrumahism is creating a ' welfare state based upon a socialist pattern of society adapted to suit Ghanaian conditions in which all citizens regardless of class, tribe, colour or creed, shall have equal opportunity and where there shall be no exploitation of man by man, tribe by tribe, or class by class ; and shall strive to promote and to safeguard popular democracy based upon universal adult suffrage and the rule of the majority '.

To me, society can have no nobler aim. Seeking to improve the quality of social life, Nkrumahism fosters high social

[1] 20 February 1964.   [2] 15 February 1964.

ideals. Freedom of worship is a principle of our Ghana
Constitution, and is protected by the law of the land. Education is being made universal at an ever-growing rate. It is
largely free. It is not a status symbol. It is not a form and
source of snobbery, promoting or perpetuating class distinctions.
Education is encouraged as a service to society, a preparation
for service to the nation. It is available on equal terms to
boys and girls, for Nkrumahism embraces the startlingly simple
truth that, if a country wants to double its brain power, equal
opportunity for women is the most certain way to do it.

Most urgent of our social ideals is stability and internal
peace. The basis of such stability is respect for law that is
worthy of respect : that is law supported by an intelligent,
incorruptible police force, law under constant review and
subject to reform so that it does not become tradition-bound ;
law administered by men and women who really understand
the meaning of service to the state.

This insistence on law as a service to society rather than a
mere livelihood for legal gentlemen always raises the hackles
of many commentators in the Western press and Parliaments.
I cite against these critics, two profound students of law.

' The judges must act in accordance with what Parliament
says . . . Judges must never comment in disparaging terms on
the policy of Parliament . . .'

' The judiciary is one of the component parts of the state,
and in the eyes of the world is associated with the Government
of the country.'

Dr Nkrumah made the second statement, Lord Denning[1]
the first. Both are saying exactly the same thing.

' Well, yes, of course ', admits the half-educated journalist
trying to echo His Master's Voice, and the rabble-rousing
Member of Parliament, too often, alas, a Labour member
who might be expected to know better. But, insular resentment that an English judge agrees with an African socialist
overcoming him, the latter thunders : ' Who appoints the
judges ? ' The answer is simple. The most important
political figure in Ghana, the President, appoints the judges
after consultation with the Lord Chief Justice. In England

[1] *The Times,* 9 June 1959.

a political figure of less importance – sometimes, indeed, of no importance, either political or legal, although always a party political functionary – the Lord Chancellor appoints the judges after consultation with the Prime Minister. This answer is too devastating. It arouses the passionate kind of nationalism that decent men abhor, and the British critic reduces the argument to absurdity by asserting that ' the Lord Chancellor does not sack judges '. Of course he does not, even when he should. The tradition, which Africans do not pretend to understand, is that judges, once appointed, are sacrosanct. However incompetent they may turn out to be, they are permitted, in Britain, to send innocent people to prison, to bring the civil law into contempt, and to spread misery and loss throughout the whole community. Then, at a respectful distance of time after their death – and all judges are ' an unconscionable time dying ' – the verdict will be pronounced that these judges ought not to have been appointed.

Thus, an eminent English barrister and witty writer on legal affairs, whose latest book enjoys the distinction of an introduction by Lord Devlin, announces : ' Mr Justice Grantham . . . together with Mr Justice Darling, Mr Justice Ridley, and Mr Justice Lawrence, made up a quartet of some of the worst judges that this country has suffered from in this century,'[1] The quartet comprised nearly one quarter of the total judicial strength of the King's Bench Division. Their inefficiencies were perpetuated by the myth and tradition boasted so often by the ordinary British citizen who knows very little about British law and nothing at all about any other law – the myth and tradition that British law is the best in the world. So, no doubt, say Americans about American law, although Mr Henry Cecil does not agree with them. So, no doubt, the French say about French law in spite of the fact that one hundred and thirty years ago the great Professor Dicey told them where they got off.

Our author makes one small reference to the most dramatic piece of politico-legal jerrymandering within living memory. ' In 1836,' he writes, 'Campbell (Attorney General) expected to be made Lord Chancellor or at least Master of the Rolls,

[1] Henry Cecil, *Tipping the Scales*, Hutchinson, London, 1964, p. 190.

both offices being vacant, but the Prime Minister, Lord Melbourne, felt he could not spare him as Attorney General. (The same situation arose over eighty years later with Lloyd George and Sir Gordon Hewart.)'[1] Now the facts about the appointment of Sir Gordon Hewart as Lord Chief Justice are stated with quite charming clarity in the late Lord Beaverbrook's last book, *The Decline and Fall of Lloyd George*.[2] Mr David Lloyd George was Prime Minister of a coalition Government in which his political opponents, the Conservatives, held a large majority over his National Liberals with whom they had joined to defeat the rising Labour Party. It was a political interest of Lloyd George to maintain the strength of National Liberal representation in Parliament. The Lord Chief Justiceship – always a political appointment of a member of the governing party with one exception : a Labour Lord Chancellor appointed on legal merit a Tory named Lord Goddard, probably the only distinguished Lord Chief Justice of this century – became vacant when Lord Reading went to India as Viceroy. Hewart, Attorney General, was the traditional and legitimate choice for the post, and was nominated by Lord Birkenhead, then Lord Chancellor. Lloyd George did not approve. If Hewart ' had been allowed to go ', Lord Beaverbrook relates, ' Lloyd George would have had to put Ernest Pollock, the Solicitor General in his place. Pollock was a Conservative. His promotion would have disturbed the balance of representation of Parties in the Government . . .' And, most important of all these profound considerations, ' Hewart's constituency, East Leicester, if opened up, might have been lost to Lloyd George's dwindling Parliamentary group '.

Hewart insisted upon becoming Lord Chief Justice. To hold him, Lloyd George was compelled to put him in the cabinet – the first breach, although not now unusual, of the British constitutional convention that the Law Officers are Law Officers of the Crown and not party politicians. Lloyd George had also to promise Hewart ' that the office of Lord Chief Justice would be at Hewart's disposal on the eve of the next dissolution of Parliament '. This pledge could be implemented only if Lloyd George had in his possession the

[1] *Ibid.*, p. 244.   [2] Collins, London, 1963, p. 35.

resignation of a caretaker Lord Chief Justice – in other words, only if the dignity and what-have-you of the British legal system were to be made the merest plaything of Party politicians and the highest judicial officer in the Kingdom were to become the puppet of 10 Downing Street. They were, and he did. Lloyd George suggested the appointment of Lord Finlay, ' a former Lord Chancellor, nearly eighty years of age and showing it. Finlay was prepared to place his resignation in Lloyd George's hands '. Press and Parliament were hostile. The Prime Minister could not defend a nominee with failing mental powers while boasting the virtues of British justice. So Lloyd George, himself a member of the legal profession, found another stooge. Sir Alfred Lawrance, although approaching eighty, was in good health and in full possession of his faculties. On Friday, 2 March 1922, the great and noble and independent Lord Chief Justice of England was travelling up to London town to hear a case that had been adjourned from the previous day. ' He read an account of his resignation in the morning paper. He went into court, finished the case, and retired with a pension of £4,000.'[1]

There is a farcical footnote to this rich comedy about how an honourable legal post was dishonourably filled. You recall Mr Justice Darling, one of the four worst appointments of this century, all four appointees being elevated after serving as Conservative M.P.'s. According to Lord Hewart's private papers, Darling made this offer : '. . . if it would be a service to me, he (Darling) would gladly take the office of Lord Chief Justice for a little time – " even for ten minutes " – and give it up whenever I asked him to do so.'[2]

Who wouldn't, to apply the materialist conception of history to these events, do ten minutes' work for a life pension of £4,000 of public money a year ?

Africans do not believe that you can divorce the law and its administration from Government any more than, in the old days, you could separate the activities of the Chief from the interests of his tribe. Africans are too busy creating conditions of stability and justice to be humbugged by such diversionary questions.

[1] *Ibid.*, p. 38.
[2] Quoted in *The Chief* by Robert Jackson, Harrap, London, 1959, p. 139.

CHAPTER SIX

AFRICA IN THE IDEOLOGICAL CONFLICT

THE ideology of a nation is probably the most pervasive single fact concerning that nation. Because it is so pervasive, it tends also to be a distinguishing characteristic, the basis of the solidity of its nation. The same given ideology, however, while refreshing to one nation or society can be repugnant to another. Ideology is enabled to be pervasive by its sources and development. It begins in the folkways and social relationships which we call tradition. Tradition provides its grass-roots and its nurture, tradition ensures its continuity. The ideology of a nation is thus that which establishes a belonging. One must carry a national ideology inside oneself, the axis around which one's social postures, thoughts, and actions revolve, in order to be of a given society. At the same time, however, ideology is influenced by history, by the upheavals of war and revolution.

The ideology of Africa may be called Africanism. Africanism is founded upon a tradition of the family whose highlights are the security, mutual aid, and affection made available for everyone. In this way every member of the African community comes to be the acknowledged responsibility of the community as a whole. But since it would be impracticable for the community to display its solicitude as such concerning each individual, the family becomes the method and vehicle of the discharge of that solicitude. A cardinal fact of Africanism is consequently the family, the extended family.

The social and moral values inherent in Africanism are very noble and must be preserved. At the same time however the ravages of colonialism upon the body of Africa have been such that, for good or for ill, the extended family system is now an inept vehicle for displaying the same communal concern about every member of society. Demographic changes alone would pose a problem. Added to these must be the greater dispersal

of members of the same family in Africa. In consequence, the
extended family is now extended not only in an anthropological
sense but also in a geographical. The location of members of
the same family is not clearly defined, and a member of any
family could turn up anywhere.

Obviously such dispersal makes it unfeasible for the family
to extend the same supervision to its members who are today
sometimes not even fully known. Though the extended family
is itself more or less out of date in the present socio-economic
formation of Africa, its concerns are not. One can still
therefore regard the idea underlying the extended family as a
basis of Pan-Africanism and continental unity which is now
within our reach.

Colonialism did disrupt the African family. It forced upon
the African family a completely new self-image. Whereas
responsibility had previously been molecular, now it is
atomic. The wealth which was held in trust by the head of
the family for all the family, could now be regarded more
narrowly in terms of private ownership and it was often
exploited for private gain and use. It could be seen that
colonialism, in thus attempting to apply the *coup de grâce* to
Africanism, forced the latter to inspire an uncompromising
anti-colonialism. This is connected with the insistence of
African statesmen on the African Personality or *négritude*, men
who have been prepared (like Nkrumah, Kenyatta, Banda) to
prefer bread and water and the company of beetles and cock-
roaches, always to be found in some abundance in colonial gaols,
to the wheedlings from Government House which also required
them to compromise their anti-colonial stand.

When African nationalism, the continental expression of
Africanism, broke the colonial yoke, we returned to the
ideology which had sustained our people during the long, dark
years. We obeyed our instincts and desires. In any event,
there was no alternative. Colonialism created no new tradition,
social or political. It did not teach democracy; for it was
dictatorial and authoritarian. It had not nourished and
expanded our heritage of culture and natural resources. On
the contrary, it had eroded them, leaving undeveloped all
that might have paid social dividends but was not profitable

in terms of capitalist enterprise. All that colonialism contributed to the art and science of government in Africa was a tiny black élite, some of whose members paid lip-service to the imperial overlords; mere hangers-on of imperial power, a feeble, futile nucleus of the Western-style class system, now in disrepute in most Western countries and always ridiculous in African eyes.

Our nationalist élite, the leaders who understand the Marxian analysis of the class struggle and are determined to spare Africa its disrupting, dividing consequences, easily overwhelmed the remnants of the colonial élite. Then they cleared the way, intellectually, for our tradition, our Africanism, to emerge and to find the fundamental answers to our problems of government. These answers resulted in democratic centralism, the one-party democratic state, and the Organization of African Unity. Democratic centralism is thus that system which to our mind offers the modern equivalent of the extended African family. Democratic centralism preserves the essential methodical democracy of the extended family. Matters seriously affecting the people are in one as in the other fully and freely discussed at the popular and basal level. The consensus that emerges is the expression of the collective will of the people, and is thus binding on all. At the same time as democratic centralism achieves an organic pattern of society in this way, it is also fully sensitive to the humanist impulses of the family system. For this reason an understanding of the Marxian analysis of the class struggle is highly pertinent. The knowledge made available by this analysis must be gainfully used to eradicate the disrupting and divisive tendencies endemic in the Western-style class system which colonialism has brought us. Unless such tendencies are eradicated, the organism and popular socialism of Africanism may be lost.

The danger posed here is one which is very well known to those of our leaders who are knowledgeable in Marxism. A clear expression of the same concern can be found in the writing of an Asian observer, Dr Fatma Mansur. Writing on ' The Education of the Nationalist Élites '[1] this observer notes:

[1] *Process of Independence*, Routledge and Kegan Paul, 1962, p. 41.

'. . . the years after the First World War were the years during
which the contemporary leaders of the new states were beginning to take stock of European ideas in the Universities and of
the political events in Europe.   The series of *coups d'état* in
Europe, the rise of fascism in Italy, the European activities of
the Communist International, the hunger-march of the Welsh
miners, the promulgation of the N.E.P. (i.e. the New Economic
Policy in Soviet Russia), were certainly the kind of events
which seem designed to throw into relief the most deadly
aspects of the class struggle. . . . It is after all the leaders of the
nationalist parties who had experienced the depression years
in the U.S.A., the friendship and encouragement of the British
Labour Party . . . the overtures and teaching of the Communist
Party everywhere.'   Our African leaders knew and understood
the world of parliamentary debate and the struggle for power.
They knew and loved the world of their ancestors, the world of
Africanism.   They dedicated themselves to the task of using
Marxism as a guide to prevent the evils of class warfare
from polluting the roots of society in the Afro-Asian
homelands.

We are, as always before, irrevocably committed to regard
every man, whatever his creed or colour, as equal in the sight
of God and his fellow men.   We are equally irrevocably
committed to an abhorrence of artificial and oppressive class
divisions.   If this is communism, we glory in the name.
Capitalists we certainly are not.   The term ' communism ' has
however come quite properly to be associated with the history
of certain societies in the present century.   The term which
can correctly be associated with our history this century is
Africanism, for only this term suggests that our views and
efforts are aimed at the release of the dynamic of the African
Personality for the redemption and regeneration of our society
in the context of modern times.

One must acknowledge that the capitalist class system is
changing in significant ways.   Compelled by its inner logic,
capitalism has in its scheme of things given a paramount
position to the productive capacity of the automated machine.
In the struggle for social power, the machine itself is neutral
and non-aligned, for it will equally well serve both a socialist

and a non-socialist society. Joined to this must be a growing commodity demand to keep mechanized capitalism going. The effectiveness of this widespread distribution of wealth, the diffusion of growing productivity revealed in fuller employment and a fuller life for the masses, is one result of modern machine development. Inevitably it will reshape the contours of capitalist society, transforming it from a pyramidal formation to a rhomboid formation in the scale of personal income. Thus Mr Mark Abrams, the well-known sociologist and statistician, whose collaboration with Professor John Boyd-Orr (now Lord Boyd-Orr), produced a dramatic exposure of poverty in Great Britain in the nineteen-thirties,[1] recently translated into economic terms a theme made familiar in America a decade ago by writers like Peter Drucker[2] and the late C. Wright Mills.[3]

Discussing the newspaper reading public of tomorrow, Mr Abrams comments: ' John Average is much better off (actually about 23 per cent over the past ten years). . . . We are moving from a pyramid shaped society (that is most incomes in the lower sector) to a diamond-shaped society (that is most incomes in the middle sector) . . . Younger, less class-conscious people spending their affluence on living and leisure patterns which were formerly social preserves . . .'[4] Societies become increasingly fluid and sensitive to change. Politics become increasingly pragmatic. Thus the harsh choice between communist collectivism and American *laissez-faire* is no longer the only choice. One alternative is based on growing realization that collective planning and free enterprise are not incompatible, as the mixed economy of Ghana is demonstrating in Africa here and now. Contact with emerging countries is teaching the West that where there is little or no private saving, public ownership is not an assertion of ' doctrinaire ' socialism. It is a social and economic necessity.

Another result of the marriage of the machine and technology with capital is that among intelligent people class divisions

---

[1] *Food, Health and Income*, 1936.
[2] *The New Society*, Heinemann, 1951.
[3] *White Collar*, Oxford University Press, 1951.
[4] Cited, *Financial Times*, 17 August 1964.

and their associated conceits and snobberies are falling into contempt. There will of course continue to be vested interests that will regard such plans as Kennedy's for war on mass poverty in America as undiluted communism. The reason of course is that the social services are financed largely from taxation on monopolies and industrial empires. It is not altogether surprising that those vested interests which stand in the way of the welfare of their own kith and kin interpret the improving social and economic policy of Afro-Asian states as communism.

Happily, this folly is passing with the passing of the cold war era. Statesmen today are beginning to understand the meaning and inevitability of coexistence between the diverse, rather than opposing, systems of social and economic organization we call societies. We can have one world or no world. There is no other choice before the nations and the continents of this earth, whatever names they apply to their forms of government.

SOCIETY AND IDEOLOGY

To appreciate fully the need for coexistence one must keep clear in one's mind the distinction between a society and the ideology which animates that society. Systems of social and economic organization vary one from another rather than oppose one another. The reason for this is that such systems are territorial, and are contained within the state framework of their territory. For this reason, such systems can coexist in the same world just as different nationalities can. But varying ideologies are very easily opposing ideologies, because ideologies often prescribe for humanity rather than for citizens. Peaceful coexistence is sincere if understood to subsist between societies. Between ideologies, it is a piece of political chicanery.

In this matter, the beginning of wisdom is that every nation has to forge its own destiny and clarify its own ideology, and may be presumed to know better where it is going than outsiders can tell it. No nation with a sense of integrity will set up a bureau of apologetics for the world at large; it is only colonialist societies seeking to destroy the integrity of nations that have to explain away their alien presence on foreign soil. The sovereign nation that makes propaganda excuses to the world is the inevitable prey of larger, more powerful propaganda machines.

Understanding this, we can see the real *malaise* of aid to developing nations in the Cold War world. Aid was an aspect of propaganda. It was thought to be a power capable of quelling the desire for freedom among the still oppressed, of inducing them to accept the values of colonial, imperial régimes. In these terms, it was an affront to the silent resistance of hundreds of thousands of villages and rural communities in the freedom struggle.

Moreover, in its organization, too much aid resembled a Hollywood film version of spying, sabotage and political warfare. Millions of pounds and dollars have been wasted on secret errands to find out who was giving what to whom and for why. The world is learning better now. All of us are freeing ourselves from the silly name-calling that accompanied the giving and the receipt of aid, from the senseless conception of assistance – or the withholding of assistance – as propaganda for Capitalism or Communism or Social Democracy or Bolshevism. We know now that aid to be aid must be neutral, mutual and non-aligned, and that reasonable facilities for trade between advanced and emerging countries make better sense in human as well as in economic relations. Civilization is not measured by a shining Cadillac or a spinning Sputnik, nor even by the provision of a holiday home. Civilization is measured in terms of the respect each one of us shows for individual honour and dignity, the level of our sensitivity to other members of our kind.

Ideology based on class and class warfare is the essence of racialism, surely the most dividing and destructive of all human weakness. One is disgusted when one reads in newspaper reports of political unrest that protesting black men look as though ' they had just come down from the trees '. It is a common, and insolent, expression of the hooligan, an exploitation of one of the pastimes of people all over the world to provide ammunition for racialists. Its sophisticated counterpart is to be found in such a phrase as ' to know a no-ball from a googly and a point of order from a supplementary question are genuinely to have something in common '. In heaven's name why ? Are cricket and Westminster-style political processes a more common human denominator than the need to eat and breathe and the desire to live in peace and freedom ? As a schoolboy in Africa, I climbed hundreds of trees and, I am glad to record, ' came down from the trees ' as often as I climbed them. What's wrong in the ambition of every schoolboy to climb trees for fun – or of men to climb trees for rubber and coconuts, or of non-African holiday-makers to seek the shade by living in houses built high in cool foliage of the great, old trees of our continent ? Or, for that matter, what is wrong with the nostalgia for cave-dwelling revealed, say, in pot holing ? Much of what passes for ' the ideological conflict ' in Africa and elsewhere is a debauchery of ideas and a mere exchange of the epithets of abuse to cover racial prejudice.

I am not to be understood, in making this plea for dignity in the use of the vocabulary of debate, as denigrating aid or denying the high quality of citizenship that has inspired many people throughout the world to protest against slavery and colonial exploitation. Africa owes much to the anti-slavery societies of the Western radicals, and to the British Labour Party which supported colonial reform, although it is fair enough to remind readers that a basic interest of Labour was to mitigate the evils of unemployment in their own country. One's regret is that too many Fabians acquired an intellectual vested interest in their own solutions for colonial problems. They have shown less sympathy than one might have expected for the idea that Africans and Asians should find their own paths to political progress – and this despite the fact that the Fabian solution of Western-style democracy and practice is now under critical review all over Europe and, even in England. Miss Rita Hinden, for example, a former leader of the Fabian Colonial Bureau, is vigorously critical of the one-party state in Africa. As editor of *Socialist Commentary*, however, Miss Hinden writes : '. . . the day will come when some future Labour Government will be faced with the inevitability of unexpected and unpopular action. To carry its followers with it, there is no alternative to showing that the need to act in certain, perhaps unpopular, ways may still be in keeping with socialist purposes.'[1]   In facing exactly that kind of problem, African states have reacted as their past traditions and present needs demanded.   They restored and applied the theory of democratic centralism.   This ensures that our people always understand the reasons for action because the process of decision-making actually begins with them.

Realism is now dropping the curtain of un-reason upon all these controversies.   The sober truth is that what is called the ideological conflict is a reflection, on a world scale, of the class struggle within those socially-sundered societies which, hitherto, have dominated the world scene.   That struggle, except in its temporary colonial manifestations, has never been a decisive presence in African life.   G. K. Chesterton's famous, worldly-wise detective, Father Brown, might have been chiding our well-meaning but not well-enough informed mentors from outside Africa when he said :

' It isn't that they can't see the solution.   It is that they can't see the problem.'[2]

A classic example is to hand in the attitude of the French Communist Party to the Algerian revolution.   Edward Behr, well-known French-American newspaper correspondent, has recorded that, while a minority of European members of the Algerian Communist Party ' threw themselves heart and soul into the struggle . . . far more European communists living in Belcourt and Bab el Oued became, almost overnight, the fervent and vociferous allies of their more wealthy *Algérie Française* fellow-settlers.   In France, the central committee of the French Communist Party adopted an ambiguous attitude towards the rebellion.'[3]

How communist failure to see the real problem appeared to Algerian eyes was revealed in a document announcing the decisions of the congress of the National Council of Algerian Revolution held on 20 August 1956, and reviewing the progress of the revolution.   ' The (Algerian) communist leadership,

[1] July 1964.
[2] *The Scandal of Father Brown.* 'The Point of a Pin.'
[3] *The Algerian Problem*, Penguin, 1961, p. 227.

bureaucratic and without real contact with the masses,' this review declared, 'was unable to understand clearly the revolutionary situation. As a result it started out by condemning what it called " terrorism " and in the first months of the rising gave orders to its followers in the Aures not to take up arms. The French Communist Party for its part played the role of yes-men and kept silent when Algeria was subjected to special Government powers. Not only did the Algerian Communists lack courage to denounce this opportunist attitude of their Parliamentary group but they have never given a word of explanation concerning their failure to take action against the waging of war in Algeria . . . The absence of unity and the resulting political confusion is based on an even more fundamental doctrinal incoherence derived from their theory that the national liberation of Algeria was impossible before the triumph of the proletarian revolution in France . . .'[1]

Realism demands the acceptance of co-existence as the primary principle of international human relations. Co-existence with freedom is the ideology which modern Africa would like to see endorsed by the community of nations. We Africans are our brothers' keepers. We are ready to defend our brothers in their time of need. In pursuit of the ideal of ' friends to all and enemies to none ', the free African countries are eager to co-operate with all countries whose aims are based upon respect for freedom and justice. This co-operation will take the form of material help when and where possible, and the thought brings me back to the problem of financial aid. I rejoice in the grand new projects envisaged by the Commonwealth and in the imaginative good-neighbourliness animating many of the schemes of assistance being prepared by many powers and groups of powers. They all support one's confidence that human relations are improving everywhere. Yet this fundamental fact remains : the resources of aid are controlled by the few.

If aid is to be freed from political strings, from the taint of neo-colonialism, all of it must ultimately be channelled through, and applied under the overall direction of, a neutral organiza-

[1] *The Freedom Fighter.* Special Issue published by F.L.N. (Algerian National Liberation Front).

tion like the United Nations. Vital to this conception is the removal of the veto, the ' right ' exercised by four dominant powers and one very ' poor relation ' to abort United Nations resolutions before they can be put into practice. Until the United Nations is reformed and made truly representative of world opinion, small countries have no chance even of survival. Their dignity is derided and their efforts at progress are hamstrung from the outset. The suspicion will persist that spurious ' assistance ' is available where imperialism is sure of its foothold ; where imperialism is unsure of itself, no aid will be forthcoming.

In order that aid should in the upshot be both consequential and neutral, it is of course hardly sufficient that its dispensers should be well-intentioned. Its recipients must already be capable of absorbing it efficiently. To be capable of so doing, however, they must have attained a constructive level of self-reliance. Without this, aid can hardly be complementary and independent. The direction of aid must be given by the recipients alone. Its framework must be provided by them. No under-developed country today can rely on self alone for its economic transformation. It would be foolish to spurn all aid. But it is necessary to ensure that aid is that and nothing else, certainly not a twentieth-century Trojan horse.

In all sincerity, I say that the United Nations, as presently constituted, is inadequate to deal with the needs of the emerging nations of Africa. In face of this, our hope lies in four conditions : our determination to stand together in the freedom struggle ; the friendship of all men of goodwill ; our will to resist new forms of imperial penetration and a fresh foreign economic or ideological scramble for Africa ; and the changing mood and spirit of the Great Powers.

Cloak for Domination

The cry of communism in Africa is merely a cloak for domination, as a look at Southern Rhodesia will show. The Zimbabwe African Peoples' Party led by Mr Joshua Nkomo was banned in 1962. Zimbabwe is an area near Salisbury, the capital of Southern Rhodesia, where the remnants of an ancient

African city are still in a fine state of preservation ; hence the freedom Party's name.

To justify the ban on ZAPU Sir Edgar Whitehead issued a White Paper in which, for the first time, an African party was branded as ' neo-communist '. What did this verbal invention mean ? That Africans in Southern Rhodesia, who cannot get into schools to learn English, were learning Russian and Chinese in secret ? That they had been issued with muskets from Moscow, probably 1806 style ? Nobody knows, not even Sir Roy Welensky ! Sir Edgar Whitehead never explained what he meant, for obvious reasons. No member of his government was able to identify any of the aims of ZAPU with communism.

In truth, the word ' neo-communist ' was meant to be rabble-rousing, to evoke fear and race-hatred. It was the dirtiest libel ever launched against Africans by any group of politicians claiming to act as responsible persons. No doubt there are guns in the hands of Africans in Southern Rhodesia. There always have been since Cecil Rhodes ' diddled ' the Matabele Chief, Lobengula, out of all mineral rights in his kingdom in exchange for £100 monthly, plus rifles and ammunition. Since nothing succeeds like success, Sir Edgar Whitehead was supplanted by the tougher Mr Winston Field who, in turn, succumbed to the fiercer regression of the intransigent, intractable Mr Ian Smith.

Not surprisingly, white sympathizers with ZAPU were tarred with Sir Edgar's racial brush. His ' neo-communist ' is the Southern Rhodesian equivalent of ' Kaffir-bootie ', ' nigger lover ', the word with which white supporters of freedom's cause are stigmatized by the proponents of apartheid in South Africa. One such is Dr Terence Ranger, an Englishman, a university teacher and a white member of ZAPU who was deported from Southern Rhodesia some time ago. Dr Ranger has written : ' When the African National Congress was banned in 1959 I felt ashamed because I had not been a member. I had known many of its leaders and had felt a greater sense of solidarity with them than with any other group of people in Southern Rhodesia.' Dr Ranger had found some aspects of white life in Southern Rhodesia repugnant. He responded, as many white people in Africa do, to the idealism and aspirations of the black community. Does this choice of the company a man will keep and of the ideals which illuminate his life justify the smear of ' neo-communist ' ? Or did his detractors really mean that he was ' anti-British ' in his views about white conduct in Southern Rhodesia ? The ' neo-communist ' smear fits every occasion ! What it readily reflects is the utter poverty of the Southern Rhodesian governing clique's policy for the problems of a tortured country now the victim of open tyranny and totalitarianism.

We Africans have other views about ideology. We despise the vested interests who use and abuse it for the purposes of political blackmail.

Our ideology, our Africanism, is our expression of social, human values drawn from our history and tradition. It gathers triumphant strength from our confidence that we shall be able to combine our wealth of tradition and democractic experience with all mankind's modern, exciting endowment of science and knowledge. So shall we win unity for Africa. So shall we make our contribution to the peace and progress of all free people in a free world, East and West.

A personal experience that will remain vivid while life lasts was the funeral of John Fitzgerald Kennedy, President of the United States of America. I attended, on behalf of my President and the people of Ghana, to affirm our affection and respect for a man moulded by the wars and struggles and human hopes of the twentieth century; a man seeking, with high courage and noble imagination, to guide the world into a new era of peace and prosperity. We mourners were men and women from East and West. We represented all nations, all ideologies, all creeds and all colours. In the unforgettable hours of softened splendour at the White House and in church, some of us wept. Ours was the unity of sorrow. It was also a unity of hope that we would be faithful to the ideals and aspirations of our dead friend and brother.

In the afterglow of these emotions, I tried to set down the simple thoughts which I, an African and a Christian, pro-foundly believe might help towards ' the healing of the nations '. I make no claim for their originality; they come from the common stock of everyman's struggle towards a civilized way of life, and from my heart. I ask the reader only to accept them as sincere.

Every country has its madmen, but no country attempts to liquidate them. Instead, madmen are sent to asylums for medical treatment. If people are judged, rightly or wrongly to possess unsatisfactory characters or characteristics, that is not a ground for destroying them. The Christian ethic calls for an effort at understanding and reform. Thus, if the West thinks that communists are ' untouchable ' – or *vice versa* – the answer is to find out the cause. You cannot find out the cause or reason by isolation, or threats, or by picking quarrels. The answer is to be found in open-mindedness, sociability and by rubbing shoulders together. Trade, and the common interest in developing it, is the most obvious way of making contact and finding understanding.

During my early days in the Gold Coast, now Ghana, I was given the impression that Russians were wicked, barbaric, and bloodthirsty. I know now that these impressions were wrong and evil. I have rubbed shoulders with Russians many times in recent years. I enjoyed this contact. I have no doubt at all that the challenge Russia presents to the world is not in the field of war. It is in the field of trade. This is a legitimate challenge in the business of increasing the wealth of the world and expanding man's knowledge of the universe. It can open doors to coexistence, to peaceful, constructive effort. This challenge does not imply the abandonment of a social point of view. Peaceful coexistence is compatible with national and ideological integrity.

Khruschev once said:

' We must see clearly that the struggle to consolidate peace will be a long one. Peaceful coexistence must be correctly understood. Coexistence is a continuation of the struggle between the two social systems – but by peaceful means without war, without interference by one state in the internal affairs of another. This struggle should not be feared. We must fight resolutely and consistently for our ideas, for our way of life, for our socialist system. We consider this an economic, political, and ideological struggle, but not a military one.'

That is my personal experience. It is also my interpretation of the conclusion reached by Mr George Frost Kennan, distinguished American diplomat and scholar, after taking his coolest look at East-West relations.[1] ' Let us remember ', he wrote, ' that the great moral issues, on which civilization is going to stand or fall, cut across all military and ideological borders, across peoples, classes, and régimes – across, in fact, the make-up of the human individual himself. No other people, as a whole, is entirely our enemy. No people at all – not even ourselves – is entirely our friend.'

I regard it as wrong for Western countries to sell wheat to Russia and, at the same time, to institute a food blockade against Cuba. Cubans, too, have the right to eat, to live, to be accepted in the world. The folly of such present policies is revealed in the fact that Great Britain and France continue to trade with Cuba and that, willy-nilly, East-West trade continues to grow. As I see it, in deciding to send wheat to Russia, the United States were moved by something bigger than a desire to sell surplus supplies at a profit. They were animated by a human feeling for people threatened with hunger. They felt that Russian *people* had a right to survive just as, under a Labour Government, the British people accepted bread rationing in order to send grain to starving India. These were expressions of Christian humanism. This is the kind of world we want, a world in which people feel for each other. It is the hope evoked by an old hymn that sunk in my memory in childhood:

> Lord let all the nations see
> That all men can brothers be
> And form one single family
> Throughout the whole world.

Africa has no wish to destroy anybody, either in the Communist world or in the Capitalist world. We wish for all the harmony we hope to achieve among ourselves.

Surely it is high time that East and West stopped talking about each other in terms of spite and horror. To refer to Africans as ' beasts of burden in the jungle ' is foolish enough.

[1] *Russia and The West : Under Lenin and Stalin*, Hutchinson, 1961, p. 369.

Please let everybody remember that propaganda and mis-representation are the wordy weapons of war – war too destructive for modern man to contemplate – and that we must still live together on this planet.

Throughout these homely meditations, I kept harking back to the words spoken by my boyhood hero, Abraham Lincoln, a century, almost to the day, before we took a sad farewell of John Kennedy.

' Fourscore and seven years ago our fathers brought forth upon this continent a new nation, conceived in liberty, and dedicated to the proposition that all men are created equal. It is rather for us to be here dedicated to the great task re-maining before us; that from these honoured dead we take increased devotion to that cause for which they gave the last full measure of devotion; *that* we here highly resolve that these dead shall not have died in vain; *that* this nation, under God, shall have a new birth of freedom; and that government of the people, by the people, and for the people, shall not perish from the earth.'[1]

Humbly, but without apology, I dare to rephrase a passage from yet another fine speech of the man whose lucidity of mind and nobility of spirit were reflected in John Kennedy's life and work.

' A world divided against itself cannot stand. I believe this world cannot endure permanently, half slave and half free.'[2]

[1] The Gettysburg Speech, 19 November 1863.
[2] Speech, 17 June 1858.

CHAPTER SEVEN

NON-ALIGNMENT: AFRICA'S FOREIGN POLICY FOR FREEDOM AND PROGRESS

IN 1964 the representatives of 56 Nations attended, in Cairo, the second triennial Conference of Non-Aligned Countries. These countries included Finland, Yugoslavia, and Cyprus, 28 African and 15 Asian States. Their numbers, growing year by year, indicate that Non-Alignment is not a vague, visionary theory advocated by a vague, visionary minority. On the contrary it is a point of view which is gaining widespread adherence. The movement for non-alignment is a world movement. It is a practical, hopeful emanation of the intellectual debate between statesmen who are seeking passionately to escape from the perpetual threat of war. It develops into a living principle of conduct described, sometimes, as positive neutralism, among world leaders who accept the Charter of the United Nations as their guiding star. It repudiates the balance-of-power policy which, having failed the people of the world twice within living memory, is heading now towards a new nuclear war.

There is comfort in numbers, according to the old adage. While there are alliances for war, the risk of war can be very great. Essentially, in an alliance for war each member pledges its war machine to any combat which involves the territory of any of its members. At the same time, however, the foreign policies of members of such alliances are not unified. This means that there is a possibility of war being provoked however peace-loving the policy of some of the members of the alliance may be. In such a situation, clearly, a great deal must be wrong.

Alliances for war can never provide guarantees of peace. Indeed, so sophisticated and devastating are the implements of war today, that accidental war is our gravest danger. The odd rifle shot, even the unintended military infringement of a country's territory can be quickly smothered down by protests, discussion or negotiation and prevented from escalating into a full-scale war. But in a nuclear age, a nuclear accident will be too disastrous to overlook. The landing of a nuclear bomb, irrespective of the motivation behind it, cannot be passed over as an accident ; it can neither be wiped out by apologies nor by compensation. It can only be paid for by a retaliatory act of war.

Alliances for war will naturally devise means of minimizing the risks of war by accident. In the very nature of the case, however, the alliance as such cannot have complete control of the total armoury and personnel of its member states. This means that any alliance for war by its very nature admits risks which the alliance itself cannot control. Non-alignment is on the agenda of world nuclear business. There, I believe, it will stay while the self-appointed power blocs learn to pursue peace and ensure it by accepting freely the sovereignty of a re-vitalized United Nations.

It must be clear that the more nations are non-aligned the fewer there will be available for military alliances, and the less will be the risk of war. The horror of war is never so stark and meaningful as when nations have to go it alone, to slip un-attended down the primrose path that leads to the everlasting bonfire.

Before peace can be real, military alliances must first accept voluntary dissolution. This return to reality will impress nations of the fatuity and ineffectuality of an independent nuclear deterrent.

First begettors of Non-Alignment, obviously, are the ' buffer ' States in the pre-war balance-of-power system. Egypt, lying athwart the Middle East, was such a state. In World War I she was a base for Allied operations, and contributed power-fully to the allied victory. Yet her hopes of national independ-ence, the fruits of victory, were denied her. In World War II, Egypt stood aloof from the conflicts raging on her borders and in her harbours. When, after that war, she determined her own future and declared for independence, she was made the victim of Anglo-French imperialist violence. Happily, world opinion, for the first time in history, adopted a posture of positive neutralism. That is to say, it freed itself from the mendacity and insincerity which military alliances breed and, taking note of fact and law, reached an independent and objective conclusion. It condemned aggression and took non-military action to end it. So Egypt remained independent to become a leader in the adventure of improving and civilizing the world's conduct of world affairs.

India's fate after World War II was less troubled. A fresh wave of radicalism had swept over Great Britain, eroding pre-war ideas of imperial domination – the wave against which, in its international manifestations, Great Britain and France sought to erect a breakwater by their military assault on Suez. World War II was itself responsible in some ways for the change in the attitude of the British Government towards Britain's colonies. The experience of the war gave radical elements of British society fertile ground for sowing their point of view. The butchery and insane destructiveness of World War I was still fresh in mind. Then, the dispossessed of the earth, those from whose ranks the war won its greatest casualties, had found themselves farther away from prosperity than they had been before the war. In order that peace should bring prosperity, a radical revolution in outlook was necessary and leftish movements began to thrive.

The repetition of destruction on a greater scale in World War II gave to the radicals the chance of translating peace into prosperity. The war had also convinced Britain, for example, that her Empire was no longer easy to defend. The Empire was too vast for the resources of Britain and Britain also had to cope with disaffected colonies bent on gaining freedom for themselves. Britain could be challenged, as the war had shown, and challenged successfully even if the challenger did not possess overwhelming power. The imperial power was no longer sacrosanct.

France was not quick enough on the uptake. In spite of the trouncing which it had received during the war, it still clung to ideas of France-overseas. It indulged in an Indo-China war in which it was defeated and badly lacerated. It also embroiled itself in an Algerian war in which it was badly mauled. Once again, France was defeated. Now it was ready to disengage from the impossibilities of Empire.

Having won their independence from reluctant ex-colonialists, independent countries cannot afford to subject their policies, their independence, to the dictation or the exigencies of ex-colonialists. To do so is to gain independence with one hand and return it with the other. To do this is to attempt to go against the dynamic of the independence movement, to oppose the tide of history, to betray the people.

Problems of development are some of the most serious problems which face an independent people. It is essential for them to conduct their affairs in conditions in which their interests are fully protected. These are the precise conditions which are negated in an inevitably unequal alliance with ex-colonialists.

Relations must always be amicable; but above all they must be non-aligned where our own interests are unaffected.

Balance of Power

Whether we look at the ' buffer ' states of Western Europe and the Balkans, or eastwards to Malaya and Burma, only one conclusion can be drawn from the twentieth-century history of balance-of-power policies: military alliance between small nations and the industrial giants availed the small states nothing. They were turned into temporary road-blocks in aggression's path. All of them were the first and most savagely mauled victims in the trials of brute strength, to be given up at once with no question of a last-ditch stand as soon as things went awry. That modern states with glorious traditions behind them and sparkling prospects before them – states like Poland, Czechoslovakia, Holland, Belgium, and Malaya – should be reduced to puppets in the war games of the Great Powers is an indictment to which exponents of the balance-of-power have no answer.

Africa was a continental pawn in this sordid, bloody gamesmanship. She was involved deeply in history's most destructive misery that followed these wars. Her territory was parcelled out in the settlements. Yet Africa did nothing to provoke these wars and had no part in making the treaties that brought uneasy peace when they ended.

I am always amazed when I read, in the correspondence

columns of British newspapers, letters supporting the racial policies of South Africa and Southern Rhodesia on the ground that these countries were inhabited by ' our kith and kin ' who fought ' on our side ' in the World Wars. Apart from the irrelevance of the argument, such letters ignore the fact that South Africa was a far from willing partner in World War II; that, indeed, there was a strong dissident minority plotting and working for a Nazi victory in the Union of South Africa. And I wonder why the letter writers never remember the black men who fought and died in a war that they had done nothing to bring about.

Sudanese soldiers performed all the army police work in Eritrea. Black brigades from Nigeria, Northern Rhodesia, Southern Rhodesia, Sierra Leone, Gambia, and the Gold Coast served in their tens of thousands in East Africa, Italian Somaliland, India, Burma, and Ceylon.[1] In the fierce long-drawn out battle for the Arakan beaches, which broke the Japanese threat to India and opened the way for the famous Fourteenth Army's advance and final victory, more than half the casualties were in the 26th Indian Division; their 4,589 dead included 431 West Africans.[2] By the end of 1945 there were 63,038 men from the Gold Coast in the armed services of whom 41,888 had served overseas – 6,000 in East Africa, 30,500 in Burma, 5,500 in the Middle East.[3] In what some military historians regard as a war operation ' without parallel in history ' Africans were a vital element.[4] This was the capture by General Cunningham, on 16 February 1940, of the line of the Juba, a feat which enabled him to travel 744 miles in 17 days, re-occupy British Somaliland then, on 23 May, force his way up hills 7,000 feet high to capture Harar. Cunningham reached Addis Ababa, 300 miles further on, by 6 April, two months earlier than he thought he would be

[1] *Orders of Battle, 2nd World War*, 1939–1945, Vol. II. Prepared by Lt.-Col. H. F. Jolsen, pp. 419 *et seq.*

[2] *The War Against Japan*, Vol. III by Major-General G. Woodburn Kirkby, c.b., c.m.g., c.i.e., o.b.e., m.c. (H.M.S.O. 1961, p. 277).

[3] G. C. Report on the Demobilization and Resettlement of Gold Coast Africans in the Armed Services, 1945. No. 5 of 1945. Cited in *Politics in Ghana* by Dennis Austin, Oxford University Press, 1964, p. 11.

[4] Chambers's Encyclopaedia, Vol. 15, pp. 696 *et seq.*

able to launch his offensive from Kenya! With one-third of the forces captured by the enemy, the Fascist grip on East Africa was broken.

On the civil side of World War II, African belts were tightened to help beleaguered Britain. Exports from Africa to England doubled between 1938 and 1944 and even school-children had to hand in their pocket money for the war effort.

Easy, then, to understand why so many African states endorse the policy of non-alignment. The wars of the West won them neither security, better living standards nor even the cold comfort of credit for the shedding of their blood. Their neutralism is positive. While they refuse to engage in war-mongering and war-making, they are active in promoting peace, as the intervention of Afro-Asian states in the Sino-Indian border dispute well demonstrates.

Proud as I am of the Afro-Asian initiative for world non-alignment, I do not doubt that its larger success depends upon the pressure of events outside the areas of Afro-Asian societies. For example, a post-war equivalent of the pre-war balance-of-power was the 'brinkmanship' associated with the name of the American Secretary of State during that period, John Foster Dulles. 'Brinkmanship' was the pursuit of policy supported by an implied threat that non-agreement might result in total destruction by nuclear attack. It put force above reason and above justice. With exactly the same facility he showed in making American aid an instrument for expanding American diplomatic influence, Dulles exploited American capacity to wage nuclear war as an instrument of policy in relation to possible or projected Russian or Communist action, and in support of an increasing number of Western defence positions. No balance, however, can remain perfect in a politically divided world.

The world is not inertia-ridden. It is dynamic. It is always on the go. It is essentially unstable. In a world in which it takes a lot of effort to keep the same position, to suppose that by speaking of agonizing reprisals or massive retaliation balance can remain perfect is to reveal a touching naïveté in surround-ings of sophistication. Less than a year after the United States tested its thermonuclear device, Russia tested hers.

From 1954 onwards, the Soviet Union was producing long-range bombers capable of penetrating the American heartland. By 1955, the Soviet bomber force had amassed enough strength to inflict severe damage on all the Nato bases on the Russian periphery. The autumn of 1957 saw Russia's break-through in rocketry, the attainment of nuclear parity, the prospect of Russian nuclear superiority. The policy of 'brinkmanship' was dead. Threats to be credible must start from a position which combines strength and advantage. Threats backed by capacity to start nuclear destruction, made by either party to the nuclear dialogue, now ceased to carry credibility. American bases in Europe lost their value. Great Britain and France, literally, abandoned their Nato alliance, although not their Nato commitments, in pursuit of independent nuclear power that provoked the new nuclear armaments race.

All, in human terms, came to issue in the high drama of the Cuban confrontation of October 1962. Mr Khruschev, in my view rightly, sustained and nourished the Cuban revolution with economic aid. Then, ostensibly to defend that revolution against American military attack, he established and manned nuclear bases in Cuba. President Kennedy saw these bases in a different light. They provided a cover for Russian nuclear striking power by creating a direct, immediate threat to the defence bases on the American continent. The myth of the 'buffer' state was exploded, finally and forever, and with it, the myth of a balance-of-power in the world today. Kennedy realized that nuclear balance is not an inability to strike. There remained only 'the balance of terror' the triumph of which involves self-destruction and utter, horrific, universal defeat.

When John Kennedy demanded dismantlement of the Cuban bases, he faced the gravest crisis ever presented on this earth with the calm courage of a man of destiny. When Nikita Khruschev acceded to John Kennedy's demand, he too faced the gravest crisis ever presented on this earth with the calm courage of a man of destiny. Fortunate world ! At the moment fraught with disaster, two giants among men acted like simple human beings. They lit a new lamp of hope for peaceful co-existence in every human heart.

Now all the pious resolutions for ending nuclear tests (in

which the equivalent of 25,000 Hiroshima bombs were exploded) have become, and are seen by all the world to have become, urgent prerogatives. By 10 October 1963, when the Moscow Test Ban Treaty took effect, more than 100 countries had signed it, the only significant exceptions being France and China.

Meantime, at other levels, non-alignment, described by writers on military and strategic affairs as ' delineation of regional denuclearized zone ' or, more simply, ' disengagement ' was moving the minds of world statemsen.

Adam Rapacki, Minister of Foreign Affairs of the Polish People's Republic, submitted to the United Nations General Assembly on 2 October 1957, a proposal to create in Europe ' zones of limited and controlled armaments ', starting with the German Federal Republic, the German Democratic Republic, Poland, and Czechoslovakia. By February 1958, the basic proposal, expanded as a result of discussion, was incorporated into a Polish State paper and handed to the diplomatic representatives of Russia, America, Great Britain, France, the German Democratic Republic, Belgium, Denmark, Canada, and the German Federal Republic.

Mr Wladyslaw Gomulka, Chairman of the Polish Delegation, told the General Assembly of 27 September 1960 that to meet criticisms, the plan could be implemented in two stages. ' The first stage envisaged the prohibition of the manufacture of nuclear weapons in Poland, the German Democratic Republic, Czechoslovakia, and the German Federal Republic and an obligation to discontinue nuclear armaments. The second stage provided for the reduction of conventional forces simultaneously with the complete denuclearization of Central Europe '. Inevitably, Mr Gomulka went on, there had been opposition from the German Federal Republic and the United States. Nevertheless, proposals to create an atom-free zone in the Balkans had been advanced by Rumania ; President Nkrumah of Ghana had sponsored a similar project for Africa ; and there had been an initiative from China in relation to the Far East.

At the General Assembly 1961 session, the Secretary General was requested to make inquiry ' as to the conditions under which countries not possessing nuclear weapons might be willing to enter into specific undertakings to refrain from manufacturing or otherwise acquiring such weapons and to refuse to receive, in the future, nuclear weapons in their territories on behalf of any other country '. This resolution was sponsored by Sweden, Austria, Ceylon, Ethiopia, Libya, Sudan, Cambodia, and Tunisia. Revised and codified the Plan was presented to the General Disarmament Conference of 1962. There it awaits the decision of every nation that it shall yield, not its security, but that fraction of its sovereignty which will ensure the peace and security of all mankind.

Let me summarize briefly, the headings of the Rapacki Plan.[1]

Its high purpose is ' the elimination of nuclear weapons and nuclear delivery vehicles, a reduction of military forces and conventional armaments on a limited territory, and thus to contribute towards a substantial reduction of the danger of conflict on that territory '.

The scope of the agreement concerning the zone is open ; other European states can enter it.

Parties to the agreement must prohibit all ' preparation of production and actual production of any kind of nuclear weapons and delivery of vehicles for them ', and they shall refuse permission for the establishment of new bases and facilities for stockpiling of servicing nuclear weapons and delivery weapons. Other states disposing of nuclear weapons and delivery vehicles for them shall be forbidden to transfer them to states included in the zone.

When the states within the zone have eliminated all nuclear weapons from their national armaments, they shall proceed to reduce to an agreed level all military forces and conventional weapons ; other states shall be required to withdraw from the zone all kinds of nuclear equipment and facilities for servicing it and to reduce foreign military forces stationed in the areas of the zone to an agreed level, with a corresponding reduction of their armaments.

Strict international control and inspection on the ground

[1] ' The Polish Plan for a Nuclear Free Zone today.' Adam Rapacki in *International Affairs*, Vol. 39, No. 1, January 1963.

and in the air will be provided, the establishment of appropriate control posts included.

' To guarantee the inviolability of the nuclear-free zone those powers disposing of nuclear weapons will undertake (*a*) to refrain from any steps which might violate directly or indirectly the status of the zone ; (*b*) not to use nuclear weapons against the territory of the zone.' A long step, this, to pulling the teeth of every war-dog, actual and potential !

Inevitably, the Plan, at its moment of birth, was bedevilled by political contention. It was launched exactly one year after Poland had revolted against the continuing horrors of the Stalin régime. Gomulka, leader of the Titoist deviationists, captured control of the Polish Communist Party and formed a national government. Russia refrained from counter-action. A dramatic contrast arose within a few days of Gomulka's triumph. Hungarians also revolted against continuing Stalinism. Nagy resigned, withdrew his country from the Warsaw Pact, and asked the United Nations to protect the integrity of his country. Kadar formed a Communist administration and invited Russian intervention. Khruschev and Bulganin responded with dismaying violence while threatening to employ nuclear weapons against their fellow peace-wreckers, Eden and Mollet, then seeking to subjugate Egypt.

Against this background, Poland appeared to the West to be acting as a pawn for the Soviet Union in proposing the Plan. Nato, since 1954, had been implementing the policy of integrating the German Army with Western forces operating in Europe. German re-armament was being translated into hard fact, despite the strains its proposal had precipitated in Great Britain and France. Thus the Plan was interpreted as a Soviet plot to impede the development of American nuclear power while Russia was still catching up in the nuclear race. Hence the dusty answer of the West : if we agree to disengagement in Europe, the relative weight of Soviet conventional arms will increase immediately and decisively. Hence, too, Gomulka's offer, in 1960, to reduce ' conventional force simultaneously with the complete denuclearization of central Europe '.

I think the march of events suggests another view. Poland

acted to avoid the darkening of prospect opening up for her and all other ' buffer ' states. Khruschev's attitude was consistent with his constant plea to the West to join in the effort to make coexistence viable.

It is clear that a country which is perplexed by the problem of lifting itself by its economic bootlaces cannot possibly hope to finance the research and manufacture of a credible nuclear force. Should it nevertheless join a military alliance, then it will be clear that it can in reality only act as a base for some major power, which makes it a first-line attack-defence post with the consequential action for such posts acknowledged in all military doctrine.

To keep up the pretence of equality, most members of military alliances have to undertake a scale of expenditure which though it is, comparatively, merely token, represents a complete loss of capital to the people. The anxiety of Poland, an underdeveloped country, is fully understandable.

The problems of underdeveloped territories should be internal ones. They should be basically the twin problems of mobilizing the total energies of the people to bring about the economic leap forward and so give a real and significant content to an otherwise paper freedom. It must always be remembered that though the gaining of independence is a worthwhile goal, it is both an end and a means. Without political autonomy, a country can never have the assurance that policies which are implemented on their behalf are really implemented for their welfare. The welfare of the people is the supreme law. As President Nkrumah correctly states in *Consciencism*, the people are the reality of greatness. They are not merely the stuff out of which greatness is made : they are greatness itself. When a nation is great, it is by the effort of the people that independence is won. And the people are those who make sacrifices and other effort for the attainment of independence. Without them, no real independence can be gained. The people have the power to win independence because it is not really possible to rule against the wish of the people. The people win independence in order that they can be more effectively and better served, not in order that they should save the colonial power the inconvenience of administration while still devoting all their effort to the needs of an alien power. Since the main problems of newly independent countries are internal, it can be disastrous to them to prejudice these problems by adopting any lopsided external postures which membership of an alien alliance will demand. Foreign policy for a newly independent country must be dictated by internal problems – problems of sovereignty and development.

These beliefs determine the non-aligned positions on such hot questions of the modern world as those of Cuba, South Vietnam, Berlin, Cyprus, and the Congo.

THE BASIC TENET

The basic tenet of non-alignment is the inalienable sovereignty of a people. Sovereignty belongs to the people alone, and it can be exercised either by the people directly or by the people through the medium of their freely chosen and approved representative.

The American attitude towards Cuba is a relic of the days of buffer states. A buffer state is really a quasi-colony. The practice of holding other territories as a shield or as a delaying agency denies the basic tenet of the incontrovertible right. The people of Cuba have, besides, a sacrosanct right of self-defence in the face of actual or threatened attack, and they have an equally sacrosanct right to appeal to the arms of those who are willing to assist in the face of actual or threatened attack. All this would seem to be a consequence of the non-aligned creed.

It must at the same time be pointed out by way of emphasis that non-alignment uncompromisingly condemns all aggression. It would equally condemn on the part of Cuba all actions which indicate a preparation to initiate aggression on another territory or all actions which indicate assistance to others in the preparation of similar aggression. A country that is prepared to be used as a jumping-off stage must expect to be treated by its opponents as a buffer state.

The same principles can guide the attitude of a Union Government of Africa to the problems of Vietnam. The people of North Vietnam constitute a sovereign state, possessed of all the attributes of sovereignty and able spontaneously to establish and pursue policies of self-development. No country in the world has the right to intervene against the right of the people of North Vietnam. Similarly, the people of South Vietnam constitute a polity, endowed with all the attributes of sovereignty, able spontaneously to establish and pursue policies of self-development. Only the people of South Vietnam have these rights in South Vietnam. No action whatever which constitutes an intervention in the destiny of the people of South Vietnam can have any justification unless it flows from the expressed will of the people themselves.

Much of the present chaos in Vietnam can be traced to the presence of alien intervention in both the North and the South. The Chinese have a decisive influence in North Vietnam and the Americans have a decisive influence in South Vietnam. Indeed the conflict between the two Vietnams should be seen as an allegorical conflict in which the South stands for America and the North for China. The two unappeased powers are really confronting each other partly directly and partly by proxy of the jungle and blood screen of South and North Vietnam. The two Vietnams thus conduct a marionette war in which the not-so-hidden activators are America and China.

The presence of America in South Vietnam not unreasonably appears as a Vietnam-veiled American threat to China. The presence of China in North Vietnam appears with equal force as a Vietnam-veiled Chinese threat to Americanism in Asia.

The sad fact, however, is that the mere physical withdrawal of the Chinese and the Americans from Vietnam will not by itself restore peace and stability in that area. For one thing, the two sections have been taught and encouraged to treat each other and behave towards each other with hostility and violence. They have themselves by now developed an inner momentum which cannot be halted by the mere physical withdrawal of China and America. For another, the mere physical withdrawal of the two powers will not mean their complete disengagement from that arena, for they will inevitably replace physical presence with teleguidance.

The consequences of the momentum of violence can however be mitigated by the presence of a neutral force composed of non-aligned states, sponsored by the United Nations, and strengthened by a mandate which is given in advance, and is both clear and comprehensive. Only a non-aligned ' police ' force will make sense in that situation, for only a force free from commitments to both America and China can have the moral authority required in any ' police ' force. It is desirable that this non-aligned force should be sponsored by the United Nations, first, in order that its costs should be underwritten, and, second, in order that the world body should be seen to be effective in a case where world peace is endangered.

It is very difficult however to prevent teleguidance. One can only hope that both China and America will come to realize that it is for the people of the two Vietnams to make their destiny, and that this right cannot be regarded as a threat to either China or America. If both powers should simultaneously give up teleguidance, conditions will quickly emerge in which the people of Vietnam can truly exercise their autonomy.

It is equally clear that peace, the indispensable condition of prosperity, cannot be attained in Cyprus unless all Cypriots acknowledge the right of the majority to rule and the right of the minority to be Cypriots. The majority is not to be construed in ethnic terms. By the majority one does not necessarily mean Greek-speaking Cypriots to the exclusion of other Cypriots. The majority must mean the political agents who have the majority of following. The agents may be Turkish-speaking or Greek-speaking. It is clear, however, that in present circumstances the emerging political agents will be Greek-speaking. But this is a fact that has to be accepted.

When one speaks of the right of the minority, one must include the right of the minority not to be fenced off, isolated and quarantined. The minority being Cypriots incontrovertibly have the rights of any Cypriot, including the right not to be persecuted.

Peace is far from Cyprus today because these rights have been infringed. The United Nations by its presence should have been able to restore physical peace by now. The main reasons why it has failed so far are, first, that other powers have been operating in the Cypriot context outside the framework of the United Nations, and, second, that the United

Nations has not seriously carried out its task of keeping physical peace in Cyprus. Unless the United Nations can be firm in excluding interlopers and adventurers, it will always be in danger of being thwarted and disgraced.

The Congo is an arena in which probably every canon of international law has been abused and set at nought. The Congo became independent in 1960. Since then, since the removal from office of its Premier, Patrice Lumumba, it is possible that there has not been one act of true autonomy in that unfortunate country. The Congo has been raped consistently by the Belgians, aided today by other Powers who ought to know better. The Congo is treated as if it were outside the frontier of international law, treated like a new El Dorado, a land of golden milk and honey, a free for all, open to bootleggers, pirates, murderers, international scoundrels of the baser sort. The United Nations has failed miserably in the Congo and appeared at every stage to be completely ignorant of the reasons why it was there, and of the consideration which led to its being sent there.

The United Nations was invited there by President Kasavubu and Premier Lumumba as legal heads of State and government, in the face of Belgian attacks and a mutiny of the *Force Publique* which was provoked by the Belgians. The purpose of the dual invitation, which was accepted, was to re-instate law and order and stop the Belgian cruelties. The United Nations, allowing its clear mandate to be compromised, permitted individual member nations to intervene directly and indirectly, even though all its members had agreed in leaving responsibility to the United Nations.

But for the determination and honesty of one man, Katanga would probably even today be in secession. This one man was quickly removed from the Congo arena, and though the territorial integrity of the Congo is preserved today, it is still as if the Congo were indeed not a colony of any one power, but a colony of several powers at once. The government of the Congo is headed by a man whom the United Nations was obliged to depose and whom the people of the Congo have never elected to office. The poor people of the Congo live in many areas in the bush, terrified equally of the barbarities of foreigners as of their own people. The leaders of the Congo are prevented from reaching a settlement by God-forsaken Mammon – wealthy foreigners who account the life of a Congolese at less than the value of one rotten banana; men who spread carnage, pillage, destruction, silence through the Congo like so many angels of death gone mad.

But the Congo will not be run by foreigners. The Congo is in Africa. It is the heart of Africa. The beat of African nationalism, the upsurge of a long-oppressed people, demanding freedom, the right to live and die in their own chosen way, in the way of their wronged ancestors, their wronged prosperity, will prevail soon. It is not really possible to rule against the will of an oppressed people however shackled. Laocoön lived in mythology. The African giant tearing his chains apart lives in reality today.

The United Nations is out of the Congo today. But the Congo is still in Africa. It remains the lacerated heart of Africa. Africa must rise like one man and in the framework of the Organization of African Unity introduce its correct solution of the Congo problems into that country; into its heart. The Congo appears today to be incapable of practising the policy of non-alignment, the only policy which can guarantee for Africa the preservation of its political autonomy and the conditions of its most rapid socio-economic advancement.

Since non-alignment is a foreign policy which offers an autonomous nation the greatest degree of all-round protection from wolfish powers, it should not be difficult for Congolese leaders who are true leaders and so are dedicated to the pursuit of the truest welfare of all the people, to accept a solution based on non-alignment. The O.A.U. being an All-African Organization committed to this policy is the only organization today which can save the Congo from its downward path to destruction.

All foreign powers must disengage from the Congo at once, and leave the solution of the Congo problem to the capable O.A.U. which solved the Algerian-Morocco war in so short a time. This was possible because foreign intervention was absent. In the same way, the O.A.U. must be left to solve the Congo problem, and it will solve it in the first hundred days.

Foreign powers which have a vested interest in the immense riches of the Congo will continue to foment tension and unrest in that unhappy country so that they can then turn round and give advice. The Congo is a natural forum for the cold war by reason of its strategic riches. This is why the Organization of African Unity must make a determined effort to neutralize all non-African private intervention in the Congo. The O.A.U. must with the consent of the Central Government of the Congo maintain an efficient army in the Congo to eliminate the negative foreign military presence in that country and maintain law and order. At the same time, the O.A.U. must introduce a negotiating machinery to assist in creating a political union in the Congo.

It should be seen that non-alignment as a guarantor of peace must imply some doctrine of peaceful-coexistence. Peace is not the solitude of the sole survivor, but the compresence of a multifarious world. Peace is the peaceful coexistence of the nations of the world. Those whose aim it is to bring about peace and sustain it must consider and make suggestions about the conditions in which the nations of the earth should and can accept their mutual coexistence.

If peace is not the solitude of the sole survivor, neither is it the complete subjection of the rest of the world to one nation or to a concert of nations. Peace is much more than the absence of war. Peace implies the individual autonomy of the nations coexisting in peace. It demands the abandonment of all acts of suppression or other acts of interference in the internal affairs of the nations. The legal and political equality of the nations is a *sine qua non* of global peace. In its absence, a rat race for influence and power systems ensues, with all the instability and potential for war which a system of clientele nations encourages.

COEXISTENCE

In our own time, perhaps the greatest single apostle of peaceful coexistence has been the great Soviet citizen and former Premier, Nikita Khruschev.

The Khruschev theme of peaceful coexistence, therefore,

demands a closer look.   Despite the Sino-Soviet dispute which,
to the non-communist observer, looks like an explosion of
verbal violence in an ideological vacuum, the idea of coexistence becomes more acceptable to more people throughout
the world.   The facts of rapidly increasing East-West trade is
one hopeful sign; trade, in which China is very eager to
participate and in which the East European countries as well
as the Soviet Union are vigorously engaged.   Another sign, as
I have noted elsewhere,[1] is the willingness of America to relieve
Russia's grain shortage; it is good to be able to believe that
hunger is no longer regarded as a weapon in the battle of
ideas.   Yet another indication which warms my heart is the
growing tendency to help emerging countries on the basis of
their needs and what they can contribute to the world's
welfare rather than on the basis of ideological affiliations.

Even more fundamental, as I have also suggested elsewhere,[2]
is the real source of increasing productivity and rising living
standards in the world of today and tomorrow.   The machine
is neutral, non-aligned.   It is not affected by the political and
religious ideas of the men and women who operate it.   It is
indifferent to their belief, or lack of belief, in Capitalism,
Communism, Socialism, Democracy, Dictatorship, Religion,
the Market Economy, or the Planned Economy.   The machine
is also colour blind.   It responds only to the efficiency and
scientific understanding of its human operators, whether white,
black, red, or yellow, and to the physical materials upon which
it works.   It runs down only when a failure to distribute its
products wisely causes markets to collapse and thus destroys
demand for these products.   Any society, whatever its social
and political form or organization, that can build or buy the
machine and operate it competently can gain viability and
survival value.

The machine, therefore, neutral and non-aligned, tends to
remove the conflict of political ideas and aspirations from the
physical plane to a more moral and intellectual plane.
Certainly, there will be continuing debate about what kind of
social and economic organization makes most enterprising use
of the machine.   That, however, is an issue *within* systems, a

[1] P. 141 above.   [2] P. 130-1 above.

problem of internal state policy. It is not an issue *between* systems which one state should settle for another, a problem for disputation in which the dangers of neo-colonialism, violation of integrity and military aggression are implicit. In other words, the machine distributes the capacity to produce more equitably, both within societies and between societies. It requires of man only that he distributes its products with the sense and wisdom that will keep the machine working on man's behalf.

What, then, is the policy of peaceful coexistence as the former Russian leader envisages it? I find, in all Mr Khruschev's speeches, the most comprehensive explanation of his theme in the following extracts:

> In its simplest expression it signifies the repudiation of war as a means of solving controversial issues. However this does not by any means exhaust the concept of peaceful co-existence. Apart from commitment to non-aggression, it also presupposes an obligation on the part of all States to desist from violating each other's territorial integrity and sovereignty in any form and under any pretext whatsoever. The principle of peaceful co-existence signifies a renunciation of interference in the internal affairs of other countries with the object of altering their political system or mode of life, or for any other motives. The doctrine of peaceful co-existence also presupposes that political and economic relations between countries are to be based upon complete equality of the parties concerned, and upon mutual benefit.
>
> Peaceful co-existence can and should develop into peaceful competition in the best possible satisfaction of all man's needs.
>
> Co-existence on a reasonable basis presupposes . . . the recognition of the right of every people independently to deal with all the political and social problems of its country, respect for sovereignty and adherence to the principle of non-interference in internal affairs, and the settlement of all international disputes by negotiation.[1]

Coexistence, as set out above, is a component of non-alignment. Non-alignment, indeed, is the effective instrument of co-existence, especially where, as in Africa, it can cover an area that is continent wide.

[1] Nikita Khruschev : 'To Avert War our Supreme Task' cited in V. Nedbayev, *Peaceful Co-existence and the Liberation Struggle*, pp. 61 *et seq.*

The peace of the world requires that Africa should be
non-aligned. Africa is a prize continent. Its potential is the
greatest in the world, and unless it remains non-aligned the
Great Powers of the world will engage in a tug-of-war with
Africa as the rope. Nothing but ill can come out of this, ill to
the Great Powers which will corrupt their own souls and
squander their own resources, for such a tug-of-war can have
no end ; ill above all for Africa, whose potential will remain
undeveloped, the good of its own people, made constantly the
begetter of other peoples' riches.

When, in May 1963, the Heads of 32 African States and
Governments assembled in Addis Ababa to establish the
Organization of African Unity, they announced their purposes
to be :

(*a*) to promote the unity and solidarity of the African States ;

(*b*) to co-ordinate and intensify their co-operation and
efforts to achieve a better life for the peoples of Africa ;

(*c*) to defend their sovereignty, their territorial integrity,
and independence ;

(*d*) to eradicate all forms of colonialism from Africa ; and

(*e*) to promote international co-operation, having due
regard to the Charter of the United Nations and the
Universal Declaration of Human Rights.

In pursuit of these purposes, the States-members agreed to
co-ordinate and harmonize their general policies in the fields of
politics and diplomacy, economic development including transport and communications, education and culture, health and
sanitation and nutrition, science and technology, and defence
and security.

Such worthy ambitions must be supported by a set of clear
principles. These, written into the Charter of the Organization
of African Unity, are solemnly affirmed to be :

(1) the sovereign equality of all member States ;

(2) non-interference in the internal affairs of States ;

(3) respect for the sovereignty and territorial integrity of
each state and for its inalienable right to independent
existence ;

(4) peaceful settlement of disputes by negotiation, mediation,
conciliation or arbitration ;

(5) unreserved condemnation, in all its forms, of political assassination as well as of subversive activities on the part of neighbouring States or any other State ;

(6) absolute dedication to the total emancipation of the African territories which are still dependent ;

(7) affirmation of a policy of non-alignment with regard to all blocs.

It is important, here to spell out the names of the signatories to this historic Charter. These names give the lie to all foreign commentators, whether biased or merely ignorant, who seek to defeat the cause of African unity and to misinterpret its purposes. I give them in alphabetical order :

ALGERIA, BURUNDI, CAMEROUN, CENTRAL AFRICAN REPUBLIC, CHAD, CONGO (BRAZZAVILLE), CONGO (LEOPOLDVILLE), DAHOMEY, ETHIOPIA, GABON, GHANA, GUINEA, IVORY COAST, LIBERIA, LIBYA, MALAGASY, MALI, MAURITANIA, MOROCCO, NIGER, NIGERIA, RWANDA, SENEGAL, SIERRA LEONE, SOMALIA, SUDAN, TANGANYIKA, TOGO, TUNISIA, UGANDA, UNITED ARAB REPUBLIC, UPPER VOLTA.

They include one-party democracies, multi-party democracies, monarchies, military dictatorships, socialist-based societies, private enterprise-based societies, every form and variety of social and economic organization known to man ! The Organization of African Unity is a mighty microcosm, an epic epitome, of the macrocosm we call the world !

Is this magnificent adventure in coexistence and non-alignment a Communist plot, an anti-Communist one or a plaything of vested interests and the Capitalist powers ? Look again at the names of the signatories – and laugh ! As, indeed, Africans do at their critics and traducers.

Note, now, in relation to non-alignment, the successes scored in the first year of the Organization's life. A grave dispute between Algeria and Morocco was resolved. Controversy between Kenya and Zanzibar over boundaries, which precipitated violence and threatened worse than violence in Somalia, was ended by the mediation of the Organization of African Unity.

God knows, in relation to the world scene, these successes are modest enough. Yet they indicate that we are acquiring experience in the arts of peacemaking, and as the Colombo

Plan which ended the Sino-Indian dispute reveals, that our African experience is valid elsewhere in the world. Above all, we have shown that coexistence and non-alignment work. They take the subject of disagreement right out of the immediate arena of conflict, where passion runs high and prejudice may run deep. They abandon all resort to arms. They transform the issue into one of independent mediation under conditions that make political settlement possible. That is exactly the aim of non-alignment, not only within the African continent, but also between the nations large and small : to create the conditions of political settlement.

The Congo Tragedy

The unhappy story of the Congo throws light on another aspect of non-alignment. The revolt against the properly constituted government following the flight of the colonial overlords was referred to in the United Nations ; in the circumstances of the time, rightly so. War, fomented and financed by alien capitalists, broke the cohesion of the new state. The United Nations, and only the United Nations at that moment, could effect a political settlement. Alas, the Congo became a tragic reflection of the disunited power blocs in the United Nations, and of the avid desire of racialist leaders in Colonial Africa to add fuel to the flames. Responsibility for the Congo disaster lies heavily on the shoulders of the Big Powers – for their mutual suspicions and their unwarranted interference in the internal affairs of the Congo, for their determination to defy and undo the conciliation efforts of the United Nations, and for the opportunities which their machination offered colonialists who were hell-bent on making trouble.

And the answer ? That, surely, is plain. An All-African Defence Force, operating under the authority of the Organization of African Unity and in accordance with the directives of the United Nations. Beyond doubt, such a Force, had it been available, would have ensured peace and security and freedom for the Congolese people. Non-alignment postulates the creation of such a police force, as President Nkrumah's foresight warned that it must. On the day it is formed, the last vestige of excuse for any ex-Colonial power or any power bloc whatsoever to engage itself in Africa's internal affairs will have disappeared.

As the Congo tragedy suggests, non-alignment is not an alternative whatever its practical application to world problems, to the United Nations. It is an instrument of the United Nations, perhaps the most powerful instrument yet devised to give effect to United Nations policy. It can resolve the situation in which a tiny minority of powers, by virtue of their overwhelming military and economic strength, can veto decisions of the United Nations or, if they disapprove of the decisions, but for political or propaganda reasons do not want to veto them, can frustrate their application. The principle of non-alignment, in fact, enhances the democracy of the United Nations by ensuring that the back-room influence of the Big Powers is rendered ineffective. Non-alignment alters the United Nations, to the Charter of which Afro-Asian countries have been very faithful, in only one respect : it ends the folly of the world's most beneficent institution being exploited as a Tom Tiddler's ground of warring political creeds. Non-alignment moves mankind a little nearer to understanding the ways and means of achieving real international co-operation.

Being involved, intimately and urgently, in the race against time to secure peace, non-alignment, and the larger idea which embraces it – the idea of Positive Neutralism – does not impose a vow of silence upon those states which practise it, nor does it give them an excuse for indolence. Africans cannot stand aside while apartheid flays and degrades their brothers in South Africa and the most brutal forms of restriction and dictatorship are imposed upon the citizens of Southern Rhodesia. African protest will not be muted while Portugal, vulture of twentieth-century colonialism, exports thousands of our fellow men every year as slave labour to the Witwatersrand gold mines. Slave labour and slave trading built great fortunes for the British and the Dutch in days gone by ; but it cannot be permitted a continuing life in order to subsidise and bolster up a ramshackle totalitarianism in South Africa.

Africans re-echo the Franklin D. Roosevelt doctrine that if

peace is disturbed anywhere, peace is disturbed everywhere. They ' ask not for whom the bell tolls '. They know ' it tolls for thee ', and for them. Everybody endorses that noble sentiment, as a sentiment. Everybody tends to ignore its truth. If I fear for non-alignment, it is because I fear that the idea which must win approval in principle will become the subject of the Big Powers' tug-of-war in practice. France, for example, is prepared to neutralize Vietnam. To ensure peace in Vietnam ? Certainly, but not solely. Another aim is to prise North Vietnam loose from its reliance upon China. This is to turn non-alignment, neutralism, into a senseless debating point and a subject of delaying dispute. It shows some understanding of the solution. It shows, as Father Brown might remark, no understanding of the problem : can we create a nuclear-free zone, a neutral zone, in the South Pacific, including Vietnam ? France, engaged in nuclear testing in the area, objects to any nuclear-free zone in the Pacific, despite Australia's angry protests. So does America, in face of the opposition of public opinion, expressed in the *Nation* of Sydney, that ' everybody knows that the United States will have to agree to some free zones, as will the Russians. And if such zones are desirable in Africa and South America, why not here, particularly while the Chinese are without nuclear weapons ? '

True, Australia, eager to keep in step with the United States, has not complained about American and British testing, now in temporary abeyance, in the Pacific. Yet winds of realism are blowing through the corridors of Canberra. Sir Garfield Barwick, Minister for External Affairs, in striking contrast to the views of Sir Robert Menzies, has stated explicitly that the policies of South Africa and other African territories ruled by minorities ' must be a matter of anxiety and concern outside Africa ' – ' concern one hopes which Australia will express in its voting at the United Nations ', observes the only important journal of opinion in that great continent. So public opinion begins to unravel the tangled web of power politics. The grand cause moves on. Slowly, too slowly, it captures the minds and hearts of men. Progress would be speeded up dramatically if, on the authority of the United Nations, the proposal for an African nuclear free zone could be referred for vetting and umpiring to the Organization of African Unity.

Our own problems press hard. They absorb intellect emotion, energy. I am sure, however, that the Organization, aligned to no power bloc, but to the ideal of non-alignment would serve proudly and proficiently the cause of a pacific Africa.

Let us reach out to the hope that the Rapacki Plan, described in some detail in this chapter, becomes a reality. Let us imagine that in the spirit of coexistence, an honest, statesman-like effort is made to neutralize the vast, rich, and varied industrial complex comprising Germany, East and West, Poland, and Czechoslovakia.

The whole world would gain immediately. Central Europe, alas, is only one source of international tension, only one of the world's sore spots, but it is a vitally important sore spot. Civilian life there proceeds in an atmosphere of military pre-paredness ; an accidental gun-shot could precipitate a crisis at any time. The closing of the military road-blocks and the banishment of the looming, gloomy frown of the Berlin Wall would, at once, ease tension in Europe and everywhere. The question of Germany would no longer be bedevilled by the allegiance of the two parts of that country to alien powers and opposed militaristic organizations. How can the problem of German unification be solved from a situation in which both sections are aligned to hostile camps ? Alignment means that the interests of the two sections are subjected to the interests of the alliances. As the latter interests are mutually exclusive, it is not in their framework that the unification of Germany can be achieved.

The first realistic step towards that solution therefore has to be the isolation of the two Germanies from the two hostile camps. Non-alignment is essential as a preliminary to German unification. It is only in the conditions of non-alignment that the two Germanies can concentrate on their loyalties to them-selves rather than those of foreign blocs. Then they will be able to consider the problems of German unification as problems of Germany and not as problems of Nato or problems of the Warsaw Pact.

Given this, the problem of Berlin immediately becomes

secondary; for once the problem of unification is solved, that of Berlin automatically disappears. Meanwhile, however, it must be recognized that West Berlin belongs to West Germany, and the guarantees which make free and unhindered access to that city possible must be resolutely maintained.

The world would also see a real prospect of solving all the vexed problems involved in air and ground inspection of nuclear armaments. The discovery of a technique of inspection free from all risks of espionage would give sanity a chance in every corner of the earth.

THE BERLIN WALL

Within the area of the Plan the clouds of suspicion that dim the people's sense of security would disappear. There would follow an increase in the exchange of prosperity-promoting trade and communication, of social and cultural contacts, and a reunion of brother with brother and friend with friend, the prevention of which has been the cruellest damage done by the division of Germany. Gradually, the administrative machinery would take shape, grind into efficiency, become understood and accepted. Millions of Germans, Poles, and Czechoslovaks would learn, what hundreds of thousands of them already know, that the things uniting them are bigger, more worthy of preservation and expansion than the age-old enmities that divide them. Vain hope, to which the Berlin Wall, that monument to the sad fact that leaders who co-operated in war failed miserably to fashion a reasonable peace, still bears ugly witness. The division of Germany is not a natural division. The road blocks and military barriers between Germany and her neighbours are not natural barriers. They are all artificial devices imposed upon people by the folly and fear of war. They have no place in a world seeking peace, as a brief glance at recent history will show. For on 5 June 1945 the governments of the United States, United Kingdom, Russia, and France assumed supreme authority over Germany. Each of the four signatories to the Berlin Declaration was given an Occupation Zone in which a Commander-in-Chief exercised full power. For 'matters affecting Germany as a whole' there was set up an Allied Control Council in Berlin, this Council consisting of the four Commanders. What was lacking in these arrangements was a written document attesting the Western Powers' unrestricted right of access to Berlin. President Truman and the late Marshall Stalin had exchanged letters referring to these matters on 14 June and 18 June 1945. General Clay, however, was sent by General Eisenhower to organize the Berlin occupation with the Russians, for reasons which appeared proper to him at the time, made no attempt to put the right of free access into written agreements; and the Russians, suspicious that 'imperialist warmongers' might build up armaments against them, were unco-operative.

The Allied Control was never effective. It collapsed in March 1948. Ten years later, the Soviet Union repudiated finally the agreements of the Berlin Declaration.

Meantime, in June 1948, America, Great Britain, and France established a central control system for the three Western Zones. The British and the French shared the view that a settlement of the German problem in co-operation with Russia was still possible. Both, for political although differing reasons, objected to the European Recovery Programme financing the re-growth of German industry and enterprise, and to the currency reforms which the Americans were proposing for Berlin. The Russian military authorities might have sought to exploit these disagreements between the Western Powers. Instead, they decided upon a *tour-de-force*. They invited West Berliners to cross the sector boundaries and register with the borough authorities in East Berlin. In return for a display of soldarity with their comrades of the East, West Berliners were to be guaranteed a ration of food and fuel. Basic human needs were made an instrument of political policy. Only 85,000 West Berliners, in a population of more than two million, registered for the Russian rations. The Russian reaction to political failure was to impose, on 24 June, a blockade upon West Berlin, to deny to a largely homeless and hungry population all access to food and warmth.

By 27 August, following two interventions by Stalin, agreement about lifting the blockade appeared to be possible on the basis of the withdrawal of the new Deutsche Mark and the acceptance of the Soviet zone currency. A month later, it became obvious that the Soviet leaders had decided that the West could not supply Berlin with food and fuel by air, especially in winter weather. In the event, the famous Berlin Airlift, at its peak, landed a plane every 61·8 seconds round the clock and delivered a total of a million-and-a-half tons of food and fuel for the relief of the city.

What dictated the Russian decision? Basically, the unending flow of refugees from East Germany to the West. This was a massive, constant demonstration of German preference for the West, a continuing political affront to Russian power, and a threat to the defence in depth presented by the East European countries to the Soviet Union against a resurgence of Nazi militarism. Thus the Berlin Wall, erected by the German Democratic Republic on 13 August 1961, appears in its true light. It was a last despairing effort to stop Germans ' voting with their feet '. By 1954 more than two million persons had moved from East to West. In the succeeding years until 1961, migration from East to West again exceeded two million, the movement in the reverse direction – that is, from West to East – being 279,000.[1]

Defeat of the blockade was hailed in the West as a military victory. Its political repercussions were profound. West Germany became reconciled with America, with Britain, even with France. German opponents of the idea of a West German State because they feared that its creation would formalize boundaries and make ultimate re-unification of Germany more difficult, were won over. The way was cleared for German adherence to the emerging European Economic Community which, besides bringing new strength to Russia's western neighbours, was regarded by many people, in the West and in Russia, as a political and a potential military threat to the Soviet Union. Stalin retired defeated; he did not even press his demand to establish the Soviet-zone currency throughout Berlin. Four days before the blockade ended officially, on 12 May 1949, the West German State came into being. In May, 1955, the German Federal Republic was elevated into an independent power and welcomed formally into member-

[1] Source : *The Statesman's Year Book*, 1963, p. 1049.

ship of Nato. Thus the Western Powers, although still concerned to contain German military ambitions, became allies of their former enemy. They converted West Germany into a ' conventional ' pistol pointed at the heart of their former ally.

Then came the nuclear age. Precisely as Russian rocketry had destroyed the credibility of American bases on the Russian periphery, American nuclear strength had made incredible the idea of Soviet safety being assured by control of East European states. The stalemate called for a fresh political initiative. That was made by Mr Khruschev on the eve of Christmas 1963. East Berlin authorities were believed to have had pressure exerted on them from Moscow ' to relax stringency regarding the Wall '.[1] Millions of Berliners were enabled to enjoy reunion with families and friends. People began to feel about people. The Wall was reduced to the status of a passport office. It is still forbidding, still a playground of too many trigger-happy gunmen, still an offence against human dignity. But a passport office just the same. Common sense must soon demand its demolition, like other walls in history.

The situation in its world setting, unfortunately, is not so clear. American suggestions to guarantee the sovereignty of West Germany under the protection of American nuclear power, that is, without the launching of a German independent deterrent, are based upon the realities revealed in the Cuban confrontation. They pre-suppose American support for a nuclear-free zone in Central Europe, to which there are reasonable prospects that Russia would agree. These hopes are endangered by the determination of France and Great Britain to possess ' independent ' nuclear deterrents, to make possible a proliferation of such deterrents, to maintain the useless balance-of-power in a balance of terror ; and, inevitably, start a new armaments race.

The situation can be summed up in these terms : Russia no longer fears either Germany or America although, together with the late President Kennedy, Mr Khruschev learned that ' the responsibilities of ultimate power may outrun the privileges it may seem to confer ' ; Russia accepts the thesis, which France and Great Britain still contest, that ' the active

[1] *The Times*, 7 January 1964.

and leading involvement of the United States in the world's affairs is indispensable for peace and prosperity ', and that this involvement implies that ' Germany must be either a partner or a peril ', and accepted as such.[1]

In this unfolding situation, the Rapacki Plan is recognized as the only constructive idea for a practical and lasting solution. The vital fact is that positive action now is possible while Germany remains without the nuclear deterrent, possession of which would make her a peril and destroy her magnificent capacity to be, what the majority of the German people want their country to be, a partner in peace. Given action now, the Wall would disappear. The threat to Germany and of Germany on her borders would disappear. The future of the beautiful city of Berlin, admired as a custodian of Europe's art and culture and as the capital which offered brave, unyielding opposition to the Hitler régime, could be debated in pacific, political language. Of course, the *status quo* would not be altered at once ; but discussion of the status of Berlin in the new Europe and in Germany would raise no threat of war. Berlin, indeed, could become the symbol of peace, and of the prospects of peace, for the entire world.

A break-through in Central Europe with the Rapacki Plan, wonderful achievement though it would be, would represent only the first decisive victory for non-alignment. It would herald a world-wide movement towards paths blazed by the Organization of African Unity and the Conference of Non-Aligned Countries.

Yugoslavia is committed already to the policy. So is Rumania. Here, then, is the hub of a nuclear-free zone in Southern Europe and the Balkans in which Cyprus, divorced from the ' peace-making ' military activities of foreign powers, would be neutralized and enabled to work out and operate a real peace formula. The big zones in Europe would mean that a vast area of continent would be pledged to non-interference and to constructive non-military action to promote peace. Organization of moral opinion would replace the exercise of military options. The basic facts of modern life would be faced realistically ; modern wars, whatever the causes that provoked

[1] *The Economist*, 4 January 1964.

them, have created more problems than they have solved ; only political settlements, hammered out in freedom and without the accompanying din of martial menace, have survival value.

These are the considerations behind my cherished hope that, soon, the United Nations will be endowed with authority to sustain peace pacts approved by free votes in the Security Council and the General Assembly. For any peace force required would not be formed by alien powers pursuing alien interests. It would be formed in the countries and by the nationals of the free zones concerned. It would act under United Nations orders. This policy, despite all doubts and difficulties, would have a real chance of success in a Latin American nuclear-free zone including Cuba, and in the area covering Malaysia and Indonesia where, otherwise, the present hostilities may drift into a long, costly conflict poisoning international relations for generations ahead. President Sukarno is amenable to the principal of non-alignment based, as it must be, upon freedom and independence. Is it impossible to believe that, if Malaysia's allies exercised their influence in a similar direction, a salve would be found for what looks like becoming the most intractable sore spot our tortured generation has ever known ?

If my faith in the quality and possibilities of the African contribution to international harmony appears to the reader to be over-enthusiastic, let me affirm the reasons that inspire it. Non-alignment is the basis of African unity. In face of the scepticism, even the sneers, of many Western commentators on the Addis Ababa Conference of the Heads of African States two short years ago, non-alignment has worked effectively as a peace-making principle in Algeria, Morocco, and Somalia. It is working with increasing speed as we develop the expertise which ensures its successful application. The decision to entrust the pacification of the Congo to the Organization of African Unity's representative, Jomo Kenyatta, is proof of that.

Moreover, the achievements of non-alignment raises the pace of our progress towards full economic and political unity in the vastest and potentially the richest populated area of this earth still awaiting development. And Africa can serve the world with clean hands. We have no non-African interests, no overseas territories to subvert ; we desire none. We have been loyal supporters of the United Nations, faithful to its purposes and decisions. Our good offices have been welcomed in India, China, Indonesia, and the West Indies.

One big problem will arise when we seek world recognition for a declaration of all Africa as a nuclear-free zone. That recognition must include Israel and Egypt. It must be accepted by these two great friends and helpmates of all emerging African countries, as I hope and believe it will be. Then the world shall hail us as worthy of the pride and dignity our fight for freedom and independence has already won for Mother Africa, and of the leadership we can offer all nations in the mighty, inspiring tasks of the future.

CHAPTER EIGHT

AFRICAN STATES IN THE COMMONWEALTH

THE Commonwealth of Nations whose ceremonial head is the Queen of Great Britain is no longer at an experimental stage. It is now a body with many organically connected limbs, whose common sensorium will be the Permanent Secretariat suggested by President Nkrumah. By this sensorium, each member nation will be able to have its finger on the pulse of every other member nation. In this way, a true and constructive mutual understanding and community of interest and sentiment will be sustained.

The Commonwealth is spread over five continents – Africa, Asia, America, Australia, and Europe – which are linked in many ways, visible and invisible. Its ceremonial head, Her Majesty, visits in succession the far-flung territories of this association. The Queen's visit to Ghana in 1959 was an experience never to be forgotten. The sincerity and scope of the reception which she received in Ghana was unsurpassed at any time. The people of Ghana had an opportunity of a living relationship with the Head of the Commonwealth of which we are such a proud member. The Queen had an opportunity of a first-hand experience of one of those countries which so notably contribute to the richness and variety of the Commonwealth.

The Commonwealth, being an organic association, is able to develop. From a mercenary fraternity founded upon a now insignificant trade preference, it has grown into one of the real forces for peace in the world of modern times. War between continuing members of the Commonwealth is inconceivable notwithstanding the periodic Indo-Pakistani sabre-rattling. The peacefulness of the Commonwealth is not merely inward. The Commonwealth today is an alliance for peace, and an external Commonwealth war is as unthinkable as an internal one. If the whole world could be portioned into such alliances, the risk of war would everywhere be minimized. In this respect, the Commonwealth emerges as a true example for the world. It represents the unanimity of peoples of different races, creed, and interest for peace, progress, and prosperity.

It is because of this will for peace and the completely non-military nature of the Commonwealth that there was no 'Commonwealth brigade' in the Indo-China fracas. Every nation has an inalienable right of self-defence under aggression; but an alliance that is founded solely on principles of peace, an alliance which is founded on discussion as the method of peace, cannot spring upon an astounded world a 'Commonwealth brigade'. It is this passionate commitment of the Commonwealth to peace which constitutes the strongest factor in Ghana's adherence to it.

The success of the Commonwealth as a force for peace can be illustrated through the Southern Rhodesian question. The present situation in Southern Rhodesia is an explosive one. Should the detonation come, its flames will engulf the whole of Africa and leap out beyond Africa's immense confines. There is a very live threat of serious war in the Southern Rhodesian situation. The press of the world, reiterating the opinion of the world, has said the same. The United Nations have in repeated resolutions made the same acknowledgement. The representative of the British Government stubbornly obstructed discussions by the world body whose sole concern was for peace and justice. The British paradoxically rejected the claim of the world whose security and peace was threatened by Britain's unjust handling of the situation to intervene. While Britain obstructed the world, world peace was more and more endangered.

The Commonwealth, however, is an association of equals who are free and sovereign. In the case of South Africa, the Commonwealth found it impossible to regard a country as free when nearly the whole of its population was disfranchised. South Africa, being an internal colony, was kicked out of the Commonwealth where it did not belong. Britain had played a constructive role on that great argument.

It was therefore hurtful and obnoxious to many to note that Britain not merely preserved a colony in Southern Rhodesia but actually permitted the colony to be administered on principles no less obnoxious than those of South Africa. The Commonwealth, being a moral force, spoke, and refused to have any skeletons stored away in reeking cupboards. The Commonwealth reiterated its principles of freedom and self-determination over Southern Rhodesia, and made it possible for Britain to undertake that that country would not become independent while its African population, the true inheritors of the territory, remained without a franchise.

If the Commonwealth is to continue then individual members, whether Republican or Dominion, must scrupulously adhere to its enunciated principles of peace and true independence. For this reason Commonwealth unity in the absence of colonialism and racialism is a keystone of Ghana's foreign policy.

The Queen is a Commonwealth axis drawing all its members together, corporate or individual, republican or dominion.

Peace is a necessary outward mark of the recognition of equality. Though peace is desirable in itself, it can be greatly enriched by a raising of the level of Commonwealth connections. An exchange of information is necessary to understanding, and understanding is a force for peace. But equitable trade is another index of the recognition for equality without which peace can be seriously endangered.

Colonialism has been perspicaciously described by Dr Nkrumah as a system whereby a metropolitan country, using political ties, subjects the economy of another country for its own gain. Colonialism has today been routed by a combination of positive forces wielding positive action. But ex-colonial countries are really threatened today by a new form of control whereby some countries still attempt to subject the economies of other countries for their own gain. One of the methods is an old one. By means of an uneven trade which is predominantly favourable to ex-colonialist powers, they attempt to ensure that the national economies of underdeveloped countries remain underdeveloped and so remain so dependent on the metropolitan economies that the underdeveloped ones can be manipulated at will.

The suggestion has been made that unless a territory can

boast a developed national economy, its people cannot really be free. Since the Commonwealth is a force for peace and freedom, it is essential that Commonwealth countries should develop a pattern of trade among themselves which shall not be inequitable.

The Commonwealth is a strong alliance ; at the same time it is faced with deep problems of political justice in Southern Rhodesia and British Guiana, and also with problems of Commonwealth trade, as with problems of discipline of certain sections of the Commonwealth press.

The recent meeting of the Commonwealth Heads of State and Premiers tackled some of the problems successfully, leaving the organization stronger and more meaningful than ever before.

The Commonwealth Prime Ministers' Conference of June 1964, met in London in brilliant sunshine under clouds of doubt.

From early in the year, politicians and the Press in Britain had been discussing, not the prospects of Commonwealth, but whether or not these prospects were worth discussing at all. Lord Gladwyn, once a high-ranking official of the Foreign Office, now a member of a firm of international merchant bankers and an enthusiast for British membership of the European Economic Community, wrote to *The Times* : ' The truth is that the Commonwealth though it has great value as a sort of inter-racial clearing house, does not exist politically, and only to a limited and diminishing extent economically.'[1] On the same day, the *Daily Sketch* took a sour look at the Commonwealth and, putting together the two most prejudice-evoking words in its vocabulary of vulgarity, hurled both at President Nkrumah, whom it described as Ghana's ' black-dictator '. Even during the sessions of the Commonwealth Prime Ministers' Conference, this newspaper continued to pour the vials of its ignorance over London's distinguished visitors.

In *The Times*, on 2 April 1964, ' A Conservative ' – said to be a former Minister with hopes of returning to high office – was permitted to write : ' The Commonwealth has really become a gigantic farce. Most people, including most con-

[1] 21 January 1964.

servatives, know this, and in their hearts they despise the politicians who keep the farce going. Not merely the non-European members, increasing at the rate of six or a dozen a year, but the so-called " Old Dominions " have no present real ties with Britain other than such as history might have left between any *two foreign* nations. Indeed, resentment against the former ruling power or mother country makes some of them less well-disposed to Britain than to Germany, China, or Israel. And why should it be otherwise ? ' The cynical admission of Colonial self-interest implied here is startling. ' A Conservative ' is saying, in effect : the pretence that Britain is really interested in the Commonwealth is now being seen through. The Commonwealth cannot be exploited any longer for our defence and profit. Let us, therefore, like the rape-and-run-thugs we have always been, try our luck elsewhere.

My personal view is that the *malaise* about Commonwealth strikes deeper and is less the product of economic greed than ' A Conservative's ' analysis admits, and I shall try to explain why later in this chapter. Meanwhile, Press and political comment meandered on inspired, with a few honourable exceptions, by that mixture of condescension and contempt some members of the British official and semi-official classes seem to feel for all ' colonial ' peoples, whether African or Australian or Arab. On its very eve, the Conference was being discussed in terms of sheer political horse-trading. The British Prime Minister, it was said, could not accept the African demand that pressure should be put upon Southern Rhodesia, however, evil the policy being applied there, without endangering his command over the most reactionary section of the Tory party vote at the forthcoming British General Election. And, of course, they added for good measure, the Africans were playing politics, too, although not very cleverly. From London they would travel to Cairo, to a meeting of the Organization for African Unity where they would ' lose face ' if they failed to stampede the Common-wealth Prime Ministers into dramatic action ! In this artificial, newspaper-created atmosphere, when an arriving African leader made a mild pre-Conference comment – and African leaders, on the whole, are mild-mannered because highly educated and civilized men – his words were interpreted as a snub for a fellow African !

NEW LEASE OF LIFE

Happily, this dreary load of prejudice and ignorance did not impede the work of the Prime Ministers. Under the heading, ' A new lease of life ', the *Sunday Times* proclaimed : ' So the prophets of Commonwealth futility have been confounded. The multi-racial Commonwealth has resolved, in effect, to gather internal strength – not indeed for joint defence or a common foreign policy, objects that have been unattainable, in truth, since the first world war – but for those less spectacular purposes which a community of widely varying sovereign states can pursue together if they have the will, as the States of the Commonwealth have shown they have.'[1]

On what did the *Sunday Times* base this conclusion ? ' Bar only the historic acceptance of India as the first republic within the Commonwealth,' the editor wrote, ' the Prime Ministers' Conference which ended last week in London was the most constructive top-level Commonwealth meeting since the Balfour Report of 1926 defined the co-equality of the then independent members.'

The *Sunday Times* welcomed the decision, in relation to Southern Rhodesia, that independence would not be granted to that Colony in the absence of ' sufficiently representative institutions ' – a decision that owed much to the determination of the British Prime Minister, Sir Alec Douglas-Home, to keep the Conference debate on a higher level than some British newspapers sought to pitch it, and to the statesmanship of the Prime Minister of Canada, Mr Lester Pearson, a persuasive voice for racial equality.

The importance of this decision cannot be gainsaid, either on the short view or on a long view. It marked a long step forward from the British position at United Nations only ten months earlier. Then Ghana and Morocco proposed to the Security Council that Great Britain should be asked ' not to

[1] 19 July 1964.

transfer to its Colony of Southern Rhodesia as at present governed any powers of sovereignty until the establishment of a government fully representative of all the inhabitants of the Colony '. The resolution also asked Great Britain ' not to transfer to its Colony of Southern Rhodesia the armed forces and aircraft as envisaged by the Central African Conference of 1963 ' which, readers will recall, followed the break-up of the Rhodesian Federation. For this resolution eight votes were cast with one vote (Britain) against and two abstentions (France and United States). Great Britain then applied its power of veto. At the London Conference, however, Great Britain agreed that Southern Rhodesia would not be granted independence without the creation of ' sufficiently representative institutions ' and also, if the Southern Rhodesian Government made a declaration of independence in defiance of that condition, no Commonwealth country, including Great Britain, would recognize the régime. Great Britain, in short, is now standing almost four-square against the continuance of colonialism in Southern Rhodesia.

The *Sunday Times* also hailed President Nkrumah's proposal – supported by President Kenyatta, a binding influence at every stage of the Commonwealth Prime Ministers' Conference – for setting up a Commonwealth Secretariat, as ' the first truly all-Commonwealth institution of the present era ' and one which ' will form a point of continuous co-ordination, and specifically, promotion of Commonwealth links '. The newspaper warmed to the proposed ' joint development projects involving several Commonwealth members, in which the British Government have offered a substantial contribution '. Finally, it endorsed the most urgent hope of all the Afro-Asian members of the Commonwealth: the idea of ' working through new and old instruments of co-operation for the objects of freer access to markets, price stabilization and balance-of-payments support ' adumbrated by a recent Geneva trade conference. Thus a Commonwealth Prime Ministers' Conference, comprising a majority of representatives of Afro-Asian countries in its membership launched broad-based plans for the modernization of an ancient, beneficent institution. I hope and believe that a few years onward, the world will look back on this Conference

A.G.R.—7

of 1964 as a turning point in the wiser, more just conduct of human affairs.

The Conference also enjoyed its small, gay triumphs. For example, on 15 July the editor of the *Daily Express* sent a memorandum to all executives: ' We should not refer to the Commonwealth as the Empire. The Commonwealth is the Commonwealth. . . .'[1]

It is, indeed!

END OF EMPIRE

Empire, whether expressed as conquest or cooperation, was based upon Admiralty. Without an efficient Admiralty able to embrace the whole world, an empire of the size and spread of Britain could not possibly be maintained. The cohesion of the Empire therefore depended upon the supremacy of the Navy in the arsenal of Britain. But the Admiralty had to go under. The Second World War made necessary the development of new military combinations in which the air arms had a preponderant importance. The new air arms which sprang up during World War II therefore also dealt a heavy blow to Admiralty. The actual moment of the death of the once all-conquering gunboat, the death of Admiralty and, with it, death of Empire is still a matter of debate among naval historians. For our purpose, I need only recall Sir Winston Churchill's recollection, three days after the Japanese attack on the United States Fleet at Pearl Harbour, of the events of 10 December 1941.

> I was opening my boxes [Churchill wrote] when the telephone at my bedside rang. It was the First Sea Lord. His voice sounded odd. He gave a sort of cough and gulp, and at first I could not hear quite clearly. ' Prime Minister, I have to report to you that the *Prince of Wales* and the *Repulse* have both been sunk by the Japanese – we think by aircraft . . .' ' Are you sure it's true ? ' ' There is no doubt at all.' So I put the telephone down. I was thankful to be alone. In all the war I never received a more direct shock. The reader of these pages will realize how many efforts, hopes, and plans foundered with these two ships.

[1] Quoted, *Sunday Times*, 26 July 1964.

As I turned over and twisted in bed the full horror of the news sank in upon me. There were no British or American capital ships in the Indian Ocean or the Pacific except the American survivors of Pearl Harbour, who were hastening back to California. Over all this vast expanse of waters Japan was supreme, and we everywhere were weak and naked.[1]

Mastery of the seven seas was not restored to the Allied Powers until the Battle of Midway Island penetrated fully the consciousness of the British Admiralty. It was a triumph for America, thereafter a dominant partner in the war against Hitler and, since 1945, the dominant power in the world. Soon after the end of the Second World War, Australian policy makers began to awaken to what has been called ' their dream of a Royal Navy which deterred all major aggressors '. Thus in 1951 Australia, with New Zealand, joined America in ANZUS, a pact to defend their mutual interests in the Far East and to which Great Britain was not a party. Already, India had gained full freedom with the goodwill of a Labour Government and in spite of Churchill's bitter opposition. Winds of change, unabated because unabatable, were blowing through Africa. The status of Admiralty offered no shield to the exposed bosom of Britain. In the re-distribution of world power, status had become a fading symbol except on these conditions: that Britain should nourish the new Commonwealth ushered in by Indian independence, should seek to unify it with the existing Commonwealth and with the emerging nations of Africa and Asia and thereby carve out a new and noble role – the role of moral leader of the progressive opinion throughout the world which rejoiced in the end of colonialism in India and Pakistan.

Faced with an agonizing re-appraisal of the re-alignments in world power, Britain, only temporarily, I believe, forgot the names of her friends. ' Formal Commonwealth consultation at the United Nations,' wrote a well-informed Canadian observer in 1964, ' ceased to have meaning years ago because of the avoidance of controversial issues.'[2] – e.g. South Africa's

---

[1] *The Second World War*, Cassell, London, 1950, Vol. 3, p. 551.

[2] John W. Holmes (President, the Canadian Institute of International Affairs) in *The Times*, 7 January 1964.

policy of apartheid. 'A similar disinclination has deprived the Prime Ministers' meetings of the authority they might have had.' Commonwealth consultation had collapsed into a mere convention.

This was the real *malaise* of Commonwealth. And so to the trauma of Suez, the final, feeble act of Imperial assertion.

I hesitate to rake over the cold ashes of the saddest episode in the history of British international relations. My purpose is to contribute, if I can, to understanding between the British people and a part of the globe of vital interest to the Afro-Asian members of the Commonwealth.

President Abdul Gamel Nasser was the new leader of Egyptian nationalism. What was forgotten at the time of Suez, and is too seldom remembered now, is that, although he has become the leader of Arab nationalism, President Nasser was not the first leader of Egyptian nationalism. Indeed, nationalism as an instrument of freedom from external domination had become a mighty force in the Middle East and, especially, in Egypt long before the President was born. It revealed its growing influence in World War I as a supporter of the British against the Turks.

When, in November 1914, Turkey entered the war on the side of Germany, the British deposed the Khedive, replaced him by a Sultan (the former Khedive's uncle) and proclaimed Egypt a British Protectorate. So arose the propaganda myth that the British occupied Egypt in the interests of the Egyptians. A month before the proclamation, the British Commander-in-Chief in Egypt had issued a statement that ' Great Britain took upon herself the sole burden of the present war without calling on the Egyptian people for aid therein '. Thus Egyptians were precluded from taking any part in a war waged on Egypt's soil ! Had the statement been observed to the letter by the local population and their leaders, it is possible to argue, the cause of the Allies would not have prevailed in the Middle East.

The complicated constitutional and other issues involved have been recorded in many books, and do not arise here.[1]

[1] *Wingate of the Sudan*, by Ronald Wingate, John Murray, London, 1955, is one of many valuable sources for the facts.

The acts, speaking louder than any words, which the Egyptian nationalists aided, were these : As direct assistance to the English Expeditionary Force, Egyptians guarded railway bridges, strategic points, and the Aswam Dam. The Egyptian Army also supplied guns and gunners for two armoured trains. It operated against the Senussi, undertook reconnaissance duties in Sinai, and distinguished itself in repulsing the Turkish attack on the Suez Canal in February 1915. Egyptian sappers, infantry, and cavalry served in Palestine. Barracks, hospitals, and other army buildings in Cairo were made available to the Egyptian Expeditionary Force. As the struggle reached its climax and resources became strained, the Egyptian authorities, in 1918, helped to recruit 123,000 men employed in the Labour and Camel Transport Corps, contributing £3 million to the cost of these troops.

The British, of course, worked through the Egyptian authorities. Yet the cooperation of the masses in a decisive contribution to the Allied effort – a contribution, I repeat, which was too speedily forgotten – would not have been possible if the Egyptian nationalist leaders, notably Zaghul Pasha, vice-president of the Legislative Assembly, had not backed the Allied cause.

And to what end ? On 13 November 1918, Zaghul Pasha told General Sir Reginald Wingate – the ' Sirdar ' – in plain words : Egypt demanded complete autonomy. Speaking with the authority of the Sultan and the Prime Minister behind him, Zaghul Pasha argued that Egypt, an ancient race with a glorious past, was more capable of conducting a well-ordered government than the Syrians and Mesopotamians to whom self-determination had already been promised. They had assisted the prosecution of the war with men and money. For them, the expected reward of victory was independence. They desired to remain on terms of loyal friendship with England.[1]

For no reason that any of the historians have been able to explain satisfactorily, the proferred friendship was refused. The sad and savage old colonial serial story was resumed ; a story of riot and revolt, of deportation, disunity and dismay.

[1] Wingate, *op. cit.*, p. 229.

So the British yoke continued to lie heavy on Egyptian necks through long years of uneasy peace and through World War II.

The events described above provide one of history's supreme examples of what has been called 'the myopia of foreign offices'. Another example is the assumption that President Nasser 'invented' the idea of nationalizing the Suez Canal Company.

In the early 1920's, as any political simpleton might have expected, socialists in Egypt regarded nationalization of the Canal as a primary objective of political policy. The proposal had been considered seriously when General Neguib took over in the revolution of 1952. It was known that President Nasser had been considering the problem since February 1956 – known, that is, to everybody except 'intelligence' – and for very obvious reasons. He was determined to build a great new Aswam Dam in order to accelerate the development of his country's resources. His existing assets consisted, in the main, of cotton, the export price of which was decided by the market economies of the Capitalist West, and the revenues of the Canal. The agreement in principle had been negotiated with the governments of the United States and the United Kingdom, to which the World Bank was party, to provide finance for 'the dam of dignity, freedom, and grandeur'. When, on 19 July, Dulles, pursuing his Cold War policy of 'brinkmanship' with Russia, then considering the loan which Egypt finally accepted, announced that American financial assistance was 'not feasible in present circumstances', President Nasser's response could easily have been foreseen. Seven days later, he nationalized his country's most important economic asset.

COMMONWEALTH CONSULTATION

Now, the Commonwealth Prime Ministers had been meeting in London only a fortnight before this grave international crisis blew up. The possibility of crisis must have been known to the British Prime Minister and Foreign Secretary; the latter, indeed, told Parliament that the British were 'consulted about the matter'. Yet neither the future of Anglo-American aid to Egypt nor the likely consequences of its abrupt curtailment, were discussed at that Conference.[1] Unhappily, this failure to consult the Commonwealth continued until the tragedy of this miserable episode reached a climax and the Anglo-French military campaign against Egypt died in the opprobrium of world condemnation.

What was the war on Egypt really about? Obviously its point was not to restore the peace which had been broken between Egypt and Israel; Great Britain and France, in fact joined in the attack on the Egyptians. Was it to force President Nasser to accept the proposed Canal Users' Association which was to receive all dues payable by ships of its members? This proposition, too, is untenable. It postulates an act of international alienation of Egyptian territory having exactly the same effect as an act of colonial piracy. Perhaps it was too ensure the efficient running of the Canal at fees which would not be onerous upon world shipping? Well, but for the act of aggression, the Canal would never have been blocked and closed. The last idea of an Egyptian government in need of revenue was to stop shipping by imposing heavy charges. Indeed, within a year of the end of the affair, there began a process of expansion and modernization of the canal which made it a living tribute to Arab efficiency and enterprise. Or was the purpose of a war which cost Great Britain more than four times its share of financing the Aswan Dam Project, and countless millions more in economic losses, ' to knock Nasser off his perch ' as, according to Field-Marshal Viscount Montgomery, Sir Anthony Eden defined the objective?[2] In other words, to deny Egyptians the right to choose their own leader?

These and other questions will remain rhetorical and argumentative until history throws up the honest answers. Certain beyond all doubt is this: although the British Prime Minister, answering a parliamentary question on 30 October, said, ' we have kept in close consultation with the Commonwealth governments ', he also, in a broadcast on 3 November, stated: ' Our friends inside the Commonwealth, and outside, could not in the very nature of things be consulted in time '.

[1] James Eayrs, *The Commonwealth and Suez*, Oxford University Press, 1964, p. 8.

[2] *The Times*, 29 March 1962.

And subsequent proceedings in the parliaments and assemblies of the Commonwealth countries revealed that there was nothing approaching effective consultation; that, in truth, the victims of the Suez aggression were 26 British and French soldiers and, according to an official British estimate, 750 Egyptian dead. Democracy in France also collapsed. The Commonwealth relationship was damaged.

An authentic Commonwealth view was expressed on 15 August when the late Prime Minister Nehru spoke: ' Under no circumstances should this issue be tackled through the use of armed force or threats ', he said, the issue being whether, in international law, President Nasser, by nationalizing the Canal, could abrogate an agreement that still had some years to run. The great Indian leader added: ' If any effort is made, even by mistake . . . to settle the Suez issue by force or by threats, then the results will be disastrous '. Only the goodwill and the constructive activities of Canadian and Asian members of the Commonwealth at United Nations prevented these solemn words of warning from becoming a forecast of grim truth.

In a House of Commons debate on 1 November, the day following the Anglo-French invasion, Sir Anthony Eden said: ' Israel and Egypt are locked in conflict . . . The first and urgent task is to separate these combatants and to stabilize the position. That is our purpose. If the United Nations were then willing to take over the physical task of maintaining peace in that area, no one would be better pleased then we. . . .'

Four years later, Sir Anthony (now Lord Avon) interpreted these words as giving birth to the idea of the first United Nations peace force, ' taken up in the General Assembly the next day by Mr Lester Pearson and others '.[1] Any author of disaster may be forgiven an attempt to salvage his reputation, and Lord Avon's efforts on behalf of the pre-War League of Nations are worthy of commendation. Nevertheless, the simple truth is that, on 1 November, nobody at United Nations was listening to the British Prime Minister. On 30 October, an emergency session of the Security Council had condemned the

---

[1] *Full Circle*, by Lord Avon, Cassell, 1960, pp. 535–6. Cited, *The Commonwealth and Suez*, p. 275.

Anglo-French strike and called upon the General Assembly to take appropriate action. All during the night of 1–2 November, the General Assembly was exploding with indignation and demanding a cease-fire. When the cease-fire resolution, sponsored by the United States, had been carried by 65 votes to 5, Mr Lester Pearson rose to explain why the Canadian delegation had abstained. ' Peace,' he pleaded, ' is far more than ceasing to fire '. He wanted the resolution to instruct the Secretary-General ' to begin to make arrangements with member governments for a United Nations force large enough to keep these borders at peace while a political settlement is being worked out '. As the morning of 2 November passed, it became obvious that the cease-fire call would be ignored, and the United States delegation offered Mr Pearson support for a formal resolution creating a United Nations force.

Mr Pearson flew home to Ottawa to rally support from his own government and to consult with Washington and London. Returning to the re-convened General Assembly, he agreed to vote for a strongly condemnatory Indian resolution and to move, concurrently, that the Secretary-General should submit, within forty-eight hours, a plan for setting up an emergency international United Nations police force with the consent of the governments concerned.

The dramatic moment of history-in-the-making came at 2.17 a.m. on Sunday, 4 November. The Canadian resolution was adopted by a vote of 57 to 0, with 19 abstentions, the abstentionists including the United Kingdom, France and Egypt, Australia and the Soviet bloc, still smarting under world criticism of its brutal activities in Hungary.

So life was breathed into the first international peace force. The authority – and the possibilities – of the United Nations were revealed proudly. Great Britain, sadly, was isolated from the Commonwealth. Yet the initiative and exertions of Commonwealth members from the Far West and the Far East ensured the Commonwealth's survival ; they set a fine example of what we Africans call ' positive non-alignment '. The Asian members of the Commonwealth did more. Faced with angry demands within their own parliaments for secession from the Commonwealth, Nehru in India, Suhrawardy in Pakistan and

Bandaranaike in Ceylon faithfully upheld the cause of Commonwealth cooperation. The independent African States shared
fully and deeply the indignation of their Asian comrades over
the Suez outrage. Great Britain alone continued to drag her
feet, to backslide.

VICTORY FOR WORLD OPINION

Nations, like individuals, react variously to psychological
trauma. The Suez disaster marked the end of colonial aggression. World opinion had rallied at once to execrate it ; world
opinion would rally again to prevent its repetition. Some
members of the British Conservative Government, reconstructed
after Sir Anthony Eden's resignation, recognized the facts,
Mr Harold Macmillan and Mr Iain Macleod among them.
On the whole, however, politicians, Press and people were
confused. Public opinion polls indicated that the nation was
divided by generations. Young men and women were ashamed
and shocked ; to be brought to the brink of destructive war for
reasons that were never made clear and to be the agents of
unprovoked aggression appalled them. The aged, while supporting the Suez adventure, were stunned by failure and
disgusted by the Government's fumbling incompetence
throughout a crisis of its own creation. Certainly, a great
nation, demeaned by its political leaders, faced an uncertain
future.

These reactions may explain both the post-Suez policy of
preparing African states for independence and the opposition
expressed, mainly and spitefully, in irresponsible newspapers,
which tended to blunt the generosity of this wise decision.
Mr Macmillan's poker-faced acceptance of Lord Salisbury's
resignation from the Cabinet in March 1957, reduced public
tension by indicating that the more raucous voices of regression
were no longer dominant in the councils of the nation. His
African visit in 1960, and the ' wind of change ' speeches
appeared to have blown away, finally, the confusion surrounding Britain's policy despite the later comments of Lord Kilmuir
(who complained that he was sacked from his job as Lord
Chancellor and from his political career with only seven hours'

notice !) that '. . . neither the Prime Minister nor the Government as a whole had ever really thought out their policy
towards South Africa . . . when he made his famous speech
Macmillan was only concerned in making the appropriate
political noises in the Union on behalf of the British people '.
Then came a new crisis, suggesting the utter abandonment of
the Commonwealth by Great Britain : the Government
applied for British membership of the European Economic
Community.

Many explanations have been advanced for a momentous
move made without any real preparation of the public mind
and without seeking the people's mandate. Great Britain, it
has been argued, needed a shake-up, a revolutionary step
towards economic planning and modernization. Mr
Macmillan, always a planner (as his book, *The Middle Way*,
with its Marxian overtones, had revealed in 1938) now proposed
revolution by inadvertence. Britain was to be dragged into
competitive efficiency via the Common Market at whatever
cost to the Commonwealth.

Whether or not this explanation fits the facts must be left to
history. What can be stated with reasonable certainty are the
arguments that brought the ill-fated issue to its prestige-
destroying conclusion.

Great Britain's distinctive role in world affairs and the
source of her influence in Europe has always been her leadership
of the Commonwealth of Nations. She was stripping herself of
her finest tradition by approaching E.E.C. without the full
knowledge and eager consent of the Commonwealth. The
new economic alliance was, and is, regarded by many observers
as sharpening the defensive military alliance against Russia and
thus increasing the difficulties of political settlement between
East and West : in plain words, Great Britain was favouring
Germany, her enemy in two world wars, against Russia, her
most faithful ally in these wars. British ' intelligence ' was as
ill-formed and as little acute about Europe as it had proved to
be about Egypt. It failed to understand the motives of General
de Gaulle, now following the gleam of ' La Gloire ' and
aiming at restoring the long-forgotten French power in Europe.
Great Britain had no defence against the humiliation inflicted

upon her when France said 'No' to her application for membership of the Community.

CLAIMS OF KINSHIP

As an African whose faith in the Commonwealth has always been profound, I venture to suggest another consideration which seems to me to be important – the bonds of kinship. In the century before 1920, millions of the youngest, fairest, and most virile of Britain's sons and daughters migrated from the Mother Country to the Dominions and the Colonies. Between the wars, millions more – representatives of the present generation of British folk – followed their pioneer forebears. Few of these millions were 'exploiters' of the Commonwealth. They were the victims of mass unemployment, seeking a better life of service and a fair reward for their labour. Letters by the million rattle the letter boxes of British homes every week from these Commonwealth citizens and their children. The link is as delicate as gold, as unbreakable as steel. For them, the Commonwealth is a commonalty of flesh and blood and friendship. As I see it, the spirit and ideals of the Commonwealth are as alive in the hearts and minds of Asians and Africans as they are in the hearts and minds of Australians Canadians, and New Zealanders. Only thus could the Commonwealth have survived Suez and de Gaulle, those 'whips and scorns of time'.

Before considering the future of the Commonwealth, I think we should remind ourselves that this mighty socio-political experiment is a vital institution as well as an inspiring abstraction. Its populations exceed 700 millions, nearly a quarter of the entire population of the world. Its independent states are in a voluntary association with each other. So they pursue their individual policies in domestic and external affairs. Their social and cultural backgrounds vary widely; all are different from, say Great Britain, in their political, social, and economic development. As Mr Duncan Sandys, former Secretary of State for Commonwealth Relations, once put it, the Commonwealth is neither an alliance nor an ideological bloc. In the realm of ideas, all members of the

Commonwealth accept the principle of non-alignment. Most Afro-Asian members apply the same principle to military matters. And despite their infinite variety, all members of the Commonwealth seek to cooperate for the purpose of promoting, *inter alia*, world peace.

The Commonwealth is described often as a ' Club '. Here are some of the factors and features of loyalty to the Club:

The Commonwealth is a free association of member countries for membership of the Commonwealth is not a condition of independence. No nation is under any external compulsion to seek membership, or having obtained it, keep it. Indeed, there are countries like Burma, Sudan, and Somalia which of their own accord declined to seek Commonwealth membership upon the attainment of independence. Membership of the Commonwealth, of course, implies acceptance of the Queen's headship; but since the Commonwealth association is essentially one of foreign relations, acknowledgement of Her Majesty's headship is compatible with a republican or dominion status. Fittingly, therefore, all members of the Commonwealth, both republican and dominion, regard Her Majesty as Head of the Commonwealth.

We live in modern times; and in modern times, isolation cannot be spendid. Isolation can only arise from a manic depressive political condition. It is never politic and always perilous. The members of the Commonwealth are therefore held together in a rational bond freely constituted.

A mere wish not to be isolated can not however of itself forge any worthwhile links. The Commonwealth is also a community of feeling and unanimous in its belief in democracy. A country in which most adults lack the franchise has no truck with democracy and has no place in the Commonwealth. The principle of ' one man, one vote ' is a fundamental law of democracy.

The member nations of the Commonwealth also have political institutions in which there are strong family likenesses. Indeed, the Westminster system has been the starting point even though this has been modified in the countries of Asia and Africa to suit better the genius and circumstances of Africa and Asia.

In recent years, more African states have been joining the Club after attaining independence. I hope and believe that this trend will continue. If it does, there will be increasing representation of our African view in our changing Commonwealth. Already, in 1960, President Nkrumah was pointing to the themes and ideas to which only a flexible, frank, and sympathetic association can respond.[1] Firstly, Ghana believes that freedom and independence for Africans are essential for world peace. Secondly, the great wave of African nationalism at present sweeping over the continent is a political fact which must be recognized. We believe that it is a force no one can hold in check. An effort must be made to come to terms with it in the best interest of all concerned.

Thirdly, we realize that territories with minority communities present difficulties. However, we believe sincerely that these difficulties cannot be side-stepped by any approach which compromises the principle that the majority of people should form the basis of government. I believe that the only genuine and permanent solution to this problem can come from the application of the principle of ' one man, one vote '.

I am convinced that the Commonwealth has an important part to play in all this by demonstrating true and concrete friendship for the peoples of Africa in the critical times that lie ahead, and by co-operating in the task of creating those conditions which will make for dignity, self-respect, and material prosperity for all those who live in Africa.

Of course, there is enormous diversity of opinion within the unity of Commonwealth purpose. Let me cite an important example.

During the Sino-Indian border conflict, Mr Macmillan offered military aid to India. President Nkrumah, on terms of deep personal friendship with Mr Nehru and having excellent relations with the British Prime Minister, objected that support to one of the parties might endanger world peace, and reminded Mr Macmillan that the Commonwealth is not a military alliance. Surprised, Mr Macmillan replied: ' When the territory of a Commonwealth people is invaded, it is surely only right and natural that we should express to them

[1] *The African Eagle*, 1960, Vol. No. 2, p. 2.

our sympathy and support in their anxiety and danger '.
What was the argument of the Ghanian leader, committed to
positive neutralism and non-alignment?

First, that you do not promote peace by giving aid for war.
Second, that the Commonwealth was harmed when the
impression was created that its members did not judge each
issue on its merits but, instead, automatically sided with a
fellow Commonwealth member when that country was
engaged in a dispute with an outside power. Third, that ' resort
to arms and the employment of power politics have been the
main source of mounting tensions in the world ', and we must
now all ' look at the problems that confront the world today
with new eyes and in a new spirit of conciliation, mutual
understanding, and unflinching respect for the preservation of
peace '. This did not mean that the apostle of non-alignment
had contracted out of the Sino-Indian dispute. Far from it.
Ghana joined the Afro-Asian group whose suggestions for
ending the conflict – the Colombo proposals – were accepted
by the Indian Prime Minister and Parliament in July 1963.

As on non-alignment, so on the subject of colonialism. The
Asian-African members of the Commonwealth will never
compromise principles for which their heroes have fought and
died and the success of which in practice, they are convinced,
will convert other Commonwealth members to their view.

Who better fitted to unfold our faith than the Head of the
Commonwealth ? Speaking during her Australian tour in
March 1963, Her Majesty said : ' There are some who see the
changing pattern of the Commonwealth as the beginning of
its end. These people forget the Commonwealth is not based
on any rigid treaty or rules of action. It is an organic association of like-minded peoples. It is an instrument of enormous
power and influence in the hands of its members, but it can
only function for their benefit if they are prepared to use it.
It is like a plough, which is quite useless standing in a shed,
but in the right hands it can cultivate the soil into productive
farm land. Properly used, the Commonwealth can help
cultivate a prosperous, enlightened civilization for all its
members : neglected, it will rust into scrap.'

To ensure that the Commonwealth shall be strong in will,

' to seek, to strive, to find, and not to yield ' – that was the high purpose behind Ghana's proposal of a Commonwealth Secretariat at the Commonwealth Prime Ministers' Conference of 1964.

' The first truly all-Commonwealth official institution of the present era,' as the *Sunday Times* described the proposed Commonwealth Secretariat, ' will form a point of continuous co-ordination and, specifically, promotion of Commonwealth links.' That is well said. The Commonwealth must achieve the unity and the spirit of a band of brothers if it is to play a significant part in creating the conditions of social peace in the world.

Today's Challenge

Let us remind ourselves, briefly, of the size and nature of the problem now challenging the quality of our human intelligence, our conscience and, indeed, our claim to be called civilized.

Between 300 and 450 million people, most of them coloured people, actually go hungry at the present time, and from one-third to one-half of mankind suffer from either under-nourishment or malnutrition or both. Thus, writes Mr B. R. Sen, Director-General of the Food and Agricultural Organization of the United Nations :[1] ' if the balance between population and food supply is not rapidly improved in favour of food supply, the number of under-nourished and mal-nourished people will be at least doubled by the end of the century, that is, roughly, 3,000 million '. Mr Sen bases his figures on the estimates of expert demographers that, during the next 30 to 40 years, world population will certainly double itself. F.A.O.'s Third World Food Survey (1963) having analyzed the quantitative and qualitative improvements necessary to provide a minimum adequate diet for the world population, stated that food supplies must be doubled by 1980 and trebled by the end of the century to ensure a reasonable level of nutrition for everybody. Thus Mr Sen sums up : 'Whatever may be done to control population, the need to increase food production remains a central issue.'

Consider, now, what Africa is doing to dispel that dark and

[1] *The Times*, 19 July 1964.

looming danger. The weapon is science. While European
countries have from 500 to 2,000 scientists per million population, Africa has about 20. At Lagos, in August 1964, 29 African
nations meeting under the joint auspices of UNESCO and the
Economic Commission for Africa, ' took a decision of breath-
taking audacity '.[1] They unanimously adopted a crash plan
to boost African science by no less than 15-fold in no more than
15 years. By 1980, they declared, Africa will need between
50,000 and 70,000 scientists, or 200 per million population –
and the need will be met. Four-fifths of new African science
will be concerned with Africa and its natural resources. The
plan includes a research institute for each African country, or
a share in a regional institute, where hydrologists, map-makers,
mineral prospectors, soil experts, agriculturalists, and their like
will be able to make a many-pronged attack on the best ways
to use the continent's natural resources.

Meantime, most African states are engaged in vigorous
efforts to improve both the quantity and quality of production
and to solve the problem of tropical agriculture not always
appreciated even by sympathetic Western commentators :
whereas in temperate zones the system of crop rotation ensures
that one crop returns to the soil the nourishment which the
succeeding crop requires, in tropical conditions much land
must still be left under bush for many years to enable it to
regain fertility before being farmed again for a comparatively
short period. In the African Freedom from Hunger Campaign
of October 1964 the theme was ' Food is Life. Grow more.
Waste none '. Ordinary people are cooperating to raise
production by avoiding loss on the farms, in storage, in markets,
and in the homes.

Here, surely, is an adventure to match the mood and spirit
of a developing Commonwealth ! And the role of the Commonwealth Secretariat ? It is to keep every country in the
Commonwealth informed about the problem, about the
successes scored and the failures faced in tackling it, about the
contribution each can make for the good of all, and to stimulate
continuing public interest among the people of the Commonwealth in what I do not hesitate to describe as 'this work of God'.

[1] Gerald Leach in the *New Statesman*, 21 August 1964.

Information – accurate, free from political bias in its presentation, up-to-date ; information on trading possibilities, on the needs and progress of education, on appropriate scientific ideas and inventions, on political and constitutional matters, on books and the arts and cultural movements ; information, its speedy collection and quick dissemination is the first, perhaps the supreme, task of the Secretariat. The agenda of the Secretariat, too, will include detailed study of growing capital investment and, before anybody complains that I am raising the cry of ' neo-colonialism ' once again, let me remind readers that, although every country welcomes, for example, private investment from say, the United States, large sections of the populations of Great Britain, Canada, and Australia are concerned to avoid the risks of ' economic colonization ' implied in all foreign investment. Indeed, New Zealand, now engaged in expanding her industry, is legislating against the take-over of domestic business by foreigners and they, writes a correspondent in *The Times*, include ' British, as well as Australian and American companies '.[1]

I would expect the Secretariat to interest itself in what Mr Harold Wilson once called ' the minuscule Department of Technical Co-operation '[2] in order to expand greatly that valuable service and immediately to coordinate effectively the work of technical cooperation. Mr William Clark, Director of the Overseas Development Institute, has suggested that there should be a Commonwealth technical assistance representative in every Commonwealth capital with the right to communicate with his colleagues in every other capital. ' This is essential ', he declares, ' because by one of the absurdities of Commonwealth protocol no High Commissioner can act for another Commonwealth country, with the result that whereas in Ethiopia the British Ambassador will gladly communicate requests for assistance to the New Zealand Government (which has no representative of its own) neighbouring Kenya can communicate only with those four or five Commonwealth countries which have set up Missions in Nairobi; there is literally no point of the contact with the rest of the Common-

[1] 10 July 1964.
[2] *Daily Herald*, 22 January 1964.

wealth '.[1] The Secretariat can study and help to eliminate the clogging rust of tradition and make communication faster, more fluid, and more fruitful.

Mr Clark has advanced other valuable suggestions that the Secretariat might be the best body to investigate. He would like to see the Commonwealth, speaking through the Commonwealth Prime Ministers' Conference, accepting responsibility for setting up the proposed college of administrative training in Britain and including on its staff such leading international civil servants as Narasimhan of India, Adu of Ghana, Adebe of Nigeria, and other Afro-Asians who have served the United Nations with distinction. Since mutual aid is replacing Admiralty as the sheet-anchor of Commonwealth relations, he favours the creation of a ' Commonwealth pool of talent with each contributing and benefiting ' to launch in every developing country of the Commonwealth at least one joint Commonwealth project – for instance, an administrative college or an experimental farm. He would also like the British people to endorse the idea ' of a period of service overseas once or twice in a lifetime as a normal part of the career structure accepted by universities, employers, and professional men alike '.

' POLITICALLY-FLAVOURED ' AID

I am attracted greatly by the ideas of Dr Claudio Veliz, the able expert on Latin American affairs.[2] His plea is that all governments – although he is writing specifically about a British Labour Government – must reject the ' mendicant philosophy and all it implies '. Financial aid, however massive, cannot solve the economic and social problems of underdeveloped countries. ' No amount of foreign money or investment can have much effect without the major part of the effort being made domestically . . . Every nation must work out her own economic salvation independently '. The end of politically-flavoured aid, he points out, is that money finds its way through intricate channels ' into the redecoration of

[1] *The Times*, 4 July 1964.
[2] *Labour's New Frontiers*, Andre Deutsch, 1964, pp. 159 *et seq*.

officers ' clubs and salary rises for army, navy, and air force '.
Dr Veliz's argument proceeds:

> Hunger is bad : infant mortality is bad : ignorance is bad :
> misery and deprivation are evils which must not be tolerated in
> London, Glasgow, Lagos, or Potosi. Britain should offer the
> best in her to fight the worst evils of our time and her assistance
> should not be conditioned by colour, political affiliation or any
> such distinction but should reach as many human beings as
> possible who are in need of it. The help which Britain offers
> should result in an absolute minimum of interference of any kind
> in the domestic affairs of the recipient nations and finally, it
> should be aid of a vital self-sufficient type which will effectively
> allow under-developed countries to solve their complex problems
> by themselves.

Remember, Dr Veliz is not a citizen of the Commonwealth.
He is an outsider looking in; and what he sees pleases and
inspires him.

> Britain has the highest municipal civilization in the world
> [he writes], one of the most sophisticated cultural traditions ever
> developed in any nation and – most important of all – it is about
> to begin a scientific and educational revolution unparalleled in
> the modern world. These are the best things in Britain : these
> are the mainstays of this country's future development and it is
> these things, magnificent, far-reaching, imaginative and vital
> which Britain should offer . . . The amount of money needed to
> finance enough scholarships and grants to bring to this country
> the best brains of a whole generation of future artists, engineers,
> economists, and scientists would be insignificant if sent abroad
> in the form of direct aid. However, spent in education of this
> type, it would represent a revolution in habits, in attitudes and
> in expectations.

Dr Veliz speaks in the accents of generous, aspiring youth.

> No new nation is in the mood to recapitulate the
> whole process of technological development undergone by
> the industrial countries. On the contrary, their first tendency is
> to move to the vanguard of technological advancement and
> establish their new industries at that level . . . The new countries
> may not want their own steel industries if they lack coal and iron
> but they certainly want to adopt the most advanced level of

industrial technology ; they want to organize their new cities according to the best methods of urban planning ; they want to arrange their systems of higher education according to the best precepts and to enrich their own cultural stream with the best other cultures can offer.

I have quoted Dr Veliz at length because his perception has been proved by our experience in Ghana. There, in the process of industrialization, men and women have learned quickly the disciplines of obeying the clock and the division of labour and have revealed great aptitude in mastering complicated tools and machinery. I agree entirely with his view that ' scientific and educational help of the type Britain can offer is dynamic aid: it will enable people to solve their own problems: it is not patronizing and it does not humiliate but gives human beings the tools to do the job themselves '. This mutual aid is mutual enrichment. His proposal that, in sharing ' the most important expansion of higher education facilities that has taken place in the world since the War ' Britain should also ensure that those who take degrees will have, back home, proper laboratory facilities to carry on high level research and experimental stations and research centres in the field, is absolutely right; it meshes with the idea of Afro-Asian scientists. He rounds off a complete conception – for which the Commonwealth Secretariat could prepare the plans – with a proposal that primary and secondary schools in Great Britain and, I would add, other Commonwealth countries should establish a direct association with schools in underdeveloped areas of the world. Finally, he links up his vision splendid with ' the genesis and development of industrial plans supported with long-term credit obtained through the partnership '. This requires a rational administration machinery which, as I see it, the Secretariat would be fully capable of defining and, perhaps, keeping properly oiled, even if the administration itself must be operated by and through friendly Commonwealth governments.

There are scores of voluntary and semi-government organizations doing magnificent work in many fields of Commonwealth endeavour. They are engaged in all forms of education and in varied research. They produce books, papers, film closed-circuit television programmes, and many other forms of uniting men and women in understanding and mutual activities. By coordinating these grand though, at present, rather diffuse enterprises, the Commonwealth Secretariat can economize and so expand their services. Yet, more important than the agenda of the Secretariat will be its ambient spirit – the spirit of brotherhood and service in the exciting adventure of lifting all men nearer to the angels.

I have no doubt about what is the most urgent task before the reinvigorated Commonwealth. It is to define, and apply as widely as possible, a viable trade policy between advanced and underdeveloped countries. The Commonwealth is better fitted to undertake this task than any other grouping in the world today. It encompasses every field of business and productive enterprise. These businesses operate under all the varied conditions of geography and climate known to man, and at every level of sophistication, from the simple to the complicated. Above all, the Commonwealth is a partnership of peoples, each with an equal right to influence its policies. It is capable of grasping, quickly and sympathetically, the real meaning of the demand now heard in many underdeveloped countries, for ' trade-rather-than-aid '.

This demand is based upon two considerations.

First, almost all underdeveloped countries are limited in their immediate export potential to one or two agricultural commodities. Between 1953 and 1961, the underdeveloped countries raised their volume of exports by an average of 4·3 per cent per annum, yet their terms of trade worsened by 0·7 per cent per annum. Ghana, which has devoted much time and money to improving both the production and the quality of the dominant cocoa crop since Independence, has found its financial returns falling steadily although retail prices for processed cocoa have increased sharply throughout the world.

Second, economic rate of growth depends as much upon what some economists call ' the higher dynamism ' as upon natural resources and investment potential and, recent researches show, the higher dynamism flows from industry rather than from agriculture. In the period 1938–61, for example the yearly growth of world production of food and raw materials was 1·9 per cent and of manufactures 4·7 per cent.

Developing countries, naturally, are eager to capture the higher dynamism and, with it, a share in world markets for their output ; upon this is based their hopes of rising living standards. They are entitled also to expect fair and stable prices for their primary products. This requires a commodity stabilization scheme, or agreements to sustain the purchasing power of developing countries over imports during periods when their export earnings are fluctuating in world markets, or better still, a decision involving all the Great Powers to negotiate ' commodity prices on the basis of equality buffer stocks and controls to deal with shortages and surpluses without exploitation of either producer or consumer '.

My quotation is taken from the Havana Charter agreed by the United Nations at the Havana Conference of November 1947–March 1948, largely under the inspiration of Mr Harold Wilson, then the delegate of the British Labour Government. Alas, economic power in those days was being forged as a weapon in the long waste of the Cold War.

COMMONWEALTH AND COMMUNITY : A CONTRAST

At times, a comparison has been suggested between the Commonwealth and the French Community. There is no real ground of comparison. The French Community was originally conceived as a unitary state representing a kind of extension of France. The Commonwealth, which is centred in London, was on the other hand conceived at its inception as a free association of free and equal partners, in which no member will in any degree be subjugated to another. This point of view has persisted and has been much strengthened since the definition of the co-equality of the dominions in the Balfour Report of 1926.

It is this equality and freedom which has enabled the Commonwealth to play such a constructive part in the development of international solidarity. The unity of the Commonwealth is a natural unity. It contains no artificial seams and

suffers no fissiparous stress. On all these points the Commonwealth stands contra-distinguished from the French Community, which has really collapsed and has now been replaced
by a mercenary relationship.

There are Commonwealth Conferences at which even
explosive issues are discussed. There is Commonwealth consultation which is a real manifestation of solidarity and cooperation. There is Commonwealth mutual assistance whose
value is enchanced by the freedom and true equality of those
involved in it. There is the real sympathetic concern which
member-states of the Commonwealth show over one another.
These are the sinew, the blood and life of a voluntary and
meaningful association.

The member-states of the Commonwealth are able to comment on Britain's proposal to join the Common Market, and
have certainly not been committed, in any sense, to association
with that Market by Britain's proposal. The French Community has on the other hand had to be associated, because of
France's membership with the Common Market, irrespective
of the true interests of the new independent members of that
Community.

The Commonwealth Prime Ministers Conference of July
1965, brought the Commonwealth Secretariat into active life.
It also created a Peace Mission to explore the possibilities
of bringing the combatants in Vietnam to peace talks. This
initiative may fail. Yet it succeeded in revealing the capacity
of the Commonwealth to act in dangerous world situations in
which no other organization is available.

The Peace Mission, which I hope will become a permanent
institution within the Commonwealth, does not supplant
United Nations. It supplements United Nations when hostility
between powers obstructs that Organization's operation. The
Commonwealth has thus assumed a positive role in world
affairs as a peace force. It must sustain the life and vitality
of its Peace Mission. This is the crowning justification for the
Commonwealth's own existence and the assurance that its
ideals will not perish from this earth.

CHAPTER NINE

UNITED NATIONS : OUR GUARANTEE OF WORLD PEACE

MY faith in the United Nations has never faltered. In writing about the United Nations, however, I find that I must recall its origin, which many politicians, publicists, and others forget too easily ; and I must set out its purposes, which its critics never choose to remember.

The idea of reviving the pre-war League of Nations in a form capable of meeting the needs of the post-war world took shape aboard H.M.S. *Prince of Wales* in August 1941. ' President Roosevelt told me at one of our first conversations,' wrote Winston Churchill,[1] ' that he thought it would be well if we could draw up a joint declaration laying down certain broad principles which should guide our policies along the same road.' Sir Winston agreed gladly. One can almost hear the great man chuckle as he adds : ' Considering all the tales of my reactionary, Old World Outlook, and the pain this is said to have caused the President, I am glad it should be on record that the substance and spirit of what came to be called the " Atlantic Charter " was in its first draft a British production cast in my own words.'

From much debate and consultation there emerged, on 12 August, a joint declaration of ' common principles in the national policies of their respective countries on which they base their hopes for a better future for the world '. And these were the principles:

First, their countries seek no aggrandisement, territorial or other.

Second, they desire to see no territorial changes that do not accord with the freely expressed wishes of the peoples concerned.

Third, they respect the right of all peoples to choose the form of government under which they will live, and they wish to see

[1] *The Second World War*, Vol. III, Cassell, 1950, pp. 385 *et seq.*

sovereign rights and self-government restored to those who have
been forcibly deprived of them.

Fourth, they will endeavour, with due respect to their existing
obligations, to further the enjoyment by all States, great or small,
victor or vanquished, of access, on equal terms, to the trade and
to the raw materials of the world which are needed for their
economic prosperity.

Fifth, they desire to bring about the fullest collaboration
between all nations in the economic field, with the object of
securing for all improved labour standards, economic advancement, and social security.

Sixth, after the final destruction of the Nazi tyranny they hope
to see established a peace which will afford to all nations the
means of dwelling in safety within their own boundaries, and
which will afford assurance that all the men in all the lands may
live out their lives in freedom from fear and want.

Seventh, such a peace should enable all men to traverse the
high seas and oceans without hindrance.

Eighth, they believe that all the nations of the world for
realistic as well as spiritual reasons, must come to the abandonment of the use of force. Since no future peace can be maintained if land, sea or air armaments continue to be employed by
nations which threaten, or may threaten, aggression outside of
their frontiers, they believe, pending the establishment of a
wider and more permanent system of general security, that the
disarmament of such nations is essential. They will likewise aid
and encourage all other practicable measures which will lighten
for peace-loving peoples the crushing burden of armaments.

Remember, when reflecting upon this momentously radical
document, that America was still, technically, a neutral power
whose refusal to give full support to the pre-war League of
Nations had weakened that organization disastrously.

This Atlantic Charter idea triumphed over all the chances
and changes of war. In 1943, Great Britain, America, China
(Formosa), and Russia recognized, in Article 4 of the Moscow
Declaration ' the necessity of establishing at the earliest
practicable date a general organization based on the principle
of the sovereign equality of all peaceful states and open to
membership by all such states '. With its basic aims intact, the
idea was approved unanimously by 50 nations at the United

Nations Conference on International Organization held at San Francisco in June 1945.

There, the agreed statement of purposes – the Charter of the United Nations – was set out as follows:

1. To maintain international peace and security, and to that end : to take effective collective measures for the prevention and removal of threats to the peace, and for the suppression of acts of aggression or other breaches of the peace, and to bring about by peaceful means, and in conformity with the principles of justice and international law, adjustment or settlement of international disputes or situations which might lead to a breach of the peace ;

2. To develop friendly relations among nations based on respect for the principle of equal rights and self-determination of peoples, and to take other appropriate measures to strengthen universal peace ;

3. To achieve international co-operation in solving international problems of an economic, social, cultural, or humanitarian character, and in promoting and encouraging respect for human rights and for fundamental freedoms for all without distinction as to race, sex, language, or religion ; and

4. To be a centre for harmonizing the actions of nations in the attainment of these common ends.

Since one of my most vital interests in the United Nations relates to Colonialism – which I want to end without war and the continuance of which is a menace to peace – I must round off this account of the Organization's purposes by quoting Article 73 of the Charter.

Members of the United Nations which have or assume responsibilities for the administration of territories whose peoples have not yet attained a full measure of self-government recognize the principle that the interests of the inhabitants of these territories are paramount, and accept as a sacred trust the obligation to promote to the utmost, within the system of international peace and security established by the present Charter, the well-being of the inhabitants of these territories, and to this end :

(a) To ensure, with due respect for the culture of the peoples concerned, their political, economic, social, and educational advancement, their just treatment, and their protection against abuses ;

(b) To develop self-government, to take due account of the political aspirations of the peoples, and to assist them in the progressive development of their free political institutions, according to the particular circumstances of each territory and its peoples and their varying stages of advancement ;

(c) To further international peace and security ;

(d) To promote constructive measures of development, to encourage research, and to co-operate with one another and, when and where appropriate, with specialized international bodies with a view to the practical achievement of the social economic and scientific purposes set forth in this Article ; and

(e) To transmit regularly to the Secretary-General for information purposes, subject to such limitation as security and constitutional considerations may require, statistical and other information of a technical nature relating to economic, social, and educational conditions in the territories for which they are respectively responsible other than those territories to which Chapters XII and XIII apply.

I never forget that the original League of Nations, in the circumstances that produced it, was a brave and imaginative effort to create the conditions of international amity. Much of the good it did was not ' interred with its bones '. The International Labour Office, for example, brought to fruition half-a-century of toilsome advocacy and struggle to improve social conditions in industrial societies. The I.L.O. survives today, proud forebear of the Food and Agriculture Organization, the World Health Organization, United Nations Educational, Scientific, and Cultural Organization, the Technical Assistance Board, and the various Commissions of the Economic and Social Council, concerned with, among other matters, Human Rights. All the limbs of the United Nations are engaged, and with devoted passion, in lifting mankind nearer to the angels. Add to them the International Court of Justice, an integral part of the United Nations since all member states are *ipso facto* parties to the Statute of the Court. Note, too, the activities of United Nations Agencies seeking to promote the peaceful expansion of atomic energy, international monetary cooperation and exchange stability and international trade.

Criticize these Organizations and Agencies as you may.
Deplore some of the policies laid down for them by their
controllers if you will.   Yet these facts remain: a world civil
service of first-class quality is in being; so too are the means
and the administrative machinery of world unity.   Their
disappearance would plunge mankind into an abyss of hope-
lessness.   Their neglect is a stain on the honour of member
states who willed their creation in response to the moral
opinion of the world, yet refuse to yield up that mere fraction of
national sovereignty which would bring their work to full success.

World Moral Opinion: Fact or Fallacy?

I am always saddened by critics who, in their dislike of the
United Nations, and, especially, of its power to give continuity
to world moral opinion, deny the very existence of that opinion.
In America, these critics as a rule are the enemies of civil rights
for black men.   In Great Britain they were and are supporters
of the Anglo-French undeclared war on Egypt.   The latter
were defeated, magnificently defeated, by world moral opinion,
and their defeat ensured a continuing life for the grand British
ideal of a Commonwealth of Nations.   The former are being
defeated in America because the vast majority of American
citizens find world moral opinion in accord with their own
thoughts and aspirations.

What is beyond all doubt is that, despite the reach and
range of modern communications, there would be neither
a world moral opinion nor the means of expressing it if the
United Nations did not exist.   It is a battle-ground of ideas,
a sounding-board of political, social, and economic theories.
It throws immediate light on evil wherever it is perpetrated,
and on good wherever it is promoted.   It puts the whole of
the world on the map.   It reveals the human fears that divide
men as well as the hopes that can unite them.   Secret diplomacy cannot survive its scrutiny.   If the entire Press of the
world, the television screens, the cinemas, and the radio
stations were dedicated to defending peace and freedom rather
than to making money for their owners, freedom could still
be murdered while good men were asleep.   The United

Nations is humanity's unsleeping watchdog, but a watchdog as yet lacking, alas, the teeth to defend us against the evils which it alone is inclined to expose, and to destroy them.

The explanation is apparent. All nations, and especially the Big Powers, welcome United Nations endorsement of their policies, but at the same time, they refuse to regard the condemnation of their neighbours in the General Assembly as a reason for departing from or changing their policies. Like the giants of the old League of Nations, they seek collective security to protect their national interests but denounce and defy that principle when it defends the national interests of others against them. National interests, in the former case, can be synonymous with profits from oil. Hence the pre-war refusal to apply the oil sanctions, which, certainly, would have stopped Mussolini's rape of Ethiopia and halted Hitler's march to war ; oil sanctions which, today, would certainly help to bring apartheid in South Africa to a speedy end.

Yet another blow to the United Nations is the formation of regional defence pacts, perpetuating the discredited pre-war balance of power on a massive scale while sustaining a potentially explosive confrontation of the major power blocs. There is also the fantastic fact that a decision by, say, Great Britain to apply for membership of the European Common Market is not simply an economic decision ; it implies a military and political decision to line up with one set of powers against another set of powers although nothing is more desired by almost every nation today than the opportunity to do trade across all borders free from political and military strings.

Perhaps the most serious, most urgent aspect of the situation (and one with which I shall deal in the last section of this chapter) is the denial of admission to the United Nations of the People's Republic of China representing 700 million human beings. Quite literally, America alone opposes acceptance of China's application. And the reason ? The American view that China committed aggression against Korea. On this view, it is possible to question whether the United States should be represented at the United Nations after the American adventure of the Bay of Pigs, or the Soviet Union should be represented after Hungary, or the British people should be represented after Suez. Here, as I see it, we reach the very heart of the problem – the veto, the use of which in the most effective organ of the United Nations, the Security Council, enables any one of five powers, acting singly or together, to ignore and frustrate the decisions of representatives of 110 member states.

The Security Council consists of eleven members, each with one representative and one vote. There are five permanent members and six non-permanent members, the latter being elected for a two-year term by a two-thirds majority of the General Assembly. On procedural questions, decisions are made by an affirmative vote of seven out of the eleven members. All other decisions – the vital decisions of principle – require the affirmative vote of seven members to include the con-curring votes of all the permanent members, any one of whom can, if it chooses, veto even a decision agreed by the other ten !

The importance of this power of veto is best measured against the responsibilities of the Security Council to maintain the world's peace and security. The Council can, after con-cluding the necessary agreements, call on the armed forces and facilities of the member states. Its Military Staff Committee consists of the Chiefs of Staff of the five permanent members or their representatives. It is in constant, continuous session.

Let us look at the names of the five – our Big Brothers – in ascending order. There is the island of Taiwan (Formosa) with 11 million inhabitants ; yes, this tiny satellite of America can hold up prosecution of the world's important business at the whim of its dictator ! Then comes France, with a popula-tion of 47 million and an association with the great French community overseas. Great Britain follows, with a population of 51 million and an influence, through the Commonwealth of Nations, covering a population as large as that of the People's Republic of China. Next is the Soviet Union with a population in excess of 200 million and one of the richest economies the world has yet seen. Finally, we have America, with a popula-tion of around 200 million and an economy undoubtedly the richest in history. Within the Security Council, these five are equal, although some are more equal than others !

Permanent membership of the Security Council is the reward of the four original powers – America, Russia, Great Britain, and the island of Taiwan (Formosa) – for their part in creating the 'peace association'. They voluntarily added France, vanquished in World War II, to their number. By virtue of Article 27 of the Charter of the United Nations, as I have noted above, this Big Five must all cast concurring votes for any majority decision of the Council ; otherwise that decision can be rendered void.

This is not dictatorship ; that would imply that the Big Five decide policy and implement it. It is not democracy ; the principle of one vote commanding a power of veto makes a mockery of all other votes. It is the anarchy of sheer farce. It means that the Big Five, including the island of Taiwan, does not have to care in the slightest about any decision of the Council and neither they nor their associates give a tinker's curse for the resolutions of the General Assembly.

The General Assembly, in October 1962, invited the United Kingdom to take steps to secure the lifting of the ban in the Zimbabwe African People's Union and the release of Southern Rhodesian nationalists then in prison. The British Government did nothing. A month later, the General Assembly, by a large majority, condemned apartheid in South Africa. The Union Government, confident that Britain would veto any positive action, thumbed its nose at the United Nations.

We are fumbling, through the United Nations, towards a viable system of world governance over matters of war and peace. I accept this fumbling as inevitable in a human institution seeking to conciliate many conflicting interests and ideas and aspirations. I do not deny that, in the callow youth of the United Nations, the privileged position of the permanent members of the Security Council may have had advantages for a world ravaged by war and in urgent need of a sense of security in the task of overcoming war's cruel aftermath. Surely, however, the Organization can be assumed to have acquired some maturity in the twenty intervening years. Certainly, the fact that one Big Power, Russia, has been able to exercise the veto on 100 occasions points to one conclusion : the longer this fumbling continues, the graver becomes the danger of stumbling into the disaster of nuclear war.

The veto must die if United Nations is to live.

The use and abuse of the veto has bedevilled and confused the continuing debate among people about the United Nations' purposes and policies – a debate which, besides being a continuing expression of world moral opinion, is essential to the clarification and application of these policies. For example, the civilized world hailed the creation of the United Nations peace-keeping force which brought the Suez threat of international conflict under control. Alas, reaction was different when, in response to the invitation of the late Patrice Lumumba, a United Nations peace-keeping force entered Katanga. The Congo, tragically, was turned into a Tom Tiddler's ground for vested colonial interests determined to thwart the will of the Congolese people and defy the growing moral force of the United Nations. A rather similar situation was allowed to develop in Cyprus. These were not failures of the Organization. They were not failures of the vast majority of its member states. They were attempts at sabotage of United Nations decisions by one or other of the power blocs.

Disloyalty of the big powers, however expressed, fosters the conception denied implicitly in every Article of the Atlantic Charter and the Charter of the United Nations: the conception that the Organization was designed to be 'primarily the instrument of the great powers'. This idea, that 105 nations have joined the Organization in order to become satellites or pawns of the Big Five, including Taiwan (Formosa), would be ludicrous if it were not so loaded with menace to the peace of mankind. Yet it is advanced seriously, together with the proposition that the United Nations 'by falling into the hands of scores of small states . . . has forfeited its central role in the shaping of world affairs'.[1]

Let me quote, in reply to this kind of argument, the view of a serious expert student of international law.

'Collective acts of states, repeated by and acquiesced in by sufficient numbers with sufficient frequency, eventually attain the status of law,' writes Mrs Rosalyn Higgins, in her authoritative book.[2] 'The existence of the United Nations – and

---

[1] Paul Johnson in the *Evening Standard*, London, 17 September 1963.

[2] *The Development of International Law through the Political Organs of the United Nations*, Oxford University Press, 1963, p. 2.

A.G.R.—8

especially its accelerated trend towards universality of member-ship since 1955 – now provides a very clear, very concentrated, focal point for state practice.' Obviously, problems of status, internal methods of determining the form of government and similar matters must be considered by the United Nations in dealing with applications for admission. To deny the uni-versality of the Organization, however, is to deny the usefulness of the long, patient and often painful progress of the world towards security and the peace in which to enjoy it.

I regard the attempt to deny the principle of universality as part and parcel of the propaganda campaign to keep colonialism and its evils off the agenda of world business. This propaganda seeks to establish the case that the tremendous human issues involved in apartheid are not a proper subject for international debate and decision, and that they have become so only through the illegitimate pressure of the Afro-Asian countries. If this were true – and *The Times* was per-sisting in assuming its truth as recently as February 1962[1] – there would be no place in the United Nations for developing countries. The Organization would deserve the sneer of 'thieves' kitchen' hurled at the old League of Nations by Communists and Nazis up till 1939.

Happily, it is not true. I cite Mrs Higgins again. ' In the early stages, when the facts still required clarification and constructive suggestions had yet to be made, reports were prepared by the United Nations Commission on the Racial Situation in the Union of South Africa, which found that the racial policies of the Union " are contrary to the United Nations Charter and to the Universal Declaration of Human Rights ".' The Assembly then noted ' with apprehension the adoption of new laws and regulations by the Union Govern-ment, which, in the Commission's view are also incompatible with the obligations of that Government under the Charter '. Thus as early as 1954 the Assembly was taking upon itself to criticize the laws of a member country – a subject normally reserved to the domestic domain – because they contravened the Charter provisions on human rights. *It might be noted also* [and the italics are mine to emphasize Mrs Higgin's statement

[1] 15 February 1962.

of the fact] *that this action of the Assembly occurred considerably before the so-called ' anti-colonial ' era – a phrase currently much in favour in certain countries as an explanation for adverse United Nations decisions in human-rights matters.* The assumption that United Nations jurisdiction in these matters is a mere political re-flection of the growing influence of the Afro-Asian bloc, and devoid of legal basis, must be rejected as facile and inaccurate.[1]

Having nailed the propaganda lie, I gladly affirm that events since have reflected the growing influence of the Afro-Asian bloc and the leadership they are giving to world moral opinion.

Our brothers in South Africa, and in all African territories still under colonial domination, are the victims of a brutal racial totalitarianism. For us to stand aside would be treason, not only to our brothers, but to the peace of our beloved Mother Africa and of all people everywhere.

THE MARCH OF EVENTS

Observe, now, the march of events which we are proud to have influenced.

In 1956 the General Assembly again denounced South African policy as contrary to Article 55 of the Charter which reads :

> With a view to the creation of conditions of stability and well-being which are necessary for peaceful and friendly relations among nations based on respect for the principle of equal rights and self-determination of peoples, the United Nations shall promote :
>
> (a) Higher standards of living, full employment, and condi-tions of economic and social progress and development ;
>
> (b) Solutions of international economic, social, health, and related problems : and international cultural and educa-tional co-operation ; and
>
> (c) Universal respect for, and observance of human rights and fundamental freedoms for all without distinction as to race, sex, language, or religion.

In 1957 and 1958 stronger resolutions were approved.

[1] Higgins, *op. cit.*, p. 120.

In 1961 the Assembly called upon South Africa to bring its conduct ' into conformity with its obligations ' and, for the first time, requested member states ' to consider taking separate and collective action . . . to bring about the abandonment of these policies '.

In 1962 the Assembly endorsed the use of sanctions. Member states were asked to break off diplomatic relations with South Africa, to close their ports to South African ships, to forbid their own ships to enter South African ports, to boycott South African goods, and to refrain from exporting goods to that country, including arms and ammunition. The Security Council was urged to take appropriate action, to apply sanctions and, if necessary, to consider the expulsion of South Africa from the United Nations.

What, then, is the world waiting for ? For United Nations leadership ? Or for honest observance by some powers – mainly Western Powers – of their solemn treaty obligations ?

The first result of the formation of the Organization of African Unity at Addis Ababa in May 1963, was that Colonialism assumed a more urgent importance at the United Nations. Under the heading, ' Africa's U.N. Year ', *West Africa* noted that the Security Council is being enlarged from 11 to 15 to accommodate three specifically African seats and commented : ' This sort of advance is typical of the results which the African nations' diplomatic offensive in the wake of Addis have produced.'[1]

West Africa went on to argue that the two votes in the Security Council on banning the sale of arms to South Africa (7 August and 4 December) brought a creditable list of nations willing to ban all arms, including America and, more recently, Switzerland. The difficulties of British ministers in Parliament over the supply of spare parts for Saracen tanks ' shows that there is more ground that can easily be taken '.

These Security Council votes are worthy of more detailed discussion against the background of our intensified action on behalf of our people in South Africa. I quote at length from the authoritative book by Colin and Margaret Legum.[2]

[1] 28 December 1963.
[2] *South Africa : Crisis for the West*, Pall Mall Press, 1964, pp. 236 *et seq.*

By 1963, impatience over South Africa's failure to respond positively to international moral pressure swelled to a crescendo. It marked the end of seventeen years of verbal condemnation and the beginning of the demand for concerted action. It also marked a new attitude to the Western nations' equivocal policies. For the first time the independent African States embarked on collective action, by making a *démarche* on the Security Council in July 1963, in support of their decisions at the Addis Ababa summit conference the previous May. The result was that the Security Council resolution of August 1963 went beyond ordinary condemnation. It called on member nations to stop selling arms, ammunition and military vehicles to South Africa. And it called on the South African authorities to release all opponents of the apartheid system imprisoned or restricted for their political views. Nine members, including the United States and Norway, voted for the resolution ; only Britain and France abstained. Britain argued that its existing defence agreements, including that for the Simonstown base, excluded the possibility of a total arms embargo ; but its delegate added that no arms were, or would be, sold to South Africa if they could be used to perpetuate apartheid. The Western nations, including the United States, emphasized that they did not regard the resolution as binding upon them. Since they refused to consider that South Africa's policies represent an actual threat to the peace, *the measures proposed were taken to* be recommendations under Chapter 6 of the Charter.[1]

A few weeks later, on 11 October, the General Assembly passed a resolution specifically related to the Johannesburg trial of African and other opposition leaders in South Africa ; it asked member states to ' make all necessary efforts ' to induce South Africa to end the trial, release all political prisoners and end the ' repression of persons opposing apartheid '. Only South Africa and Portugal voted against ; and this time there were no abstentions. Two months later the General Assembly again considered the South African question. It asked all member states to carry out the provisions for sanctions referred to in the Security Council's August resolution and to provide aid, through the United Nations, for the victims of apartheid and their dependents. Again, there were no abstentions, and again only South Africa and Portugal voted against.

[1] Chapter 6 provides for the Pacific Settlement of Disputes by Mediation, Conciliation, etc.

Meanwhile, on 4 December, the Security Council had passed a unanimous resolution with a dual purpose : to increase international pressure upon South Africa, and to reassure white South Africans that the United Nations was concerned for their security in a future non-racial state. This dual formula, presented by Norway, was inspired by the five Nordic countries. They had embarked in the middle of 1963 on a significant role in international affairs by taking a Western initiative in the South African problem. The resolution widened the existing scope of sanctions recommended, to proposing the banning of exports to the Republic of machinery for the manufacture of arms. It also appointed ' a small group of experts to examine methods of resolving the present situation in South Africa through full, peaceful and orderly application of human rights . . . to all inhabitants of the territory as a whole . . . and to consider what part the UN might play in the achievement of that end '. The United States announced it had already extended its ban to include machinery for the manufacture of arms : but Britain and France again drew a distinction between arms (and machinery) for use in enforcing apartheid which they agreed they would not supply – and those needed for external defence, which they proposed to continue selling to South Africa.

Thus the point is long since passed when it is useful to argue whether or not the United Nations has a ' right ' to condemn South Africa's domestic policies. The world community has decided that apartheid is part of its business. What is not yet agreed is whether the situation in South Africa constitutes a threat to world peace . . . more than two-thirds of UN members take the view that apartheid represents a threat to peace, and that Chapter 7 should be invoked.[1] They argue that apartheid is a constant provocation to all coloured peoples, that its outcome must be a race war, and that such a war could not be confined to South Africa. The Asian nations, the Soviet bloc, Yugoslavia, most of the Latin America countries, several Western nations (notably the Scandinavian countries) as well as the African states, see this incipient race war as an active threat to world peace, and one which can only escalate with time. Despite their majority, Chapter 7 has not been specifically invoked because the Security

---

[1] Chapter 7, Article 42 provides, as a last resort that the Security Council ' may take such action by air, sea and land forces as may be necessary to maintain or restore international peace and security '. Such action is subject to the veto.

Council has not found it expedient to risk a Western veto if it is pressed. It has preferred instead to strike bargains, the West giving a little more each time, and to rely meanwhile on recommendations.

Most dramatic of our 1963 successes was in arousing the nations to a realization of the prospect that the reactionary administration of Southern Rhodesia, following the breakdown of the Central African Federation, was likely to secure its independence from the United Kingdom Government. Fortified by the requests of the General Assembly that Great Britain should secure for people under its authority in Southern Rhodesia the elementary right to vote and by the demand of the Addis Ababa Conference that Britain should not transfer to a foreign racial minority in the Colony ' the attributes of sovereignty ', my country raised the question at the Security Council. Only one vote was cast against our resolution. The British delegate, routed factually, logically and morally in the debate, was completely isolated.

At the United Nations Economic Committee International Conference on Trade and Development, in June 1964, the redressing of the balance between the ' haves ' and the ' have-nots ' among the nations strode on to the world stage as the problem of problems.

And the principles of action upon which these victories were scored ? They were set out in proposals for the reform and strengthening of the United Nations approved by the Addis Ababa Heads of State Conference as follows :

> Believing that the United Nations is an important instrument for the maintenance of peace and security among nations and for the promotion of the economic and social advancement of all peoples ;
> Reiterating its desire to strengthen and support the United Nations ;
> Noting with regret that Africa as a region is not equitably represented in the principal organs of the United Nations ;
> Convinced of the need for closer co-operation and co-ordination among the African State Members of the United Nations ;
> The Summit Conference of Independent African States meeting in Addis Ababa, Ethiopia, from 22 May to 25 May 1963,

(1) *Reaffirms* its decision to the purposes and principles of the United Nation's Charter and its acceptance of all obligations contained in the Charter, including financial obligations ;

(2) *Insists* that Africa as a geographical region should have equitable representation in the principal organs of the United Nations, particularly the Security Council and the Economic and Social Council and its Specialized Agencies ;

(3) *Invites* African Governments to instruct their representatives in the United Nations to take all possible steps to achieve a more equitable representation of the African region ;

(4) *Further invites* African Governments to instruct their representatives in the United Nations, without prejudice to their membership in and collaboration with the Afro-Asian Group, to constitute a more effective African Group with a permanent secretariat to bring about closer co-operation and better co-operation in matters of common concern.

In Unity, indeed, is our strength.

Confirming Our Faith

Let me now place on record the quiet, almost unobserved movement of world opinion which finds expression in the Organization and which confirms my unfaltering faith in its future.

In 1948, when there were only eight Asian and three African members[1] of the United Nations, India forced upon the attention of the first session of the General Assembly the racial discrimination under which Indians were suffering in the Union of South Africa. The first resolution relating, in general terms, to apartheid, was passed in 1952 ; that was eight years before the independent states of Africa began to acquire any real voice in the affairs of the Organization. By October 1963, there were on record 27 General Assembly resolutions and two Security Council resolutions condemning apartheid.

Early in the long debate, Sweden argued that the Assembly had no right to request alterations in the domestic laws of a

[1] Egypt, Ethiopia, and Liberia.

member state. The United Kingdom went further ; it denied
the Assembly's authority even to discuss such matters. By
1958, Sweden was agreed that the United Nations had both a
right and a duty to discuss racial discrimination in South
Africa. In that same year, moreover, a group of states which
had hitherto abstained from voting, now supported resolutions
condemning South Africa – America, Peru, Italy, New Zealand,
Argentina and, in 1959, Finland.

At the 1959 Assembly, former opponents of the resolutions
– Australia and Belgium – became abstainers.

At the 1960 Assembly, the United Kingdom deployed a
change of line. It decided that, while its previous objections
had lost none of their force, the situation on apartheid was now
sufficiently *sui generis* for draft resolutions to be considered on
their merits: the United Kingdom might even see its way to
abstaining on a moderate resolution! Of course, the United
Kingdom and France, faithful to their unity over Suez, stood
together and alone in voting against the Security Council's
condemnation of the horrific Sharpeville shootings.

Back at the Assembly in 1961, South Africa had only one
public friend – Portugal, its fellow felon in the practice of racial
totalitarianism.

So world moral opinion acquires the force and fervour of
moral law. To speed up this process, above all, to translate
moral law into legal, political action – that is the task upon
which all our activities, our energies, and our passion must now
be concentrated.

This giant's task requires the removal of the built-in weaknesses of the Organization and the end of conditions which
enable recalcitrant powers to ignore and defy its policies.

THE VETO: VEHICLE OF DISTRUST

Most important of these built-in weaknesses, as I have argued
above, is the veto, available to the five ' permanent members '
of the Security Council. They can, and do, walk out of the
Council and return according to whim. They appear to
determine issues in terms of their conflicting ideologies.
Appealing nations presume that their propositions have to be

represented in relation to the national and ideological idio-
syncrasies of the Big Five rather than on their merits. These
suspicions, I believe, are unfair and unjust to men as devoted
to the cause of peace as any other group of men. Yet they are
encouraged by the existence of the veto which adds a ridiculous
dimension to votes and voices that should be making decisions
as equals with their non-permanent colleagues. The veto, far
from being an instrument of power and stability, is a vehicle of
distrust damaging to the United Nations and all its works.

I endorse without equivocation the view that, if the Security
Council is to be effective, its decisions must be made quickly.
To pacify a situation that has arisen is more important than to
discover and observe meticulously any traditional law about
the matter in dispute. I agree, therefore, that there must be a
substantial majority for any resolutions committing all member
states to a course of action which might involve military action.
The established principle of a two-thirds majority should
supplant the veto, and give the Security Council real authority
and dignity in the discharge of its responsibilities.

The intemperate use of the veto is gradually but surely
lowering the dignity and command of the Security Council.
It has brought about situations in which the General Assembly,
impelled by dissatisfaction at this reactionary system, has
reclaimed certain matters from the ambit of the Security
Council, and decided them itself upon the resolution of an
adequate majority. Whereas the veto could compel thorough-
ness in the discussion of certain important issues, it has increasingly been used as an instrument of partisanship to
thwart and frustrate the will and action of the nations of the
world. The increasing misuse of the veto is already beginning
to raise in many minds doubts concerning the practical value
of its retention. From the point of view of the theoretical
equality of member states of the United Nations, its retention
is indefensible.

Second only to the veto as a dividing element is the refusal
of admission to China, a mighty republic now carrying out all
the world-wide obligations of a great state, and a state whose
exclusion means that the Organization is not, and cannot be,
fully representative of world opinion. The Chinese application

was not assisted by the fact that, in proposing it, the Soviet bloc demanded also the expulsion of Formosa. Formosans, like the rest of us, are people with a right to live and to be heard among the nations of this earth. I cannot believe, however, that the passage of time has not erased many of the emotions which, fourteen long years ago, were inflamed by China's aggression against Korea. That aggression was not cancelled out by the later aggressions of the four of the permanent members against Egypt, Hungary, and Cuba. It was not even mitigated by the truth that, whereas the permanent members aggressed while professing to be pillars of the United Nations, China owed no loyalty to the Organization and Korea had no valid claim to its protection. Yet these are vain quibbles in the face of humanity's urgent need to wipe the slate clean in a new bid for the world unity to which China, like the other great powers, can contribute so greatly.

Emphatically, the passage of time has settled the paramount consideration of entry to the United Nations: the consideration that the People's Republic is the effective government in China. It is in complete command of all the resources of the area for which it seeks representation. While – and I mention this fact reluctantly and only by way of contrast – the Formosa government is among the perpetually tardy payers of their budget contributions, the Organization, in its dealings with China, has found the People's Republic a satisfactory collaborator. Certainly, United Nations opinion, as I can testify from first-hand knowledge, is convinced that the participation of China is essential if ever disarmament is to be achieved. It is agreed, too, that the United Nations cannot deny for all time to come the legality of revolutionary changes throughout the world; a finally successful internal conquest clearly changes title to a territory.

There is a problem of national prestige involved to which only China can give the answer. Both the Republic and Formosa have found unacceptable the proposal that, since both exercise jurisdiction in their territories *de facto*, both should be recognized by the United Nations as exercising jurisdiction *de jure*. *De jure* recognition would leave for further consideration the problem of deciding which government is the legal successor to the pre-1949 China and, consequently, which China should sit among the permanent members of the Security Council with the right to exercise the veto. Removal of the veto would help to answer this controversial question.

I am persuaded that China inside the United Nations would never have contemplated diverting the resources she needs in building her new society to the manufacture of nuclear weapons. I am confident that, within the Organization and playing her full part in its many constructive agencies, China could even now be induced to renounce that vile deterrent.

Yet another problem, which caused a miserable deadlock in the 1964–5 meeting of the General Assembly, is the political management and financing of the United Nations peace-keeping forces. The Organization's magnificent initiative and triumph in the Suez crisis revealed that these forces are absolutely indispensable. Experience in the Congo and elsewhere reveals that the operation and control of these forces still presents unsolved problems. My plea for reform would be unnecessary if member states would be faithful to the purposes of what is called ' the international army '. The agonizing fact, alas, is that some powers refuse to recognize and obey the United Nations line of command even when they accept in principle the employment of the peace-keeping forces.

We in Africa believe we have found an answer. The Organization of African Unity is ready to create its own peace-keeping force within the African continent and to operate it faithfully in accordance with the principles of the United Nations. This proposal, however, requires that machinery must be devised at Security Council level to ensure that the Council's rule of law shall be observed by all other member states and that, once a decision is taken, there shall be no interference by non-African powers pursuing their aggressive policies against Africa and the peace of nations.

The independent states of Africa are fully prepared to make their African Defence Force the instrument of United Nations authority. There is encouraging evidence that other nations are willing to do likewise – i.e. to yield up a fraction of their national sovereignty in order to render effective the power and influence of the United Nations to stop local conflict that might develop into widespread war. Surely the grand contributions made by Canada, Sweden, Norway, India and other nations to peace-keeping activities since 1956 must rank in the history of these troubled times as a gesture of dedication to the ideal of collective action for collective security. The will for peace exists. Power to exercise that will must be rendered realistic through the Security Council. Power to stop the supply of arms to peace-breakers and to ensure their supply, in full measure, to the peace-keeping forces ; power to withdraw from mercenaries in search of private gain and from political wire-pullers the protection now afforded them by the civil law of states not involved directly in the conflict but eager to subvert the policies of the United Nations.

Modern science is conquering all the problems involved in the detection and inspection of nuclear weapons. Inspection and control of conventional arms, if the Security Council is equipped with the necessary authority, will become a matter of administration – and of the life of the Organization and everything that it represents. I regard this matter, in some respects, as of more immediate importance than the control of the deterrent.

The nations have gone a long way towards unifying mutual aid and technical assistance for developing countries. They are readier than ever before to formulate joint policies for stimulating the growth of trade which would enable developing countries to command the resources to the extent which will make their progress feasible. As I have said earlier in this book, I want to see all these great schemes funnelled through and administered by the United Nations. Some of the machinery is there. An international civil service is in being. Coordination would be economic. It would speed up help for the hungry, galvanize the whole, the inevitable, world process of raising living standards. No question of national sovereignty arises in directing the world's generosity through the one supra-national Organization already capable of doing the job.

These reasons are cogent and compelling. Even more important, they enable us, by making mutual aid, technical assistance and cooperation in finance and trade a principle of world policy, to smother and destroy the danger of their exploitation as armaments in the idiotic ideological conflict.

On the eve of the 1964 General Election in Great Britain, Mr R. A. Butler, then Foreign Secretary, made a noble plea to his fellow citizens to intensify the war on want – in order, he said, to prevent the spread of Communism. What an ignoble reason for a noble plea ! The business of abolishing hunger is part of the human adventure of freeing men and women everywhere to choose and follow their own way of life. The starving child does not ask : Is this a Red glass of milk ? Is that a Red, White and Blue bag of meal ? My own people – and they are typical of people everywhere – would sooner starve in freedom than be the affluent pawns of ideological overlords, whether they call themselves Capitalists or Communists or Flat Earthers or anything else. We have not fought and died to destroy Colonialism in order to become the subjects of neo-Colonialism. And neo-colonialism is the shortest name for the ideological subjugation of one people by another. Our problem in Africa is not that we do not know what to think. We have no need of anyone exporting ideology to us. Our problem is one of action, of carrying out those innumerable, complex, and co-ordinated acts which will transform us into a prosperous society.

I pose this question to the developed nations as a test of their morality and conscience. Do they desire to relieve hunger in order merely to serve their own national interests or is it in order to alleviate human misery ? Is their attempt to relieve human poverty merely a not-so-clever act of spreading their alien ideology, or a human deed aimed at the reduction of that colossal misery and despair still persisting in the lives of a majority of the children, women, and men now inhabiting our world ?

I know the answer every good citizen of every country will give. To them, the United Nations is the keeper of everyman's conscience. Yes, it is that, or nothing.

THE SUPREME ISSUE

For Africans the supreme issue of the immediate future is the racial totalitarianism of the Union of South Africa.

Some non-African commentators see this as a make-or-break issue for the United Nations itself. Colin and Margaret Legum, for example, argue that ' if the United Nations were to retreat over South Africa it would repeat the rout which followed the League of Nations' abdication over Ethiopia. Appeasement on great moral issues can only weaken the world along all the fronts where the battles for human rights are waged.'[1]

Certainly, when the citadel of terror in South Africa falls – a terror as corrupt and degrading as Hitler's treatment of the Jews in Nazi Germany – the pip-squeak dictators in Salisbury and Lisbon will also collapse, and all Africa will be free. I do not doubt that the end of apartheid will be welcomed by hundreds of thousands of white South Africans, of Dutch as well as British origin. Thousands of them are identified with freedom's cause now. Thousands more do not wear proudly the badge of the ' skunk of the world ' – to quote *Die Burger*[2] pinned on them by the villanies of the Verwoerd régime. All are in the grip of a tiny political and economic bureaucracy as mad and bad as the clique that went snarling to its death with Hitler. Once that grip is broken, I believe the vision described by Chief Luthuli in his Nobel Peace Prize speech of 1961 will be realized and without violence:

> In government we will not be satisfied with anything less than direct individual adult suffrage and the right to stand for and be elected to all organs of government.
> In economic matters we will be satisfied with nothing less than equality of opportunity in every sphere, and the enjoyment by all of those heritages which form the resources of the country which up to now have been appropriated on a racial ' Whites only ' basis.
> In culture, we will be satisfied with nothing less than the

[1] *South Africa : Crisis for the West*, op. cit., p. 257.
[2] 24 March 1960.

opening of all doors of learning in non-segregatory institutions on the sole criterion of ability.

In the social sphere we will be satisfied with nothing less than the abolition of all racial bars.

We do not demand these things for people of African descent alone. We demand them for all South Africans, White and Black. On these principles we are uncompromising.

I am confident that, while some member states will drag their feet, the United Nations as a whole will refuse to falter before the responsibilities it must face within the next few months. Why, even the British at the General Assembly, have described apartheid as ' abhorrent ', although Sir Alec Douglas Home, former Secretary of State for Foreign Affairs and former Prime Minister, reflecting the mood and spirit of a seventeenth-century feudalist, argues that the threat apartheid offers to world peace is not the fault of its perpretators but of its victims! To Americans, apartheid is ' toxic '; to Indians ' hateful '; to Belgians ' thoroughly repugnant '; to Bolivians ' the negation of all social purpose '; to Japanese ' fundamentally immoral '. These words and phrases were all used in the General Assembly debate of October 1963. Tanganyika, on the same occasion, summed up the situation for all Africans in these words: ' a catalyst of violence '.[1]

Apartheid is a ' catalyst of violence ' not only because it sentences millions of Africans to live and work in brutish conditions but also because it seeks to perpetuate these conditions and to destroy all human hope of amelioration and progress. The many generic groupings of Indian, Malayan, Zulu, Xhosa, Hottentot, British, Afrikaner, and so on matter little in South Africa. All important is the answer to this question: *Are you White, Coloured, or Native?* It settles forever a man's status and way of life. The system of classification was given force of law by the Population Registration Act of 1950, which provided that

(*a*) A ' White ' person means a person who in appearance obviously is, or who is generally accepted as, a White person, but does not include a person who, although in appearance obviously a White, is generally accepted as a Coloured person;

[1] Cited in *South Africa : Crisis for the West, op. cit.*, p. 235.

(*b*) ' Native ' means a person who in fact is, or is generally accepted as a member of any aboriginal race or tribe of Africa;

(*c*) A ' Coloured ' person means a person who is not a ' White person ' or a ' Native '.

In 1956 it was found necessary to pass an amendment as follows:

' A person who in appearance obviously is a member of an aboriginal race or tribe of Africa shall, for the purposes of this Act, be presumed to be a Native unless it is proved that he is not in fact and is not generally accepted as such.'

In 1959 the Coloured sub-groups were classified in greater detail. In 1960 the word ' white ' had to be redefined and, finally, in March 1962, a bill was passed declaring as White ' a person who is obviously White in appearance and not generally accepted as Coloured, or one who is generally accepted as White though not obviously White in appearance.'

The Minister of the Interior is reported to have said of the original definitions set out in the Registration Act of 1950 that until then, many people had passed ' all their lives in a state of unease because it was uncertain to which racial group they belonged. But now, after the enactment of the Population Registration Act certainty had been given, and the clouds which hovered over them had disappeared.' The need for so many changes prove that the clouds of uncertainty are still very much in evidence. The classification system is closely linked with the Immorality Act prohibiting mixed marriages, and a cause of extreme hardship for the children of illegal unions. A child so born is classified as Coloured. While young, he will be brought up with his mother, presuming she is an African, but once he reaches the age of having his own identity card, he is forced to live with his ' own ' people in a Coloured area. He has no roots there. He becomes one of ' God's step-children '.

In November 1961, a family of eight appealed against being classified as Coloured. The six children, aged between seven and eighteen years, were paraded in court before Mr Justice Snyman, who remarked : ' This is an unhappy position for a judge to be in . . . I am in no better position than any other South African to judge whether people are obviously white in appearance.' Until they were classified, this family had been accepted as white. The children went to white schools. The father was served in public bars, and had been treated in hospital as a white man. The Classification Board case, however, was that young children who appeared to be white were apt to become more coloured in appearance as they grew older ! The judge, contemptuous of the argument, demanded : ' How dare I say so ? How do I know this is so ? Have you anything to assist me ? Any authorities ? ' The attempt at legalized blackmail failed, and the family was declared to be white. White, also, according to a judicial decision noted by *The Times* of London in a leader entitled ' Whiter Still and Whiter ' on 27 November 1961, are the Japanese ! This although the Chinese are classified as Coloured !

The effect of the Immorality Act in promoting racial purity may be assessed from the facts of convictions in the eleven years following its passage. These numbered 3,980. It is known that, after serving sentence, most of the victims of this horrible Act re-unite to enjoy their illegal consortium openly and defiantly, although within the lowest classification group open to them.

No facet of life escapes the rigid application of apartheid. Directly, it affects movement, residence, the right to own land, education, employment, trade unions. Indirectly, it affects family relationships, crime and delinquency, health and mortality rates.

Africans are detribalized, shifted and shunted from one Reserve to another, from one township to another, torn from loved ones to undergo forced labour hundreds of miles from their shacks. Their lives are surrounded by inhuman vexations and maddening regulations. Take, for example, the pass laws, re-inforced by the Natives' (Abolition of Passes and Co-ordination of Documents) Act, 1952. This made it necessary for all Africans over the age of 16 years to carry a ' reference book ' containing documentary evidence such as tax receipts and employment contracts. The Act extended the pass system to women. Failure to carry his pass on his person and produce it on demand renders the African liable to summary arrest.

Between 1951 and 1962 convictions under the pass laws totalled 4,272,000 ! Few Africans pay the fine or serve the imprisonment prescribed. Instead, convicted persons are 'offered' the chance of 'tholing their assize' by working for starvation rates of pay on farms. South African newspapers abound with accounts of these hell-holes or slave farms and the sub-human level of existence that obtains on them.

An African must live where the authorities determine. In some 'white areas' Africans are an economic necessity ; they may reside in such areas as long as the economic need persists and the Africans themselves are capable of work. Frequently, the worker is confined to 'Bachelors' Quarters'. His wife may be permitted to visit him for 72 hours if she can convince the authorities that she is anxious to conceive. Uneconomic Africans are relegated to the Reserves. These Reserves cover approximately 12 per cent of all the land in South Africa 'saved' from the rapacity of the 'Whites' and allocated to the rest of the population. The 'Bantustan' philosophy, legalized by the Group Areas Act, 1950, provides for the proclamation of certain group areas which are then the 'home' of a particular group of people, classified by race. No member of another race may own immovable property there, or live there. Areas already occupied by Africans are often not recognized, but proclaimed group areas for other races. Then the Africans are forced to leave, without compensation for the losses, of property and trade, entailed in their uprooting.

The Bantu Education Act of 1953 is the personal creation of Dr Verwoerd. It reflects an image of the man who believes paradoxically but, no doubt, sincerely, that he himself was created in the image of God. Its purpose is to teach all Africans in the future to accept and applaud the wisdom of the doctrines of separateness. When steering his Bill through Parliament, Dr Verwoerd said :

> I take full responsibility for the pegging of the (state) subsidy to native education at £6,500,000 . . . While the European is prepared to make heavy contributions to native education, the native community will have to shoulder their share of the responsibility . . . We do want to indoctrinate the teachers (and children) – if we must use that term – with our spirit, and that is

the belief that they must serve their own people and they must not think that once they are educated they can leave their own people and seek equality with the European . . . The native teachers must be trained in training schools under our control.

In 1954, this leader who claims to walk in the steps of the Man of Sorrows declared that ' the Bantu teacher . . . must learn not to feel above his community, with a consequent desire to become integrated into the life of the European community '. His most infamous utterance, made in 1953, was this : ' What is the use of teaching the Bantu child mathematics when it cannot use it in practice ? That is quite absurd . . . Education must train and teach people in accordance with their opportunities in life, according to the sphere in which they live.' If Dr Verwoerd lives in history, it will be as the man who tried to blow out the lamp within the Bantu brain. If I did not feel personally and acutely the sufferings of the parents of African children, I would address him in the agonizing, haunting words of Robert Browning :

> ' Go practise if you please
> With men and women : leave a child alone
> For Christ's particular love's sake ! '

Education of African children is not compulsory. Only 30 per cent receive any kind of formal education.

The Extension (*sic*) of University Education Act, 1959, provided that, after 1 January 1960, the only universities open to Africans are the Xhosa College, the Zulu College, and the Sotho Tswana College, where only tribal languages are used as the medium of instruction. Separate colleges are to be established for Asians and Coloured. Education syllabuses are vetted according to the role the ' privileged ' students are expected to play in later life as indoctrinated followers of apartheid. There is scant hope of any student receiving a passport should he be offered a university place outside the Union.

So all is clear. The purpose of Bantu education is to condition Africans to accept without question their inferior status, to accept without protest a wage permanently below subsistence level, to accept exclusion by statute from certain types of work and all the more skilled professions and occupations. An African can be born in a manger, but he cannot be a carpenter. The pass system prevents movement from job to job, frustrates the inevitable desire to flee the economically overburdened Reserves and rural areas in the hope of finding employment in the cities. The large number of poor whites embarrasses the government and is one reason why Africans are excluded from an increasing number of semi-skilled and unskilled jobs. Industrialists are forbidden to increase African wages, as many of them would like to do, because the whites measure their superiority by the gap between their standard of living and that of the Africans; a rise for Africans would mean a rise for the whites.

I can think of nothing closer to my idea of hell than growing to manhood as a detribalized African in South Africa, especially in a shanty town, probably the only place where one could live. All the savage hurts of oppression are intensified by starvation, bodily, mental, and cultural. The shanty town is really an open prison. The boy growing to manhood there is a native of an alien-occupied country. He is made to feel that the sooner he is out of the way, either in work or in the grave, the better it will be for his peace of mind.

Yet noble men and women, by the thousand, rise above the degradation that is South Africa today. They give their people leadership to a free and better future. Their faith and sacrifice, and their assured triumph, gives glory to the human spirit.

The crunch must come soon. The question at issue will be the future of South West Africa, of which South Africa was the mandatory power under League of Nations auspices following the defeat of Germany in World War I. South Africa exploited the disappearance of the League of Nations to claim that, since the second party to the mandate agreement no longer existed, South African responsibility to the international community had lapsed, and that the Union alone would decide the fate of the former German territory. As long ago as 1950 the International Court of Justice gave the first of one advisory and two supplementary opinions on the points in dispute.

These opinions stated that South Africa was not obliged to place South West Africa – where the Union was the first imperialist power to resort to mass-terror bombing of unarmed populations – under the trusteeship system. Nonetheless, the Court decided, South Africa was not entitled to alter the international status of the territory except with the agreement of the United Nations, and the Organization has the right of supervision over the administration of the territory as long as it does not exceed the supervision formerly exercised by the League of Nations Mandates Commission.

The Union has ignored these opinions and pieces of advice. It has terrorized the Herreros. It has perpetuated the German plunder of tribal lands and reduced the area of land available to the local inhabitants. It has imposed upon all of them the evils of apartheid.

Now the compulsory jurisdiction of the International Court has been invoked by Ethiopia and Liberia, both former members of the League of Nations. In 1960, they asked the Court to declare that South Africa must cease forthwith the practice of apartheid in South West Africa. The procedure chosen makes the Court's judgement binding on both parties and places upon the Security Council the task of enforcing the judgement. The case stated by Ethiopia and Liberia is summed up in the following extracts from their reply to South Africa's counter-memorial and submitted to the Court in October 1964.[1]

> . . . under apartheid, the accident of birth imposes a mandatory life sentence to discrimination, repression and humiliation. It is, accordingly, in violation of Respondent's obligation, as stated in Article 2, paragraph 2 of the Mandate, to promote to the utmost the well-being and social progress of the inhabitants. The policy of apartheid, moreover, is repugnant to the objectives and requirement of Article 22 of the Covenant of the League of Nations.

Ethiopia and Liberia also argue that the territorial apartheid projected by South Africa for the mandated territory:

> is not, in any meaningful sense, based upon consultation with, or consent of, the governed, whose well-being and social progress

[1] *The Times*, 15 October 1964.

form Respondent's sacred trust.   Such failure of consultation or consent achieves an even more pointed significance in the light of Respondent's failure and refusal to consult with the United Nations, or in any other manner to report to the international organ vested with supervisory authority by the Mandate instrument.   Even more, Respondent has rejected the overwhelming consensus of the United Nations membership that its policy of apartheid in general, including ' territorial apartheid ' (i.e. Bantu homelands), its most extreme form of application, is unsound, inhumane, and incompatible with the obligations of the Mandate.

If the Court decides against South Africa, the Security Council must act.   If South Africa answers by clearing out of South West Africa, its policy of apartheid will fall into disarray, an admitted as well as an obvious failure.

VERWOERD'S WAR-MONGERS

All the signs are that the Verwoerd clique, in defiance of world opinion and of the overt and covert disapproval of very many whites within the Union, and despite the eagerness of all African states to solve the problem by non-violent means, will fight to the bitter end.

Every hope expressed in the optimistic theory of ex-Foreign Minister Eric Louw is being rendered vain.   Hope that the Cold War would intensify; that the Afro-Asian nations would become estranged from the West; that the African states would fail to unite and, instead, attack each other or that their economic problems would so absorb their energies that they would lose their zest for the freedom fight.   In truth, the Cold War has abated.   The West is realizing that it needs the economic and political cooperation of the Afro-Asian countries as much as they need and desire cooperation with the West. The African states are steadily building up their strength and commanding increasing support from their own populations. All of them are committed, although in varying degree, to the idea that the peace and freedom of each of them is endangered while slavery persists in South Africa.

The Verwoerd reply to these stark facts has been to turn

the Union into an armed camp. Defence expenditure increased
five-fold between 1960–1 and 1963–4 ; it stands now at
£125 million a year. A voice of sanity, the Johannesburg
Financial Mail, discussed the 1964 Budget and all its sad
implications in these terms :

> The Minister has resisted pressure group claims for widespread
> tax concessions and has applied most of the current surplus to
> helping finance the bigger spending, mostly on defence, planned
> for next year . . . What does the budget do for the non-white
> group as a whole ? Very little. Yet this group is the poorest
> and weakest. One could have expected a substantial grant out
> of the £44 million surplus towards improving the material lot of
> the non-whites. If anything, the reverse is true. Take the case
> of African education in areas other than the Transkei. There
> the educational subsidy has been severely cut by £1·55 million
> from £8·8 million in 1963–4 to £7·25 million. In a sense, it is,
> ironically, the African who is thus partly paying for the further
> increase in national security expenditure, which has reached a
> massive £124·5 million, made up of £102 million for defence and
> £22·5 million for police. Instead of using part of the rich tax
> harvest to expand educational facilities . . . for the African, and
> to re-invest in him a small part of the great wealth he is helping
> South Africa to produce, the concessions and allowances provided
> for in this budget will benefit primarily white men, business men,
> shareholders, and property-seekers.[1]

The Union, quite deliberately, is seeking to start a race war,
a war from which the world dare not stand aside. In these
conditions, only two alternatives present themselves : international intervention outside the framework of the United
Nations, or collective action – that is, the rigorous application
of economic sanctions – through the United Nations.

Colin and Margaret Legum, both of them South African
born, describe the lurid prospect with which international
intervention outside the framework of the United Nations
might bring the world face-to-face and, although I do not
endorse all their views, especially about the possibility of
the Cold War spreading to Africa, they must be respected as
well-informed and honest witnesses.

[1] 20 March 1964.

Such intervention, they argue,

holds great dangers for black and white South Africans, for Africa itself, for the United Nations, and for the West . . . The non-white underground in the Republic will become stronger and violence will mount. The African states will increase their economic and military support for the underground, while at the same time intensifying their pressures on the West in support of international action. Much of the effective military and financial aid will come from Russia and China, each pursuing its own separate interests . . . When the situation reaches the point where the black underground can begin to operate effectively, the chances of arranging a truce to discuss a reasonable basis for settlement will have been lost. The African military leadership's demand for ' all or nothing ' will be irresistible, as it was in Algeria by the end of the seven-year war there. There would be little chance of a peaceful settlement in which the country's three million whites could rebuild their lives in a non-racial society . . . The second alternative open to the world – acceptance of collective action against South Africa through the United Nations – may be the only way to avoid catastrophe. The major Western countries who are alone in obstructing this solution should actively support such a policy. Whatever transitional losses might result, especially for Britain, will be marginal compared with what they stand to lose by fiddling with their cash registers while the faggots of South Africa's pyre are being stacked.[1]

The British stake in South Africa is substantial. I do not refer to the Simonstown naval base which, in the nuclear age, retains very little of the value it once had. I refer to the financial investment, estimated at around £900 million, which British big business refuses to understand is threatened seriously by apartheid and by everything the Verwoerd régime represents. In 1963 the South African Foundation, an apartheid propaganda agency, induced the National Association of British Manufacturers to address to British businessmen a booklet entitled ' The British Stake in South Africa '. The argument runs : ' Whatever view of South Africa's political and racial problems is held by the individual, one fact he cannot escape : the large industrial stake the people of Britain

[1] Legum, *op. cit.*, pp. 258–60.

hold in the Republic. This booklet . . . is also intended to emphasize the damage that could befall the peoples of Great Britain and South Africa if the demand from certain quarters for a trade boycott was satisfied . . . in any case, the first to suffer would be those a boycott is supposed to help – the non-Europeans.'[1]   This anxiety for the fate of non-Europeans, a vast number of whom are starving and rotting in the reservations, is a touching, even heart-rending excuse for making profits from what Lord Lucas told the House of Lords is ' a fascist state ' where ' three-quarters of the population are living in a police state '.[2]

What British business must understand is that Afrikaner investment amounts to one-tenth of all investment in South Africa, and that Verwoerd is gambling with British and American money.   If he is allowed to bring South Africa down in ruins, the ruins will not be Afrikaner, they will be British and American.   On the other hand, a change effected with the least possible violence and disruption means this : rising living standards for ten million Africans and a growing mass market inside and outside the Union ; a sharp reduction of fantastically high overheads involved in separate public building for Whites, Indians, and Bantus and the segregation of human beings in factories and workshops, to say nothing of a reduction in the heavy costs of maintaining an armed camp ; a rise in productivity as African skills develop to enrich South Africa and, indeed, the entire Continent.   The National Association of British Manufacturers is a purblind Argus, all eyes and no sight.   Or is it really racialist, using its shareholders' money to support its stupid belief in white superiority ?

The purpose of sanctions is to induce the South African government to prepare, in consultation with all the communities in the Union, a constitution acceptable to all.   The application of sanctions has been worked out in detail by economic, political, and military experts.[3]   They would close down exports and imports, nearly three-quarters of which are bought and sold by Great Britain, America, and Japan.

---

[1] Cited, *South Africa : Crisis for the West, op. cit.*, pp. 247–8.
[2] *The Times*, 13 April 1962.
[3] Papers read to the London Conference on Sanctions, April 1964.

They would stop supplies of oil to the Union which produces only one-seventh of the country's needs. If the blockade were rendered unbreakable – as it could be, given honest observance of the United Nations' decisions – victory for human decency would be won within six months. Unless the moral opinion of the world is set above the deadly sin of avarice, the issue, inevitably, will be resolved by force. Force is loathed by the Afro-Asian nations. All of them would seek to avoid the spread of the Cold War to the African Continent, as they did while giving their full support to their African brothers during the seven terrible years of the Algerian war. Yet they cannot shirk an issue which sears the soul of every man and woman in my homeland, harsh and long though the struggle may be.

China's Isolation : A Threat to World Peace

The threat of war will however remain with us until those engines of war which make men think and act aggressively are contained and destroyed. In this connection, one must reckon with China. The situation must not be allowed to develop in which the rest of the world seek to destroy nuclear stocks while China is left free to develop them – handed a nuclear monopoly on a silver platter. But the continued exclusion of China from the United Nations gives China some moral justification to seek its own security as best as it may. How can a country of seven hundred million inhabitants, which year after year is spurned by the United Nations, entertain the illusion of being embraced in the collective security which the United Nations promises ? It is imperative that China should be admitted to that world body now without scrutiny of its national ideology, creed, race, or other belief – as enjoined by the United Nations Charter. The United Nations must not be driven into taking up a partisan ideological position vis-a-vis China, but must recognize the hard fact that there is an effective and indeed important Government in Peking, in full and complete control over the territory which it claims to represent.

My own confidence in Chinese integrity was fortified during

recent visits to the East. In Peking, I found Chou-en-lai a believer in the principles of non-alignment and eager to see other states follow the example of Afro-Asian countries in endorsing them. I noted that instead of promoting military action against Hong Kong and Macao – as they could with certain success and at little cost – the Chinese leaders were allowing these areas to flourish as centres of the international trade which I regard as a sedative to the ideological conflict.

In Moscow, too, Brezhnev, First Secretary of the Communist Party, Prime Minister Kosygin, President Mikoyan, and Foreign Minister Gromyko revealed full understanding of non-alignment and its relation to the principles of peaceful coexistence. Through every conversation, in both countries, there ran a strongly expressed desire to prevent present conflicts from escalating into nuclear war and to find a peaceful path towards settling all the outstanding issues between nations.

The admission of the People's Republic of China to the United Nations has been favoured and supported by a majority of members of the United Nations. The Government of that country is even in diplomatic relations with some of the countries which vote to keep her out !

This issue is as big as the ideological conflict. The question of the admission of China should not be made an ideological question, for the exclusion of China makes it more ideologically intransigent than it needs to be. China has closed her ranks and may well accelerate to that position in which membership of the United Nations is no longer of practical use to her.

The same error of judgement has led many to prolong the hunger and destitution of the poorer countries as a way of affecting their way of thinking. Poverty of course makes people do incomprehensible things. It makes them act at times against their own real conviction. Africa however is not devoid of ideas concerning the nature of society and man's place in it. Africa is neither an ideological desert nor a mart open to whoever bids the highest. There is no question in Africa of acquiring the ways of thought of another people. Foreign ideologies will never fill the minds of Africans, though they may suggest to us paths of development. Poverty may make Africans appear to acquiesce in foreign ideologies, but this seeming aequiescence is bound to be disrupted. It is better to assist a people's development through fair trade than to try to enslave their minds by bribing them. Poverty does not inquire about the capitalist or communist origins of money. It only sees it as a means of exchange making it possible for some human needs to be satisfied. The attempt to buy the minds of hungry people is a major cause of the Cold War and of the ideological conflict.

The ideological conflict is a concomitant of partisanship, and this, like the abuse of the veto, has been reducing the effectiveness of the Security Council. The United Nations is not ideological. It is not ' anti ' any nationality, but is founded upon the highest principles. Though it is not ideological, it is committed to all those lofty ends enshrined in its Charter.

Its discussions must always be guided by those ends, since they have received the voluntary affirmation and endorsement of member states. Discussions which are guided by those ends and brought to a conclusion, must command the allegiance of member states on pain of making a mockery of the Charter of the United Nations.

It is astonishing that responsible nations can vote for a course of action in the Security Council, which they admit there to be necessary, and at the same time say that the resolution only has the force of a recommendation, meaning in fact that it will be ignored. It is this same cavalier attitude to the United Nations which makes it possible for some countries to use their own troops to further their own ends under a United Nations umbrella and then call upon others to share the cost with them.

The United Nations can be so misused because it lacks a standing force of its own. This compels it to rely upon *ad hoc* musterings of troops of many nations. If the United Nations had a standing force of its own, its authority as an arbiter of peace would be more definitive, and it would pre-budget for the use of its own standing force. It would also gain in efficiency and be less liable to be deflected if there were a kind of *troika* system to supervise the implementation of its major decisions. One man is easier to browbeat than three. A *troika* system would ensure that the implementation of major decisions takes place through a machinery. It is too much to expect of one man to supervize thoroughly the implementation of every major United Nations decision.

If the United Nations had its own standing force, it would not have been compelled by financial straits to pull out of the Congo. The United Nations found itself in such straits because the provision for such actions as the Congo operation is not a normal one in the United Nations budget. If there were a standing force however, then this would be automatically budgeted for in advance, and the margin of unbudgeted expenditure would be correspondingly reduced.

Had the United Nations possessed a standing force which it could deploy in the Congo, it would have been unnecessary for the Belgians to operate militarily in the Congo in the descent on Stanleyville with all the dangers latent in such an act.

It is not only Africa which is at the moment fragmented with all the dangers for world peace which fragmentation, atomization, encourages. Fragmentation is separatism ; it encourages the underlining of separatist and provincial interests. Provincialism is utterly unrealistic, for it ignores the fact that even a province, however well integrated it may be, is still a province of the world, and cannot out of its own inner resources fully ensure its insulation from the rest of the world. Provincialism, therefore, must take cognisance of internationalism.

A Continental Union Government in Africa, combining in its unitary ambit dozens of states of Africa, must strike the whole world as one of the most significant conciliatory acts of all time.

The world must eventually gain from the unification of Africa, for the world then will include a great and noble union. It will be unthreatened by the selfishness of a balkanized continent and blessed by a unified continent which, because of its sheer size and variety, is eminently able to absorb shocks and achieve quicker progress and stability than so many client puny states striving to outdo one another in their profession of love for their enemies.

Remember, this Government will be non-aligned. It will be the faithful friend of the United Nations. It will cover more than 250 million peoples dedicated to the abolition of war. It will threaten nobody who refrains from invading its soil and threatening its integrity. It will have neither new imperial ambitions to assert nor old scores to settle. It will be a cool, continent-wide refuge from all the conflict between East and West, a hospitable retreat for the mediation and conciliation that all the statesmen of the world seek and desire.

CHAPTER TEN

ALL OUR TOMORROWS

I BELIEVE sincerely that swift, far-reaching progress in Africa, tomorrow and for all our tomorrows, depends upon Union Government now. African nationalism aroused our sleeping continent to so keen a sense of urgency that it swept away colonial rule with dramatic speed. The idea of African Unity, child of Nationalism and Independence, has become practical politics at a pace pointing to only one conclusion : it is the will of the African people ; they demand its immediate implementation. Who would have imagined seven short years ago, when Ghana's independence heralded the new era in Africa, that an Organization of African Unity would now be operating successfully and commanding, in ever increasing measure, the confidence of all Independent African States ? In these seven years we have survived the first and most critical of the seven stages of man. The way ahead is clear.

Many topical factors, external as well as internal, have influenced this general acceptance of Pan-Africanism. Harsh events in Algeria and Egypt taught us that our only assurance against the extension of the Cold War to Africa was our united determination to keep it out of Africa altogether. We found that even United Nations support for Congo independence could not avail against the betrayal of peace and human decency by the Union Minière of Haut Katanga and its satellites like the Société Commerciale et Minière du Congo, the Brussels Society for Finance and Industry, the Société Générale de Belgique and those other capitalist interests of the West which work on the principle that economic penetration of foreign countries, or neo-colonialism, must not be allowed to fail anywhere lest it fails everywhere. The Congo problem, we were driven to understand, is a problem that only Africans in Africa can solve. Before the Independent

African States really began to create the instruments of effective Unity, we had to suffer the shock of a nuclear test explosion in the Sahara by an alien power, France. In world economic affairs, we discovered that only our united pressure on the agencies of the United Nations sufficed to force attention on the necessity of a fair price for the primary producer in world commodity markets ; a necessity that is now recognized but far from being achieved.

Internally, of course, our dominating problem remains. It is apartheid as practised in South Africa, Southern Rhodesia, and Portuguese Africa. The moral opinion of the world is unanimous in condemning apartheid, and Africans are grateful to the fine men and women, of every race everywhere, whose ardour and advocacy have helped to achieve that result. Apartheid, however, still offers business at high profits to many vested interests in the nations of the East and West, and it is these nations alone who can apply the international sanctions called for by the United Nations to remove this stain on mankind's moral escutcheon. For us, unity in Africa means freedom for Africans, and without the power represented by a Union Government our initiative against apartheid must fall short of success. The enemies of all people in South Africa are preparing to precipitate a race war which could plunge the world into a decade of violence and misery. We aim, through Union Government, to become strong enough to prevent a clash of colour while the West rallies its overwhelming economic forces to destroy apartheid ; and we hope the West will not leave us to ' go it alone ', as we will if we must.

We know that vast natural resources are waiting to be exploited in Africa. We know that their development means rising living standards for our people, a tremendous expansion of global commerce and prosperity, and a contribution of supreme value to world peace and progress. Nevertheless, we have many economies that are not viable and cannot be made viable without Union Government.

Countries like Nigeria and Ghana, Egypt and Algeria, are about to ' take-off ' into exciting agricultural and industrial growth. Countries like Malawi and Zambia, Morocco and Tunisia, Guinea and Ivory Coast, are close on our heels.

One major explanation of their advance is that they have struck, or are discovering, sources of power – oil, natural gas, hydro-electric power, and so on – which can speed the mechanization of agriculture and are the essential prerequisite of industrialization and industrial diversification. All African countries are agreed that, while they want to bring to fruition important areas of economic strength inside their own national boundaries, all Africa must be enabled to share in and contribute to the increase of new wealth. That means Union Government.

We are realizing faster than ever before that one of our greatest enemies is poverty. Our poverty will breed more poverty unless we mount a joint offensive against it. Paradoxically, we are too poor to wait. This haste, however, which, in the absence of a Union Government, forces us to compete against one another in the world money markets, raises the interest rates and in fact reduces the benefits of loans to us. It appears, therefore, that the absence of a Union Government makes it more difficult for us to raise the loans which are necessary for our economic progress.

Africa is rich in natural resources ; but these resources are not spread evenly over the Continent. This unevenness causes an inflation in the costs of development in some areas and involves a loss of foreign currency which we need to amass rather than disseminate. If there were a Union Government, the cost of development would not entail this particular setback.

If there were a Union Government, it would not even be necessary for every present state in Africa to feel obliged to engage in the whole possible gamut of industrial development. For Africa would then be one country, and production by any one part of it would be production by the whole continent, and would be available to enrich and ameliorate the conditions of life in the whole continent. This would also greatly relieve the pressures on international finance for which our disunity has been in large measure responsible.

Granted that there are huge natural resources in Africa, it is not necessary that they should all be developed simultaneously. Take bauxite deposits as an example. The world is often said to be on the verge of a glut of aluminium. There are huge deposits of bauxite in Africa ; but no African country has a monopoly of them. Naturally, therefore, every country with considerable deposits thinks of mining and developing those resources. The result is that some benefit will accrue to each country that does so. But the possible benefit is reduced by the fact that there are too many like-minded countries in Africa willy-nilly combining to keep the market over-supplied.

If, now, a Continental Union Government were responsible for the development of Africa, it would not need to oversupply the available market for aluminium. It could ensure that the world price of aluminium did not become uneconomic. Another consequential benefit would be that the loans used in proliferating bauxite mines would be largely saved and made available for the development and exploitation of other resources. Finance would become easier in relation to every kind of development programme. The development of Africa would be greatly speeded up.

The mighty strength of a Union Government would represent and underwrite the economic viability of the entire continent. It would enable us, largely through coordinated banking arrangements and a common currency, to prove the credit-worthiness of every part of Africa. We are too poor to go through the long, slow processes of the pre-automation age. The very fact that Africa is the greatest undeveloped and under-developed land mass in the world today offers splendid prospects to us precisely because it offers new frontiers to mankind's mounting equipment of science and technology. We need a plan for all Africa. We need the Union Government which, alone, can apply the plan.

When I refer to planning, I can say honestly that Africans know a great deal about it. The Economic Commission for Africa, the Afro-Asian Organization for Economic Cooperation and many other agencies have been building up a library of statistics and information and acquiring sophisticated skills down the years. So have the many Commissions set up by our various groupings now amalgamated in the work of the Organization of African Unity. A wonderful wealth of talent has been harnessed to the tasks of mapping our resources and charting our courses. Individual states have recruited world experts to join with African national planning boards in analysing our problems and proposing solutions. It is probably true to say that one of the attractions we have been able to offer to the international repertory of science is that African economic thought is not inhibited by the traditional economic philosophies of the West.

African Planning : Its Achievements and Possibilities

Let me give brief details of some of our recent planning developments, in many of which the Economic Commission for Africa, a United Nations Agency, working in harmony with the Organization of African Unity, is a leading spirit.

An African Development Bank is now in being and in active business. Its headquarters are in Abidjan, capital of the Ivory Coast. Its first President is a Sudanese. It will help to channel and administer capital investment to meet continental rather than state needs. We have begun the process of pooling all our airline services, most of them of high quality and efficiency, on a sub-regional basis. The West African states have agreed in principle that, instead of a proliferation of steel plants, there shall be three such plants catering for all these states. Similar schemes of coordinated economic action are being projected for the sub-regional areas of East Africa and Southern Africa. A new Central Equatorial African region is under consideration.

Many individual African States have launched well-conceived plans capable of being integrated with sub-regional and all-African development.

Ghana's Seven Year £1,000 million Development Plan provides an interesting example. It is more than a survey of every economic, financial, social, and industrial year until 1970, when we shall leap into the twenty-first century. It is also an exercise in operational research describing, almost literally, every detailed step in the process of building up industries and servicing them with labour, power, transport, communications, housing, schools, and the facilities that add up to a good national society and a good human condition. We have not provided for the land shark and the land speculator. We have arranged to leave both out ! Now plans like these stimulate our sense of urgency, not only because we are eager for their fulfilment. They have aroused great expectations in the youth of our nation – expectation of using the varied talents and expressing the high idealism nurtured by our, relatively speaking, very heavy expenditure on education. To have shirked these costly education programmes would have been a betrayal of our children and of the revolution. And this, the investment of ordinary men and women in their own and their children's future, must soon begin to pay off. In Ghana, we anticipate we shall absorb the ' bulge ' of school and university leavers when, this year, the Volta Dam begins to feed a growing number of hydro-electrically powered industries, as our magnificent timber supplies come into greater and more diversified use, as our agriculture responds to mechanization and intensive research, as we process more of our products for export and as we expand our airways, shipping, and transport. In short, all over Africa there is a growth of skills and of the qualities of initiative and enterprise. How shall we ensure their full and economic use ? Our young pop singers know the answer. It ' is blowin' in the wind '. It is a Union Government presiding over and directing a Union plan for economic and social growth.

I do not underestimate our difficulties. I do not want the friends of Africa throughout the world to underestimate them. Our continent has harboured men of all races and religions and, except where greed has interfered, many people of all colours and many ideologies have fused peacefully and without rancour. Nevertheless, we have still to jump linguistic barriers encouraged by colonial rule. We have tribal traditions still essential to our way of life which we want to harmonize in our forward march. For years ahead, many parts of the continent will remain comparatively inaccessible to all existing means of transport, and barter will continue as the only practicable form of exchange. These people, living happily in their own environment, without the faintest notion of nuclear warfare or the vaguest desire to obliterate America or Russia or any other place on God's earth are not stigmatized by us, as they were by our recent rulers, as ' backward ', and they must be encouraged rather than forced to join in our advance and at their own pace.   The hitherto haphazard progress of our continent has encouraged dangerous snobberies and, among some sections of the ex-colonial élite, myths of ' superior races '. These are problems of racialism within the over-riding problem of multi-racialism.   Their solution will require all the goodwill and diplomacy and humanity all of us can muster.   Within all our states there is conflict of opinion about the way ahead, about forms of government and administration; differences that are inevitable when men are free to engage in the search for better and more humane application of the controls exercised by government and law.   Our study of the political progress of the West, where methods of government, even of parliamentary representation are still regarded as far from perfect by many thinkers, teaches us that parties of reform and revolution must acquire a radical integrity if their victory is not to be sullied by corruption and self-seeking.   Our confidence springs from the revelation of our, as yet, brief experience within our independent states and between them, that men can be induced to move in unison, not because they are animals or a mob, but because they can be induced to think in unison.

Discussing Africa in the ideological conflict, I tried to make clear that we are not part of that conflict, that we want no part in it, that we are, physically and intellectually, non-aligned.   Instead, we are committed to the enormous, historic experiment of compounding a society out of all that is valuable in our continental tradition and out of all the experience, triumphant and tragic, that modern industrial civilizations can contribute to the cause of human betterment in our class-free conditions.   Apposite to this argument, especially in the former British colonies, has been our departure from Westminster-style democracy, a departure that has provoked criticism as bitter as it has been ignorant.   Yet the truth is obvious to all who seek it.   Many of our one-party states, including Ghana, tried to make Westminster-style democracy work.   Even so ' independent ' a critic of Ghana as Mr Dennis

Austin[1] admits that, in the 1956 General Election, it was not the Convention People's Party but its opponent, the so-called National Liberation Movement, which spurned the constitutional proposals of the Colonial Administration to safeguard opposition rights on the Westminster model; that the Convention People's Party Government provided every facility for such an opposition to operate; and that, instead of acting as a ' loyal opposition ', our political enemies sought to prevent parliament from functioning at all even to the extent of resorting to violence. This resort to violence, indeed, was implicit in the National Liberation Movement election platform. Their purpose was to prevent democracy being made usable. The Convention People's Party found a way of making democracy usable in the one-party system, the guarantee of true democracy in the circumstances of Africa; and Ghana's experience has been and is being repeated elsewhere in Africa. African states have a deep faith in democracy; it is in consonance with much that lives in African tradition. African states seek a method of democracy that is usable. We are not bound by ideologies, whether of East or West. We are capable of developing our own ideology, and within that ideology, which expresses the African Personality, we are pragmatic and experimental.

For the majority of thinking Africans, our sense of what is right and just and of lasting value for our people is indicated in these facts:

All members of the Organization of African Unity have entrenched individual human rights and the integrity of the state in their Constitutions.

All members will eventually cede to the Organization important supra-national powers in relation to defence and foreign policy.

Some members have declared as a primary purpose of their development plans the prosperity of all Africa, north and south of the Sahara.

All members accept the political proposition that until all Africa is free, no individual African state is free.

If and when these states, or a sufficient number of them,

[1] *Politics in Ghana*, 1946–60, Oxford University Press, pp. 277 *et seq.*

cede to the Union Government of Africa supra-national powers to guide and control continental economic activity in addition to defence and foreign policy, we shall enter upon the adventure of creating the most radical and enlightened constitution the modern world has known.

The interdependence between African states, which Union Government will nourish and express, is the real source of our strength, our peace, our freedom, and our influence upon world affairs. Influence is a two-way progress. One cannot have influence unless others are in a position to be influenced. Impact, like quarrel, calls for two. Influence also entails a community and an integration or correlation of interest. Both the West and East can be of promise to Africa. We are therefore interested in the attitudes of the West and East towards the future of Africa. One hopes that these attitudes will be mutually beneficial and will make possible the increase of fair trade, cultural relations, and cooperative enterprise of international organizations and institutions; for out of these various impacts arises the feeling of people for people, whoever and wherever they may be.

These contacts, however, take place in formalized relations. As long as Africa remains fragmented into several countries and states, the ability of the West and East to react fruitfully will be considerably stretched. With a Continental Government, a Union Government of Africa, one government will be able to act on behalf of over 250,000,000 men and women, and relations will be easier. All nations of the world which have an interest in world peace and world fraternity must for this reason (among many) welcome the coming of a Continental Union Government of Africa.

INTERDEPENDENCE : THE BASIS OF WORLD COMITY

This theme of interdependence reaches right down to the roots of world comity. Of these roots, the most sensitive and the most vital, is economic cooperation.

When Great Britain faces economic problems, all the vast machinery of world trade comes into operation – the International Monetary Fund, the General Agreement on Trade and Tariff, Britain's partners in the European Free Trade Association, the European Economic Community, and the Organization for European Economic Cooperation and Development. America and Canada are involved at once with all the nations of the Sterling Area. The reactions on governmental debt-holders and the inter-actions on world currencies are felt in Asia, India, even Russia and, indeed, throughout the world. At the moment of crisis, every move is directed towards harmonizing economic action. The alternative is widespread disaster affecting every nation, large and small.

This is the heart of the argument for harmonizing world economies, not only to conquer crises, but to avoid them and promote world prosperity and international unity. Economic cooperation offers the only solution for the difficulties of smaller states – that is, the majority of states – whose individual problems may make little impact upon global trade, yet may precipitate distress and unrest which could, in the end, draw even the biggest powers into political conflict. Just as in the modern world serious war anywhere means war everywhere, so poverty anywhere means poverty everywhere. It is as true in economic terms as in military terms that we can have ' one world or no world '.

Economic cooperation removes political discontent. It promotes political freedom and harmony within states and peace between states. It offers the best hope of ridding the world of the crushing economic burden of armaments now running at £50,000 million a year, the equivalent of 9 per cent of the world's total output of goods and services. There is no scientific or technical barrier to disarmament. The barrier is political. Only economic cooperation can destroy it.

The settlement of an issue between different countries will always seem to be a political problem in the first instance, for every nation will be anxious lest it should become worse off in an international settlement. This is a political anxiety, but the solution to the problem is not necessarily political. Any arrangement can quieten the anxiety if it promotes and preserves understanding and unity in that respect between the nations.

I am suggesting that trade is such a sedative. Trade cannot take place against the wishes of people. A country which can trade successfully with another is a country which makes the satisfaction of another people its concern. This alone can be a bond, a bridge of understanding between the peoples. Trade is therefore an instrument of foreign policy, and so of national policy. Unless the United States of America thought so, it would probably not permit trade with Poland and Yugoslavia especially. Obviously the United States of America hopes to gain political popularity in these countries, and that is why its trade effort is most intense in these of all socialist countries.

Trade can and should be used as an organ of world fraternity ; but it will be such an organ only if it is fair. At the moment, the poorer nations are having to work more for less because of an international conspiracy to keep them mere producers of raw materials. World trade becomes for them progressively unfavourable. They are forced to live as it were in a Lewis Carroll looking-glass world where they have to run faster and faster in order to stay in the same place. In what sense can the advanced nations be said to be assisting a reduction in poverty when they in fact promote unrewarded effort in the poorer countries ? If one takes cocoa as an example one will find that, though the world output of cocoa has multiplied, the gross revenue has been almost static.

It is facts like this which make it imperative that the United Nations should set up machinery which will correlate world trade and ensure fair returns to the producers of primary commodities. Survival of a nation will, then, as it ought to do, rest upon the sweat of a people's own brow. The world can be regenerated and advanced by work, and work must be allowed to earn those benefits which will regenerate and advance the world.

Uneven trade is a root cause of a great deal of the political animosity which threatens our world. Political animosity cannot all be dispelled by political negotiation ; but a correction in the terms of world trade can often ensure true political equality.

In this connection, the world must condemn all restrictive trade practices, even those which take the form of exclusive marketing groupings. An observation of Europe is pertinent here. Europe at sixes and sevens has demonstrated the political motives underlying trade associations of the kind of the E.E.C. and EFTA. The Common Market can be seen as a group of countries who do not want the Anglo-Saxon nations to have too much policy in Europe. The Anglo-Saxons used to have undisputed sway over the North Atlantic Treaty Organization. The Common Market, if it continues to exclude Britain, has the effect of drastically weakening Britain's political influence in Europe. It is not surprising that Britain's projected entry into the Common Market should have been beset by seemingly intractable problems.

The Common Market is an economic organization concerned with trade and its conditions, but as an instrument it is political. It is hardly surprising therefore that the negotiations involved in its setting up were conducted not primarily by economists and civil servants, but by top politicians of whom one is now a Chancellor, two are Foreign Ministers, one a potential leader of a political party, and so on. The Common Market is addressed to a single political problem, that of the complete political integration and autonomy of Europe. De Gaulle reveals more candour than many when he says openly that to his mind the Common Market is a step towards the political integration of Europe. Any Association of African States with it therefore raises difficult questions. Are some African States preparing themselves for the role of satellites of an integrated Europe ? It is evident that the anxiety of European nations to have primary producer countries associated with their organization is due to the European need for a continuous supply of raw materials at low prices for its own industries as well as the ensuring of a ready-made soft market for its industrial products.

The European members of E.E.C. employ an unrealistic threat, but an apparently successful one : that of raising the tariff level against African states who do not join the Market. But they are countries which *import* raw materials necessary for their industrial life. There can therefore be no real question of the Common Market countries jeopardizing their industrial life by *reducing* their ability to import the necessary raw materials.

This is precisely the effect which the elevation of duty would have.

And yet every single problem of Africa can be solved quickly by a comprehensive unity in Africa itself. World trade, as it affects Africa, will never be rationalized or liberated as long as African countries permit themselves to be economic sitting ducks.

African countries are less viable as economic units than were European countries at the end of World War II. It took Marshall Aid to revive the economies of Europe, but not even Marshall Aid could guarantee European economies. The military war might have ended, but an economic one was in full swing in its place. So serious was it that Chancellor Adenauer was able to say half in earnest, half in jest, that the error of Britain was to have won the (military) war !

Nationalism has up to a point been a positive, constructive force in Europe. But in order that nationalism should not become destructive of nations, it is essential that it should not overshoot its targets. This is as true for Europe as it is for Africa. Europe brought nationalism to new heights in the nineteenth century, and was in the twentieth century almost annihilated by it. In a world which has become more truly interdependent, rabid nationalism is suicidal.

Africa has had to wield the full force of nationalism in the twentieth century. But its full force has been directed at well-chosen targets. The force of nationalism had to be brought to bear on colonial powers in order that formal independence should be won. Indeed, nationalism was a pre-condition of that struggle. As the well-chosen targets are captured, the relevance of nationalism contracts ; and if it is given un-controlled dominance, it can endanger a people whom it once saved. This is a lesson which Europe has bitterly learnt. Let us in Africa make sweet the uses of the adversity of Europe.

The need for Pan-African contact is in principle admitted throughout the continent. But the essential forms which this contact should take in order to be meaningful or fulfil its promise is made a subject of difference where none is called for. It is actually held by many that Pan-African institutions can be created merely as institutions, standing divested of a political directorate. And yet, even in the case of Europe, which developed nationalism par excellence, the Common Market is ' a political as well as an economic issue '. Thus Harold Macmillan, addressing the House of Commons on 31 July 1961, said of the European Common Market :

> This is a political as well as an economic issue. Although the Treaty of Rome is concerned with economic matters it has an important political objective – namely to promote unity and stability in Europe, which is so essential a factor in the struggle for freedom and progress throughout the world . . . In this modern world the tendency towards larger groups of nations acting together in the common interest leads to greater unity and this adds to our strength in the struggle for freedom.

Change the geography, and these words could have been spoken by any far-seeing African leader. The political issues however are not issues of the future. They are those of the present, for if the common interest is to be effectively served, it must be protected and administered in a unitary system. There must be a supra-economic directorate, ensuring that economic trends in the Market Area continue to serve the agreed common interest.

There was a Greek philosopher called Xenophanes who thought that living things were not created in any particular way, but that there were all sorts of limbs and organs which joined in all possible ways. For example, a bovine head might join on to a human neck or a bird's feet. The idea is that those parts which joined in the right combinations survived while the others perished.

This is the kind of nightmare which will quickly overtake Africa if an attempt is made to collect diverse national institutions in the hope that they can be harmonized into Pan-African institutions. The only unity possible here is the unity implied by the sheet of paper on which they are collected. To suppose that an organic unity can grow among institutions collected in this way is to suppose that an organic unity can grow in Xenophanes' nightmare. Harmonization of institutions does not mean anything if it does not imply an adequate organic unity. And how can independent African nations accept such a unity of their institutions without a body which has executive and directorate powers ? What is such a body but a political one ?

A CONTINENT AT SIXES AND SEVENS

One can verify these ideas in the history of the European Common Market. To do this, one must pose and suggest answers to a number of questions : What circumstances inspired the creation of the Six and Seven ? What form did their rivalry take ? Why did the Seven fail to join the Six *ab initio* ? Why did the effort made by Mr Harold Macmillan to fuse the two in 1961 fail ? Why was trade and the organization of the Common Market chosen as the instrument of the political policy of European unification ?

To answer some of these questions, it is necessary to reflect on European geography and history of the last thirty years.

The Rhur Valley is the very heart and life blood of Western Europe. This vast complex of coal and steel is a magnet for a myriad ancillary industries and fertile ground for great enterprises in electricity and chemicals. Its raw materials and semi-manufactures feed shipbuilding as well as shipping northwards to the Elbe and eastwards to the brilliant electrical engineering skills of Italy. It is part of, and vitalizes, the industrial centre of France, next to Russia the biggest land mass in Europe. It is essential to Belgium, exporter of nearly 40 per cent of all the produce of the hard-working Flemings and Walloons. Its gateway to the markets of the Western world is Rotterdam ; the lower Rhine is the fluid backbone of Holland. A vast network of road and rail and air transport makes the Rhur Valley the trading centre of Europe. Thus, despite the fierce nationalistic antagonisms of pre-war Europe, there arose a European Steel Cartel with which even the reluctant British were linked.

This cartel survived World War II to become, in 1952, the European Coal and Steel Community (E.C.S.C.), first and pioneer organ of the E.E.C. E.C.S.C. had its own Consultative Assembly wielding executive political power over its six members – Germany, France, Italy, Belgium, Holland, and Luxembourg.

In 1953 this Assembly was merged in the larger European Parliamentary Assembly, supervising the European Atomic Energy Commission (Euratom) and the E.E.C. Addressing the European Parliamentary Assembly on 19 March 1958, Dr Walter Hallstein, President of the E.E.C. Commission, made crystal clear the aims of the vast consortium which was soon to influence profoundly the future of Western Europe and the world. The Treaty of Rome, the Charter of the E.E.C., then in process of being signed by the Six, he declared, did more than pool the economies of the Six; it pooled the ' economic policies of the participating countries . . . it is not the citizens who are making a sacrifice to the Community (and therefore becoming less free than before as a result of the creation of the Community) but the Governments. The merging of the national economies themselves is merely an outcome of this and in this sense of secondary importance. The significance of our Community lies in this political aspect in the institutional set-up of our Community, no less than in the practical regulations relating to the conditions of administration.'

Without political guarantees there is absolutely no way in which the economies of independent nations can be pooled. To pool economies is to pool economic policies. To pool economic policies is to accept a common political governance of economic policies. To accept the latter is to institute a political set-up for the communities involved.

It is very often thought that the European Common Market is conceived as a customs union. Nothing could be farther from the truth. While the market embraces a customs union it is not identical with one, for it not merely provided for reductions of mutual tariffs and the establishment of uniform tariffs on trade external to the market countries; it provided also for the progressive elimination of quotas of political guarantees protecting the Market countries. Dr Hallstein went on to say:

' We are striving to bring about a transformation of society. We want our citizens in so far as they think of themselves as political beings to think of themselves . . . as belonging to her great European family.'

This as a description of what the European Economic Community was striving to achieve goes far beyond a Customs union.

Also important to an understanding of the role of E.E.C. is the fact that it was intended to be the counterpart of a European Defence Community; a fact which explains Russian suspicion of it and many of the subsequent diplomatic moves on the European chessboard. In 1954 the French Parliament refused to ratify the proposed European Defence Community. The Six then sought an alternative in the Western European Union, which Great Britain joined, under the umbrella of the North Atlantic Treaty Organization.

Two other developments fostered the idea of economic-political unity. In London, in September 1944, while the outcome of the war was still at hazard, Belgium, the Netherlands, and Luxembourg concluded a convention creating Benelux, the customs union which became operative in October 1947. These three ' buffer states' quickly realized the need to integrate their economies and to eliminate the ' economic frontiers' still keeping them apart. By 1956 they had worked out and applied a common trade and payments policy in relation to all other countries and were proceeding to coordinate their investment, agricultural, and social policies. They brought into being both a blueprint for E.E.C. and a working model for the Common Market. The second development was initiated in 1947 by the French National Railways. Its officials began the preparation of timetables unifying the rail and road transport systems of the Six, including Austria if Russian opposition to European integration abated. They revealed the economies that rationalization of rail traffic could achieve in terms of lower costs and increasing speed and mobility. They produced the plan upon which the much admired transport facilities of Western Europe are now based.

Now, all these enterprises had stemmed from a political ideal nourished by European leaders who, during the war, found refuge in London: the ideal that military liberation of Europe would lead to political unity in which Great Britain would be a partner. The British War Cabinet encouraged this theme of political unification. Sir Winston Churchill was regarded as its leading exponent. When in 1951, Sir Winston returned to 10 Downing Street as Prime Minister, the initiative was still within his grasp. He did not seize it. Why? This remains the historical enigma wrapped within the mystery of British post-war policy. We know that, in adumbrating the Atlantic Charter, Sir Winston was careful to safeguard the economic interests of the Commonwealth and Empire. Were these interests still paramount in his mind? Only one fact is known. Great Britain remained in but not of Europe. Thus it is a reasonable argument – and the argument must be admitted, whatever one's personal view of E.E.C. and its development – that without the force of political ideas and ideals, E.E.C. would never have been brought to birth and, without E.E.C. Europe might have failed to recover so speedily from the ravages of war.

Following the rejection of the European Defence Community by France in 1954 and the intensified drive of the Six towards economic integration, the Organization of European Economic Cooperation, established to administer Marshall Aid, became the sounding-board of European opinion outside the Six. O.E.E.C. suggested that the United Kingdom and other countries not desiring to join E.E.C. should form a free trade area with the Six, thus constituting an All-European Free Trade Area. By January 1957, it was agreed that such an area could be superimposed upon the Common Market. During this debate there grew among the Six a strong suspicion and distrust of British intentions about European unification. More positively, European opinion had become convinced that trade liberation required, not free trade, but the organization of all trading activities to contribute to the integration of a wider community with common institutions. There was, too, a growing belief that Common Market policies of mobility of capital and labour, joint investment funds and harmonization of social plans – in economic terms, equalization of competition by equalization of important overhead costs of production – were much more vital to the liberation of trade than the application of the nineteenth-century theory of free trade, now regarded as an outdated obstacle to modern planning techniques.

In November 1959, the United Kingdom, Sweden, Norway, Denmark, Switzerland, and Austria – who were joined later by Portugal – signed the Stockholm Convention setting up the European Free Trade Association. The Seven had arisen to protect their trade against the competition of the Six, and, if possible, to force the Six into political negotiations and concessions. There now opened a tremendous tariff war, aimed primarily at weakening the position of Germany within the Six. EFTA introduced preferences which, naturally, were denied to a substantial and politically vocal section of German Big Business. The Six retaliated by revising and speeding up tariff changes scheduled to begin at the end of 1960. These changes were advanced to 1960. Their general result was that E.E.C. would be reducing tariffs at a faster rate than EFTA could contemplate ! The result was a boost to the morale of the Six.

AMERICA ABANDONS NEUTRALITY

The next step in the struggle was taken by the United States. Professing anxiety about increasing tensions in Europe and concerned about the American balance of payments problem, the State Department abandoned its posture of neutrality and initiated reform of O.E.E.C. to enable America and Canada to join it. The idea was to give the Organization – now renamed the Organization for Economic Cooperation and Development (O.E.C.D.) – a new lease of life in the form of additional responsibilities for coordinating Western trade policy and aid policy in developing countries. A parallel Committee of Twenty-one was formed, including a representative of E.E.C., to study trade problems. Great Britain welcomed this step. She hoped, within O.E.D.C., to revive the proposal for an All-European Free Trade Area. She sought, especially, to induce America to apply pressure on E.E.C. to halt the acceleration of Common Market tariff revision and reduction. United States policy, however, took a very different course. What the State Department wanted, according to Mr Emile Benoit,[1] was to get both blocs to lower

[1] Emile Benoit, *Europe at Sixes and Sevens*, Columbia University Press, 1961, p. 93.

the general level of tariffs to each other's and America's products, if possible without America having to make fully reciprocal concessions ; to head off any tariff concession from which American business would not benefit ; and to induce all these countries to bear a larger share of the burden of mutual defence and foreign aid.

In all the debate and discussion in the Parliament and Assemblies of the West, there was revealed time and time again the truth I have tried to underline in these pages. When trade is exploited for political purposes, its sedative qualities are reduced ; instead of harmonizing relations trade becomes an agent of conflict and of ideological controversy.

Before returning to the African attitude to these European issues, attention must be paid to other important considerations. The economies of the Six, unlike the economies of the Seven, are competitive with each other. This competition is a powerful beckoning condition towards efficiency. Yet its dangers are obvious. The buoyancy of trade, both internal and external, tends to be geared to specialized manufactures like motor cars and machinery. Any slump in these great but specialized industries with specialized markets could menace seriously the prosperity of every member of the Six. They must look to the developing countries, therefore, as potential markets and customers rather than as partners in their industrial progress. Thus while the Common Market ideal has captured the imagination of Latin America, Central America, and Africa, trade relations between the E.E.C. and the developing countries have done *less than nothing to* meet the urgent needs of the latter. In 1959, for example,

the EEC was buying its imports from outside the Community at prices 8 *per cent lower* than in 1957, but it was selling its exports outside the Community at prices 12 *per cent higher* than in 1957. Between 1957 and the middle of 1960 EEC industrial production rose 26 per cent and trade among EEC members rose 41 per cent in value. But imports from overseas associated countries and territories rose only 7 per cent and imports from the less developed countries generally rose only 4 per cent. Had these latter imports risen in line with EEC industrial output, they would, on a rough estimate, have netted the less developed countries an extra 2 billion dollars a year in foreign exchange – and a rise proportional to EEC intratrade would have netted them an extra 3 billion dollars. These sums, of course, greatly exceed EEC foreign aid contributions.[1]

Mr Benoit, who vouches for these estimates indicating that the poor nations are subsidizing the galloping prosperity of the rich nations, does not criticize E.E.C. for the slow rate of economic growth in America which has depressed world commodity prices. Nevertheless, he writes, ' neither the E.E.C. nor the United States can take pride in their aid programmes in support of developing countries when the programmes merely restore a part of what is lost to these countries through a deterioration in their terms of trade and a decline in the imports of their products '. And the effect of all this on developing countries ? Mr Benoit spells it out in hard economic facts. ' Commodity exports of less developed nations (which typically generate a fifth or more of their national incomes) showed year-to-year variations averaging over 12 per cent a year during 1948–57, leading to numerous and drastic cutbacks in their imports : seventeen such cuts of over 20 per cent in a single year may be found in the record of these years. These cuts bore heavily, and even predominantly in most cases, on capital goods, industrial materials, and fuels, thereby disrupting development programmes.'[2]

This process of attrition of the resources of young nations goes on and up. It is an affront to the moral conscience of all the industrial countries of the West. It is a condemnation of all who play politics with trade instead of seeking to harmonize the economics of the world for the progress and social peace of the world.

When, in 1957, France entered the E.E.C., she associated her African territories with the Common Market, ostensibly as her associates. Such development as would be permitted them would be decided in Paris and in accordance with French metropolitan interests. Now, as I have noted above, approaches are again being made to African states offering them association with the Community while denying them a voice in the policy of E.E.C. Whatever the intention of these approaches, the

[1] *Ibid.*, pp. 261–2.   [2] *Ibid.*, p. 262.

results must be disastrous to any African state beguiled by them. They are certain to precipitate strains and stresses within a continent that is, politically and militarily, non-aligned, a continent that wants no part in the Cold War. They must provoke division within the proposed African Common Market which is a major objective of the Organization of African Unity. While offering any state which chooses association the bribe of temporarily higher prices (at the expense of its African neighbours) for primary products, the proposal must perpetuate its former colonial role of supplier of low-priced primary products and raw materials and buyer of high-priced manufactures. As a result, such a state will be denied the capital accretion which its natural resources and hard labour ought to command, and its independence will be converted into a sham, indeed, into a shameful betrayal of its freedom and its birthright. Certainly, there is no prospect of harmonizing social and economic conditions in Africa with those of any country in the Six !

Meantime, world economic problems and political stresses proliferate. These problems have not been provoked by the rise of E.E.C. although they have been intensified by its success. And they demand solution at higher levels than world statesmen have yet contemplated.

Consider these facts. The Six occupy a land area of 450,000 square miles, small in comparison with the land mass of the United States. Assume, however (as I do not!), that the former French Community in Africa seeks to accept association with the Six. Then the area of E.E.C. becomes nearly six million square miles, two-thirds larger than America's customs area. The population of the joint E.E.C. area as just defined is nearing 250 million, that of America just over 180 million. E.E.C. is still second to America in terms of industrial output, although enjoying a faster rate of growth. It is, however, ahead of the Soviet Union. Only two years after the Treaty of Rome was signed, E.E.C. steel production was at the rate of 63 million metric tons a year compared to 85 million in America, 60 million in Russia, and 21 million in Great Britain, and E.E.C. was already a larger import market than America. E.E.C. – especially Germany and Italy – is attracting a steadily increasing proportion of American investment capital and although Great Britain is not a member of the Six, there are many millions of pounds of British capital invested in Europe while lack of capital investment in Great Britain itself has for long been a major headache of every Chancellor of the Exchequer.

THE CHANGING PATTERN OF POWER

All these facts underline the importance of Africa to E.E.C. and to the future of world economic and political movements. They indicate also, a vital change in what might be called the modern economic balance of power.

When, in 1947–8, Mr Harold Wilson, now Prime Minister of Great Britain, was winning the support of 54 nations for the Havana Charter, which would have tackled the problems of developing countries and world hunger in such a way that they would have been well on the way to solution by now[1] the Charter provided for an International Trade Organization capable of removing trade barriers and taking positive action to harmonize trade between primary producers and the great industrial nations. Indeed, an International Commission of the International Trade Organization was in being, fully armed, to make the Havana Charter effective. Alas, the United States refused to ratify the Charter, and turned it into a dead letter. Under American pressure I.C.I.T.O. was reduced to a mere instrument – the Organization for Trade Cooperation – of GATT. America, then the biggest single market offering the biggest tariff privileges then available anywhere in the world, became the dominating partner among countries accounting for four-fifths of world trade and commerce. Now America faces, in E.E.C., a rival bloc of almost equal strength; a bloc in the integration of which America has invested great capital resources. GAAT has outlived its usefulness. The recent Kennedy Round was an attempt to pump fresh vitality into a procedure under which the Organization for Trade Cooperation argues more and more about less and less. In African eyes, the Organization

[1] See Chapter Eight.

has become an instrument of delay in dealing with the real problems of young countries.

Meantime, the difficulties of currency liquidity and the restrictions these difficulties impose upon natural economic growth everywhere, become more clamant; problems summed up succinctly by M. Pierre-Paul Schwitzer, managing-director of the International Monetary Fund, on 21 January 1965, in these words: 'It is my firm belief that without growing cooperation in the provision of mutual support the world economy might quickly run into serious trouble. Today more than ever before, world prosperity is indivisible. It is, therefore, in the interest of all that the major trading countries of the world should act together to prevent crises from creating depressive conditions for world trade.'

The way ahead, as I see it, is clear. We must return to the principles of the Havana Charter. We must create an effective World Trade Organization operating under United Nations auspices and fully equipped to deal with all questions relating to trade and development. We must translate into practical policies the United Nations' declared ideal of offering every country equal access to raw materials and access on equal terms to world markets. Africa offers such access to its raw materials. Africa requires access to world markets on terms that will ensure to Africans reasonable living standards and the opportunity of building Africa in accord with the wishes of Africans. The claim I make for Africa is also the claim of Asia, Latin America, and Central America. It is the one promising solution for the recurring economic crises afflicting the great industrial powers. It is the only way to prevent economic competition from degenerating into ideological conflict.

As my readers are aware, all the developing countries prefer trade to aid. Throughout this book I have sought to translate this theme of relating the massive goodwill of the rich nations to the need of their neighbours for cooperation without the taint of patronage and political bribery into the fine, energizing idea of mutual aid. Hence my plea that all these goodwill enterprises should be funnelled through the United Nations. An effective International Organization would be exactly the medium through which an inspiring, fertile partnership between all nations could be promoted. Our demand is in truth a call to the noblest, most exciting adventure that has ever moved the mind and heart of mankind: the release of the majority of the world's population from poverty's prison. To satisfy our need is an immediate imperative of the continuing economic growth which the world economy requires if its continuing prosperity is not to be halted and frustrated.

The simplest, most elementary motives for co-operation between people are security, peace, and prosperity. Their cooperation, as all mankind is learning slowly, is rendered sterile, even destructive, when it is directed towards conquest, whether military or ideological.

Happily, there are no longer fundamental differences in the economic objectives of the world powers, whether expressed in E.E.C., EFTA, GATT, or in the Comecon groupings of the Soviet bloc. All seek to increase trade with all nations. All seek to encourage, internally and externally, acceptance of trading procedures of compulsory arbitration and an administrative rule of trade law. The United Nations Organization has made giant strides towards establishing a rule of law in the most difficult of all relationships – the political relationships between sovereign states. Is it impossible to believe that United Nations can formulate and apply a reasonable rule of trade? Not, I assert, if the task is tackled in the mood and spirit of General Marshall's momentous appeal to the nations to agree to a policy ' directed not against any country or doctrine but against hunger, poverty, desperation, and chaos '.

Africa in her economic plans is unavoidably concerned with a policy directed not against any country or doctrine but against hunger, poverty, desperation, and chaos. The solution cannot however be in the putting together of nationalistic institutions, for these have not been designed for Pan-African purposes.

Many in Africa today think along lines of economic co-operation entailing such things as a Customs Union, as if this could be an end in itself, a be-all and end-all. Consider, however, the following passage from a United Nations document summarizing studies of the League of Nations on Customs Unions:

> For a customs union to exist, it is necessary to allow free movement of goods within the union. For a customs union to be a reality, it is necessary to allow free movements of persons. For a customs union to be stable it is necessary to maintain free exchangeability of currency and stable exchange rates within the union. This implies, *inter alia*, free movement of capital within the Union. When there is free movement of goods, persons, and capital in any area, diverse economic policies concerned with maintaining economic activity cannot be pursued. To assure uniformity of policy, some political mechanism is required. The greater the intervention of the state in economic life, the greater must be the political integration within a customs union.

When sovereign African States are canvassed or seek to ' associate ' with the E.E.C., they are required to cede sovereign rights to an alien organization pursuing political as well as economic aims, and they will be denied any right of influencing the policies to which, henceforth, such power as they possess will be committed. Thus they become the mere lackeys of their former colonial masters for the precise purpose of the colonial system which the African nationalist revolution destroyed; to sell raw materials cheaply to the industrial powers. For African states to accept association on such terms is a betrayal of the revolution. It is also a threat to the full realization of African freedom and independence. Association does not even imply a share in the present and potential prosperity of Europe which no African begrudges that war-torn continent.

No, Africans must not subordinate their fight against hunger, poverty, desperation, and chaos, in Africa to what is simply European aggrandizement in a new shape.

The Organization of African Unity is the most spectacular institution devised by us today in order to solve our common problems – The OAU envisages definite fields within which those problems can be solved. It accordingly provides for political and diplomatic cooperation, economic cooperation, including transport and communications; educational and cultural cooperation; health, sanitation, and nutritional cooperation; scientific and technical cooperation; and cooperation for defence and security.

The great weakness of the Organization however lies in its chronic inability to fit the remedy to the ill. What form can cooperation take in each of the above cases? What can be meant by political and diplomatic cooperation in the absence of well-defined and devotedly pursued political objectives and diplomatic policies? How can economic cooperation be possible on a continental scale when our economies are largely competitive, if there is no one economic policy for Africa to which we are all subject and which protects all of us? How can we cooperate for defence and security when we have not in reality made ourselves subject to the same diplomatic policies? Fine words merely brighten up our will 'o the wisp. They hide from us the realities in which we are caught. They push further away from us the objective solutions which will deliver us.

The OAU now propose an African defence organization, to which African states will allocate units, which will, however, stay in their respective countries. These units, it is claimed will be kept ready for operations decided upon by the Council of Ministers of the Organization of African Unity.

Let us assume then that an African country has been aggressed from outside. So a meeting of the Council of Ministers is called. By whom? Let us assume that the Ministers meet. They all condemn aggression and issue blood-chilling threats. And then? And then each Minister begins to be wary about committing his Government. It turns out that they all *in principle* are committed to counter-action, but the situation obviously has to be studied by experts, for it is only then, is it not, that we can really know how much we want and what contributions each state can make. Of course, these contributions, it must be understood, are entirely voluntary but in the spirit of African Unity each Government will be prepared to send troops. On no account, however, will they be commanded by others than their own officers.

By the way, can we induce the United States government to pay? Or, perhaps, the United Nations?

Meanwhile, the aggressed country has been completely over-run in spite of the thunderclaps by distant friends. So the next item on the agenda is inevitably negotiation. Negotiation with whom? Oh, Africa!

The essence of war is as much time as courage and armoury. Many victories have been lost through the initial loss of time. If the defence of Africa is to be real, Africa must make herself capable of instant reprisal. The only defence there is is instant defence.

An OAU Defence Organization cannot be successful unless the defence of the continent is planned as one. This will require adjustments in the present military installations and dispositions in Africa. It will call for the integration of units which will take joint exercises and fit into one defence conception which is continental in scope and in participation.

But all this is not possible without a permanent political body with directorate powers. A nation may possess educational and cultural cooperation; health, sanitation, and nutritional cooperation and the lot will still be in a state of anarchy if it has no government or supreme political directorate. What we need in Africa is not cooperation but mutuality. The arrangements provided for so far by the Organization of African Unity still leave us in a state of Pan-African anarchy. African unity first and foremost imposes duties upon us. It is with the fulfilment of the duties that the benefits of unity will begin to accrue. Cooperation is not a duty but a kindness. And when do we cooperate? When the Council of Ministers says so? On the particular occasions when cooperation is of national benefit? To what principles or interests do the Council of Ministers appeal when each Minister represents the principles and interests of his own state and has often to defend them against those of other African states?

Cooperation is not the answer. Its credibility is too low, for technically it involves too great a degree of disorder and institutional lack of uniformity. Mere cooperation is bound to stand in the way of the really important commitments. If on the other hand there were a Union Government, then this government would itself have to equate the social and economic and political and security interests of the continent as a whole.

African Unity is a question of framework. And the framework of a continental government is the only one which can make it real.

The point can be further stressed by a consideration of one of the Pan-African institutions. There exists today an African Development Bank. This Bank will be regarded by each African not as a national bank, but as an additional thin-on-the-ground bank from which it may not be able to expect much that is substantial. It is hardly surprising therefore that its African capitalization is low, and that much of its capital will have to come from non-African countries like Britain, United States, France, Czechoslovakia, and the Scandinavian countries.

If the larger or even a substantial proportion of the capital of the Bank is subscribed by foreign governments, they will acquire not merely a stake but an influence in the direction of the social and economic development of Africa. The African states are bound to regard such a Bank so constituted as no more than a source of loans and for social commitment will still look to their own local efforts.

In this way, the African political aim of the Development Bank will be defeated. If there were a Union Government, then the Bank could be used as an instrument of social economic development in African designs selected and approved by the Union Government on the ground of greater feasibility. There is not one single economic project in Africa today whose feasibility will not be much greater than it can ever be at present, given the framework of Union Government. Investing for a guaranteed African market is not the same thing as investing for a national market. The really huge economies of the world are based on large home markets or otherwise guaranteed ones as in the case of France and ex-French Africa. The United States, the Soviet Union, and China cannot avoid being great economies. The only single factor that prevents Africa from becoming a great economy is its political disunity. There is only one path to greatness for us. That path lies in unity.

The African Development Bank requires an African Common Market to sustain it. Trade must sustain the Bank, and the

Bank must accelerate trade. This means that an African Common Market area is called for, in order that the Bank may be fortified. The Bank will derive a continuing income only through the flow of capital which buoyant trade guarantees. But trade can only remain buoyant and settled in the vast expanse of the continent if the political problems raised by economic development are solved. An agreed and settled trade policy for all Africa cannot be reached by a committee of economic experts, for as long as the African states involved remain politically independent of one another, the economic problems of Africa cannot be given a purely economic solution. Accepted policies are bound to be politically affected. The considerations which make an international trade agreement possible are not all economic. Among the most important are political ones.

Within the framework of a Continental Union Government however the political determinants of economic policies will be general and common to the different states involved, and economic problems can then obtain their optimum economic solutions.

This emphasis on the importance of a Union Government is not intended to suggest that the state must or even can do everything. It would be wrong for the state to attempt to do everything. The state, however, is obliged to guarantee the essentials of life including health, education, communications, housing, employment. The state must for the rest provide a framework for the individual initiative and development of its citizens. A state that destroys individual initiative by trying to do too much will destroy itself, for each of the functions that it takes over must still be performed by individuals.

In Africa, we must ensure that overall agreements are for our benefit. But then we must let nothing stand in the way of those agreements and policies clearly required for our development. It is equally essential to avoid entanglements such as those of association with the European Common Market which are harmful to us.

Trade, in order to be an instrument of pacific diplomacy, needs to be fair. Fair trade will assist in the removal of political animosities and bring the world closer to the beatific ideal of permanent world peace. Yet peace will not be brought about by trade alone while there continues to be a proliferation of weapons of mass destruction. This is why I welcome the initiative of Great Britain to end the proliferation of nuclear weapons throughout the world. I am convinced that as the threat of an arms race recedes, America and Russia can be persuaded to contain and restrict and control the engines of destruction they now command and then to reduce and, one hopes, finally to destroy them. The British initiative is political ; but its effect is economic harmony which will end poverty's grip on mankind and ensure to all people the prospect of a fuller and freer life.

Political animosity can even less be removed by war, for sometimes animosity is not groundless. In any case, even lunatics are not destroyed for having entirely groundless beliefs. Is there any reason why sane men, adopting political beliefs on some grounds, should be destroyed by an act of war ? War as a political solution is repugnant to all enlightened, ethnical systems, all rational religion, and all forms of humanism. In a non-aligned world, war will be difficult and almost impossible ; for the unbiased judgement of the world will condemn international injustice which is inevitably involved in any war. In this way, all our tomorrows will be bright and will usher in the millenium.

CONCLUSION

Africa's Golden Road is opening up noble and inspiring vistas for all who travel it. Leaving exploitation, war, and internal divisions far behind, it leads on towards strength, justice, and brotherhood. It lifts man, in fact, nearer to the angels.

But only through unity can Africa achieve these goals. Union Government Now can bring a bright tomorrow and still brighter tomorrows beyond. It can mean a happier future not only for Africa but for the world.

APPENDIX ONE

Article 1 – Name

The name of the Organization shall be the 'All-African Students Union (in Europe)'.

Article 2 – Membership

Membership of the Union shall be determined in the following manner :
Only one 'All-African Students' Organization' in any European country shall be entitled to membership of the Union.

Article 3 – Parliament

(a) There shall be established a Parliament for the Union which shall be convened once every two years and shall meet at such place and time as shall be decided by the Parliament.

(b) Each member organization shall be represented in the Parliament by not more than two delegates.

(c) Observers may be invited from youth movements in Africa, women's organizations in Africa and other friendly organizations, at the discretion of the Parliament.

(d) Each member organization may submit proposals to the Executive Committee concerning the agenda for the meeting of the Parliament not later than one month prior to such a meeting except that the time limit may be waived in case of emergency.

(e) The proceedings of the Parliament shall be conducted in such a manner as to secure the widest possible measure of agreement. However, when a vote is called for the decision of Parliament shall be by simple majority except that in the case of proposals for the amendment of the Constitution or the expulsion of an organization, it shall require a majority of two-thirds of the votes. Each member organization shall have only one vote.

(f) The standing rules of procedure of the Parliament shall be laid down by the Parliament at its first meeting.

(g) The expenses of the delegates attending the Parliamentary sessions shall be borne by the respective member organizations.

Article 4 – Heads of Delegations

Heads of delegations to any meeting of the Parliament shall be the governing body and shall, among other functions :
(a) elect a chairman,
(b) determine the agenda,
(c) appoint committees,
(d) consider financial reports.

ARTICLE 5 – PERMANENT SECRETARIAT

(*a*) There shall be established a permanent secretariat for the Committee which shall be temporarily located in London and a representative office which shall at the same time operate in Prague.

(*b*) The Secretariat shall consist of the Secretary-General and other members who shall comprise the Executive Committee.

(*c*) Both the Secretary-General and the other members of the Executive Committee shall be appointed by the Parliament.

(*d*) The members of the Executive Committee shall hold office for one year and shall be eligible for reappointment on the expiration of their term of office.

(*e*) The Secretary-General shall be responsible for the smooth and efficient administration of the affairs of the Union. He shall in particular :

(1) collect materials for discussion in the Committee of the Parliament ;
(2) notify member organizations of the development of the activities of the Union ;
(3) administer the funds of the Union in consultation with the other members of the Executive Committee ; and
(4) do all such other necessary things as may be calculated to further the aims and objects of the Union.

(*f*) The Secretary-General and the other members of the Executive Committee may be removed from office by the Parliament by a two-thirds majority before the expiration of their terms of office if the interest of the Union so requires.

ARTICLE 6 – FINANCE

(*a*) The funds of the Union shall consist of donations without strings from African States and other African organizations, institutions, and individuals who agree and subscribe to the aims and objectives of the Union.

(*b*) Member organizations shall pay annual contributions to the Fund, the actual amount of which is to be determined by the Parliament.

ARTICLE 7 – TRANSITIONAL PROVISIONS

(*a*) The members of the Praesidium of the All-African Students' Conference in Belgrade 1960, shall be responsible for taking all necessary steps towards the birth of the All-African Students' Union (in Europe).

(*b*) The first Parliamentary session of the Union shall open on the date of promulgation of this Constitution.

FINAL COMMUNIQUÉ OF THE BELGRADE CONFERENCE, 1962

The first All-African Students' Conference on the general theme of 'African Unity Now' was held in Belgrade, Yugoslavia, from 29 August to 1 September 1962.

In addition to the sponsoring organizations, a number of African Students' Federations participated as delegates and observers (or visitors).

After four days of deliberations both in plenary sessions and at four Commissions (viz. Political, Economic, Social, Cultural and Constitutional) the Conference unanimously agreed to make the following declaration :

The Conference views with indignation the continued existence of dependent territories in Africa in the face of the demand of the African peoples for independence and unity, and absolutely condemns colonialism, imperialism, and neo-colonialism in Africa.

(1) The Conference, noting that the people of Africa have repeatedly demanded the end of colonial and imperialist subjugation in Africa, and unanimously sanctioning these demands, deplores the continued existence of colonial territories in Africa.

(2) The Conference views the continued existence of colonialism, neo-colonialism, and imperialism in Africa as a threat to the peace of the world and an affront to the personality and dignity of the African people.

(3) The Conference recognizes and endorses the Resolutions of the United Nations Organization calling for the granting of independence to dependent territories.

(4) The Conference recognizes and endorses the Accra Assembly as a major and decisive effort on the part of Africa for a lasting world peace, and congratulates the sponsors of that Assembly.

(5) The Conference, noting the danger to the integrity of the Independent African nations represented by neo-colonialism, recognizes the establishment of unity in Africa as a crucial instrument of the security and independence of Africa.

(6) The Conference in this connection notes with satisfaction the efforts being made by the African statesmen to achieve African Unity.

(7) The Conference recognizes the dominant role of foreign policy, military arrangements, economic planning and cultural factors in international affairs, and accepts a unified political direction in economic planning, foreign policy, and military affairs as a minimum content of African Unity.

(8) The Conference holds that in Africa today there are factors delaying the achievement of even this minimum Unity, and cites as examples of such factors, the continued existence of colonial territories in Africa, the attempt at balkanizing Africa, the existence in Africa of groupings which

are favourable to foreign nations holding colonialist and imperialist interests, the agreement of military pacts and alliances with foreign non-African Governments, the disadvantageous association of African countries with foreign and imperialist economies.

(9) The Conference views the removal of all such factors as necessary for African Unity and security.

(10) The Conference recognizes the promotion and growth of inter-African trade and markets, aimed at freeing and developing the African economies, to be a necessary instrument of African Unity.

(11) The Conference recognizes the creation of an agreed African foreign policy, which shall be truly independent and shall not be sub-servient to any foreign non-African interests, as a necessary instrument of African Unity.

(12) The Conference views the co-ordination of African economic policies as a means of defending African economies against domination by foreign economic powers. The economies of Africa are competitive ; similar natural resources and economic problems exist in a number of African territories. And in order not to be weakened and drawn apart by these similarities, the African territories must reach an agreement on production and market control in order to maintain a strong internal and export market ; they must also reach an agreement on levels and methods of industrial development in order to rationalize the supply of capital and skill.

(13) The Conference notes the existence of an aggressive colonialism and imperialism in Africa, especially in the so-called Union of South Africa, the second doomed Central African Federation, Angola, Mozambique, the Congo (Leopoldville), and the Spanish colonies in Africa, and views the achievement of Unity in military affairs by the independent African states as indispensable for the defence and security of an independent, liberated, and united Africa.

(14) The Conference affirms that a united Africa is more than a Union of African Governments, and recognizes the role of students in the forefront of the youth of Africa in the struggle for African Unity.

(15) The Conference affirms that to maintain their role and strength the movement for African Unity students must create an instrument of contact and continuity.

(16) The Conference holds the creation of a Permanent Pan-African Co-ordinating Secretariat as essential for the above purpose, and as a concrete testimony of the dedication of students to the ideals of African Unity.

(17) The Conference condemns the European Common Market as a closed discriminatory bloc aimed at perpetual economic domination of African countries.

(18) The Conference urges those African States already associated or in the process of becoming associated with the Common Market forthwith to withdraw therefrom in the imperative interests of the African continent and its producer economies.

(19) The Conference implores the independent African States to decolonize their economies by :

    (a) freeing themselves from imperialist organic and institutional links which compromise their independence ;

    (b) co-ordinating their economic and financial policies in order to bring about the speediest economic development through the creation of an African Common Market with agreed policies on ranges of production and credits ;

    (c) instituting a systematic planned economy to ensure the proper exploitation of natural resources and capital accumulation for the financing of state industries, which shall include this bulk of the mining industries, other heavy industries, and export agricultural industries ;

    (d) implementing a proper agrarian reform in which all African Governments should ensure an equitable redistribution of land to the peasantry through proper controls on acreages and types of crop production, and furthermore, through the encouragement of co-operative farming for local consumer crops.

(20) The Conference states that the realization of a united Africa will come about through concerted struggle by all the African peoples for a true national and democratic independence based on the political, economic and cultural independence of Africa.

The Conference resolves :

(1) that the people and Governments of Africa cannot be indifferent to the possibility of a third world war ;

(2) that the people and Governments of Africa must unite in support of the active movements for peace, support the proposals made in the United Nations for banning war and for a general and complete disarmament ; and support the conclusions reached by the Accra Assembly ;

(3) that African states must pursue in foreign matters a policy of non-interference and peaceful coexistence based on the interests and sovereignty of the African Continent ;

(4) that all African states should sever connections with the French Government if it persists in its determination to carry on atom-bomb tests in the Sahara, and that all nations shall desist from giving any support which might assist the French Government in this criminal practice ;

(5) that all African Governments should declare and maintain Africa as the world's first atom-free zone ;

(6) that African states should carry out fully the decisions of the Belgrade Conference of Heads of State or Government of Non-Aligned countries, and the decisions of the Accra Assembly.

(7) that all African states should abrogate existing military pacts and alliances with non-African states, and desist from concluding such military pacts and alliances ;

(8) that the Colonialist Governments of Britain, Portugal, Spain and South Africa are hereby asked to grant national independence to the

African peoples of their dependent territories as a matter of gravest urgency ;

(9) that the sombre and explosive situation prevailing in the Federation of the Rhodesias and Nyasaland, which has been caused and sustained by the uncivilized, racialist, and colonialist misdoings of the white minority settlers there, enjoying the protection of the metropolitan government of Great Britain and the goodwill of the American Government must be redeemed ;

(10) that the British Government is hereby called upon to dissolve the Federation of the Rhodesias and Nyasaland forthwith, and furthermore, to grant national independence to the African peoples of the constituent territories as Zambia, Zimbabwe, and Malawi, in any case not later than June 1963 ;

(11) that the British Government is hereby called upon to grant national independence to the African people of Kenya, Zanzibar, Swaziland, Basutoland, and Bechuanaland not later than June 1963 ;

(12) that the Government of Portugal is hereby called upon to put an immediate end to its obscenities in Angola and Mozambique, and further-more to grant national independence to the African people of Angola and Mozambique, in any case, not later than June 1963 ;

(13) that the Government of Spain is hereby called upon to put an immediate end to its barbarities in her African colonies and, furthermore, to grant national independence to the African people of the territories, in any case, not later than June 1963 ;

(14) that in full realization of the importance of an educational re-orientation which shall suit and express African conditions and traditions, the people and Governments of Africa must correct the denigration and dislocation of indigenous African cultural and historical achievement, caused by colonialism and its educational policies ;

(15) that new educational syllabuses, more suitable to the needs of Africa than existing ones, must be rapidly set up to underline the necessity for scientific and technical education ;

(16) that African Governments must set up technical institutes in their territories for the promotion and spread of scientific and technical education ;

(17) that the African countries should encourage the study of African languages in their schools and encourage the growth of literature in these languages ;

(18) that African Governments must initiate and carry out schemes for the total eradication of illiteracy from Africa ;

(19) that all African Governments must set up teacher training institu-tions in adequate numbers for the final assault on illiteracy ;

(20) that all African Governments should give full assistance in the revival and promotion of African Art and Drama, through the establishment of art schools, drama workshops, and permanent and itinerant exhibitions ;

(21) that immediate steps should be taken to record African music and folklore, ballads, songs, and chants, for preservation, study, and circulation ;

(22) that all people who respect democracy and human dignity should co-operate in obtaining the de-colonization of Africa in the shortest time ;

(23) that a Pan-African Conference on African culture be urgently convened and that all African Governments be approached to finance such a Conference ;

(24) that all the people of Africa and their Governments should co-operate in the systematic frustration and destruction of the anti-democratic measures of colonialism and imperialism ;

(25) that all the peoples of Africa and their Governments should make available to African freedom fighters systematic, diplomatic, financial, and material aid for the combat and overthrow of colonialism and imperialism in Africa ;

(26) that such material aid should be channelled through the central clearing house as shall by agreement be instituted for the purpose ;

(27) that in order that democarcy in Africa should be real it is necessary that political, economic, and social democracy be geared on to the interests of Africa's popular masses ;

(28) that in order that national independence be safeguarded, neo-colonialism put to rout, and an adequate standard of living secured for the people of Africa, the policies of independent African states must be based on real democracy, furnished with an effective arm against reactionary imperialist and neo-colonialist re-agents.

The Conference :

(29) expresses its support and solidarity with the struggle of African Trade Unions to establish a dynamic All-African Labour Organization ;

(30) asks all African states to give their support to the fight against foreign trade union federations which seek to perpetuate neo-colonialism through African Trade Unions ;

(31) asks all African states to recognize and give their support wholly to the All-African Trade Union Federation which is the continent's only true independent and Africa-orientated Federation of Trade Unions ;

(32) notes with gratification that the 1st of September 1962, which is the final day of deliberations of the 1st All-African Students' Conference, Belgrade, is also the 1st Anniversary of the Belgrade Conference of Heads of State and Government of Non-Aligned countries ;

(33) considering the stand that conference took on current world issues and problems, considering the important role the non-aligned states and Governments played in the convening and deliberations of the recent Cairo Conference :

    (a) congratulates all participants in the Belgrade Conference on its first anniversary ;

    (b) re-affirm its solidarity with the decisions taken ;

    (c) urges all African states to adopt and identify themselves with the principles laid down by the Belgrade and the Cairo Conferences ;

(34) calls for the establishment of unity among African states and proposes as instruments for its attainment the following measures :

(a) the establishment of an African Common Market which shall be free of domination by foreign economic and imperialist powers. The imperialist countries, faced with the strenuous struggle of colonial peoples for their national independence, are being successfully forced to withdraw their political control over the former colonies. Imperialism, is however, essentially a régime in which exploitation of nation by nation is the overriding objective and imperialist countries, politically thwarted, are frantically looking for new means and methods of existence. They are seeking to retain an economic domination of African countries. An African Common Market will keep economic imperialism at bay ;

(b) the creation of a unified and rationalized industrial plan for Africa to ensure the proper exploitation of natural resources and accumulated capital for the financing of State industries ;

(c) the implementing of a proper agrarian reform, on a continental basis, by means of which land can be made ready for optimum farming in an African context ;

(d) the creation of an African Continental Bank and other financial and monetary institutions to support major economic projects based on a nationalized industrialization programme of continental dimensions ; and the establishing of a common currency for Africa rigorously controlled by an African Continental Bank of Issue ;

(e) the agreement of a common foreign policy, inspired by the principles of positive neutralism ;

(f) the establishment in Africa of a unitary institution in the higher levels of military command for the systematic defence of the Continent ;

(g) the establishment of a permanent and constitutional forum for joint consultation and joint decisions by the African Governments, which shall be binding and sanctioned.

APPENDIX THREE

National Liberation Struggle

The Manifesto drawn up at the All-African Students of Europe Conference, London, 1963

Conference resolves :

(1) that concrete steps be taken by All-African States to implement the resolutions of the African and Afro-Asian Conferences on the colonial territories in Africa and that the African states call for a definite date when the remaining dependent countries on the continent must achieve independence ;

(2) that all African states should jointly set up three centres, one in North Africa, one in West Africa, one in Central and East Africa through which full assistance particularly in the form of military training and military supplies, can be rendered to the freedom armies of Africa ;

(3) that All-African countries should set up African volunteer armies to be put at the disposal of the African Liberation Struggle ;

(4) that different political organizations in each colonial territory in Africa should form a united front ;

(5) that all African states should :

    (*a*) cut off migrant labour to South Africa, Southern Rhodesia, and Fernando Po ;

    (*b*) deny all forms of transport facilities and implement trade sanctions against the countries of Portugal, South Africa, and Spain ;

(6) that African states should jointly take measures to positively influence those African states which do not actively support the National Liberation Movements ;

(7) that the immediate release of imprisoned freedom fighters be demanded ;

(8) that African states should grant political asylum to refugees from colonialism ;

(9) that African states must condemn the French nuclear tests in the Sahara and take collective and decisive measures against France ;

(10) That the African countries must be vigilant of the neo-colonialist policies of Japan and West Germany and of the role of Israel as a tool in the hands of the imperialist powers headed by the U.S.A. ;

(11) that since the struggle of the peoples of Africa is part of the struggle of the suppressed peoples of the world the African states should support and co-ordinate the struggle of the Afro-Asian and Latin American peoples. We therefore welcome the proposal of the Moshi Conference that a conference of the peoples' organizations of Asia, Africa, and Latin America be held.

African Unity

Conference resolves :

(1) that institutions giving expression to African Unity be created as a matter of urgency ;

(2) that methods of information and telecommunication including the setting up of a Pan-African News Agency, a Pan-African Radio and Television Service and a co-ordinated Postal System be established ;

(3) that a Pan-African Assembly, Executive and Public Service be established ;

(4) that a Pan-African Army under a joint High Command be created from national contingents in order to safeguard the integrity of the continent and the sovereignty of its people, and to defend Africans against tyranny in South Africa, Angola, Portuguese Guinea, Mozambique, Southern Rhodesia and other areas temporarily under colonial subjection ;

(5) that Africa should be free of all foreign military bases, nuclear and atomic testing facilities, and foreign millitary missions, or pacts ;

(6) that while complete African Unity is still being achieved, the activities of the separate delegations to the United Nations Organization and to other international bodies, as well as of national diplomatic missions should be co-ordinated ;

(7) that Africa should claim a seat in the Security Council ;

(8) that all African countries should have a co-ordinated foreign policy which shall be guided by principles of positive neutralism and on the basis of Bandung ;

(9) that African countries must therefore free themselves from partnership in any foreign groupings which are not compatible with African positive neutralism ;

(10) that fraternal relations and solidarity with peoples of African descent in the Americas be encouraged, nurtured, and maintained and avenues should be created for fruitfully channelling their skills and talents ; that solidarity with Afro-American students fighting for equality in the United States of America be expressed ;

(11) that African Governments raise from time to time in the United Nations Organization the issue of racism wherever it exists.

Economic Development

Conference resolves :

(1) that efforts should be concentrated on the development and continuous growth of heavy industry, and that a careful location of these industries be undertaken on a continental level ;

(2) that full exploitation of internal resources must be a prime aim of African states ;

(3) that the African states should adopt a co-ordinated policy for diversification and mechanization of agriculture ;

(4) that land reforms and reforms necessary for full scale industrialization of Africa be carried out without delay ;

(5) that Africa should have a planned economy ;

(6) that the European Common Market be considered as a neo-colonialist organization which perpetuates the economic exploitation of the newly independent states of Africa and undermines African Unity ;

(7) that to protect the growing African economy, African Governments must exercise strict control on foreign imports and exchange, and favour mutual beneficial trade ;

(9) that African states should only accept economic aid without strings and such aid should not be used for prestige projects but should be invested in productive enterprises ;

(10) that as far as possible investment capital be raised from within and that the need for such internal capital accumulation calls for austerity, self-help and the abandonment of a false standard of life by educated members of society ;

(11) That an African Common Market be established to promote intra-African trade ;

(12) that Pan-African Banks (particularly investment Banks) be established and research be conducted into the possibility of introducing a common currency ;

(13) that a comprehensive statistical survey of Africa be undertaken ;

(14) that African trade unions should become affiliated to an All-African Trade Union Federation ;

(15) that an intra-African transport and communication network be built up and that airways and waterways be run on a Pan-African basis ;

(16) that since electrical energy is of great importance for the future development of African industries, a serious examination for the harnessing of the great African rivers should be undertaken collectively.

CULTURAL AND SOCIAL PROBLEMS

Conference resolves :

(1) that a vigorous programme be embarked upon by all African states to effectively put into operation a planned programme of de-colonization by a radical overhaul of curricula and other materials. Further, a thorough elimination of illiteracy among the populations of African countries be undertaken ;

(2) that African Governments should exercise vigilance to prevent foreign dominated religious and cultural bodies from recapturing and recolonizing the African mind ;

(3) that a vigorous programme be devised to provide basic and technical education to workers and peasants ;

(4) that the teaching programme in the Universities be broadened so as to include studies on African history, music, and culture ;

(5) that the major African languages, such as Swahili, Hausa, Arabic, be taught in African Universities and encouraged and popularized ;

(6) that in order to facilitate understanding it is necessary to devise and implement a programme of student and teacher exchanges between African Educational Institutions ;

(7) that the various Universities of Africa should aim at co-operating with one another by making available results of research in all branches of studies ;

(8) that a Pan-African printing house be established to deal with the publication of results of research in all fields of study ;

(9) that a Pan-African Students' Union be established with a permanent secretariat on African soil to foster closer relationship among the students and youth ;

(10) that in view of the fact that sports can be a potent medium for the effective assertion of the African Personality, a Committee for the organization of Pan-African games be set up ;

(11) that wherever necessary, the Governments of Africa should endeavour to award financial assistance to all their nationals studying abroad to avoid hardships and that the Union of African Students in Europe being the vanguard of the African students overseas be financially supported by all African states ;

(12) that in view of the chronic need for cadres African Heads of State should encourage African students to study abroad wherever scholarships are available ;

(13) that African students from *dependent* countries be given every assistance by the independent African states in the form of scholarships and travel documents ;

(14) that African Governments co-operate with the Secretariats of African Students' Organizations abroad to arrange for student participation in the self-help and community development projects ;

(15) that the Heads of African states take progressive measures to discourage polygamy in African society today ;

(16) that women of Africa should be enabled to lead an active public life ;

(17) that women of Africa must enjoy full respect as equal members of African society ;

(18) that women must have an equal right with men to all public and social services, especially education.

INDEX

A.M.L. *See* Front de Liberation Nationale

Abraham, Willie, 8

Abrahams, Peter, 103

Abrams, Mark, 131

Accra, demonstration by housewives, 104

Accra Conference, 47, 50

Achimota, 5

Addis Ababa Conference, 55
  purposes of, 162
  resolution on United Nations policy, 219

Africa, present state of, 246

Africa Report 1963, 43

Africa Unity House, 14

African Common Market, need for, 47, 273

African Consultative Assembly proposed, 19

African Cultural Committee, 19–20

African Defence Force, 224

African defence organization, 270–1

African Development Bank, 272

African Eagle, 194*f*

African Economic Committee, 19

African grouping, 16

African Interpreter founded, 102

Africanism, 127

African One-Party States, 64*f*, 82*f*

African Personality, 48, 111, 128

African Political Committee, 19

African Political Parties, 70*f*

African Political Systems, 71*f*

African States, interdependence, 252
  products, 28, 40–1

African Students' Association of America and Canada, 102

African Unity, 53–5
  Nkrumah and, 110

Africans, in both world wars, 147, 148

Afro-Malagasy Union, 49

Aggrey, James Emman Kwegyir, 5, 101
  at Lagos, 53

Agriculture, tropical, African plans, 197

Aid, 133, 134, 136, 137
  ' politically-flavoured ', 199
  with strings, 47

Akintola, at 6th Pan-African Congress, 103

Akosomba Dam, 69

Akuako, Antwi, 23

Algeria, defeat of France in, 145
  French Communist attitude, 135–6
  revolt in, 3
  riot at Setief, 4

Algerian Problem, 135

All-African Defence Force, 164

All-African Peoples' Organization, Accra meeting, 17

All-African Students' Conference, Belgrade, Final communiqué, 277–82

All-African Students of Europe Conference, Manifesto, London, 283–6

All-African Students' Union (in Europe), Constitution, 24, 275–6
  Parliament of, 26

Alliances, 143–4

Aluminium, over-supply of, 247

Amis de Manifeste de la Liberté, becomes F.L.N., 3

ANZUS, 183

Apartheid, first United Nations resolution, 220
  origins of, 37
  world opinion, 218, 228

Armah, Kwesi, attitude to Algeria, 5
  comes to London, 5
  dedication to African Nationalism, 2
  on one-party democracy, 81
  view of Russia, 140

Arsene, Dionje, speaks on Congo, 14

Atlantic Charter, 1, 120, 205–6

Atom-free zones, proposed, 150

Atomic weapons, in China, 239–40. *See also under* Nuclear.

Atta, (Sir) Ofori, 5

Austerity, 2

Austin, Dennis, 251

Australia, and nuclear-free zones, 166

Avon (Lord), 186–8

Awolowo, 7

Azikiwe, Nnamdi, 7
  on future of Pan-Africanism, 10, 11
  speaks at Lagos, 52
  statement by, 9

Balifry, Ahmed, at Casablanca Conference, 51

Banda, Hastings, speaks in London, 13
  statement by, 9

Bandung Conference, on sovereignty, 4–5

Bandung Declaration, 16
  Casablanca Group adheres to, 20

Bantu Education Act, 231

Bantustan philosophy, 231

Barker, Ben, statement by, 9

Barwick, (Sir) Garfield, 166

Bauxite, 246–7

Bechuanaland, report on, 29

Behr, Edward, 135

Bennett, Frederic Mackarness, 70

Belgian Congo, industrialism, 41

Belgrade Conference, Final Communiqué, 277–83

287